Heartwarming true stories of
kindness, faith, innovation & joy

The remarkable life of
Rabbi Kalman Packouz

Inspired by the teachings of
Rabbi Noah Weinberg

RABBI SHRAGA SIMMONS

Book design and cover concept by
Shraga Simmons / Emesphere.com

Prepared from manuscript to press by
Estie@EDPressSolutions.com

First edition published in October 2023

ISBN 978-0-9992880-2-3

Published by Shabbat Shalom Fax of Life Inc.
www.shabbatshalom.org

Printed in Israel

"Concerning the Jews"

by Mark Twain

Harper's Magazine, 1899

If the statistics are right, the Jews constitute but one percent of the human race. It suggests a nebulous dim puff of stardust lost in the blaze of the Milky Way. Properly the Jew ought hardly to be heard of; but he is heard of, has always been heard of. He is as prominent on the planet as any other people, and his commercial importance is extravagantly out of proportion to the smallness of his bulk.

His contributions to the world's list of great names in literature, science, art, music, finance, medicine, and abstruse learning, are also way out of proportion to the weakness of his numbers. He has made a marvelous fight in this world, in all the ages; and has done it with his hands tied behind him. He could be vain of himself, and be excused for it.

The Egyptian, the Babylonian, and the Persian rose, filled the planet with sound and splendor, then faded to dream-stuff and passed away; the Greek and the Roman followed, and made a vast noise, and they are gone; other peoples have sprung up and held their torch high for a time, but it burned out, and they sit in twilight now, or have vanished.

The Jew saw them all, beat them all, and is now what he always was, exhibiting no decadence, no infirmities of age, no weakening of his parts, no slowing of his energies, no dulling of his alert and aggressive mind.

All things are mortal but the Jew; all other forces pass, but he remains. What is the secret of his immortality?

Dedicated
in loving memory of

Rabbi Kalman Packouz zt"l

He started me on my spiritual journey
with the *Shabbat Shalom* weekly.
Eternally grateful,

Jeremy Goldstein

May this book bring honor to:

HaRav **Yisrael Noah** *ben*
**HaRav Yitzhak Matisyahu
Weinberg** *zt"l*

הרב **ישראל נח** בן הרב **יצחק מתתיהו** זצ"ל

Rabbi **Kalman Moshe** *ben*
Reuven Avigdor Packouz *zt"l*

הרב **קלמן משה** בן **ראובן אביגדור** זצ"ל

זכות הספר מוקדש

מעומק ליבי, תודה נצחית
על כל מה שאת עושה
בשמחה וטוב לב
עבורי ועבור משפחתנו,
שתגדל ותפרח כשאיפתנו.
את עלית על כולנה.

Dedicated to

Rabbi Shraga Simmons

With deepest appreciation for
your hours of research and commitment
to share Kalman's life,
challenges and accomplishments.
Thank you!

And Dedicated to

Rabbi Yitzchak Zweig

Kalman's friend, confidant and
hand-holder for thirty years.
You brightened his every Wednesday!

Shoshana Packouz

To

Rabbi Kalman Packouz zt"l

who called us when it was least expected,
but most needed.
And for the blessing
of our eight grandchildren.

Dr. Stuart and Elizabeth Schnider

Contents

Preface

CELEBRATION OF LIFE

Rabbi Naftali Tzvi Yehuda Berlin, known as the Netziv, was an influential leader in nineteenth-century Lithuania. He mentored ten thousand yeshiva students and wrote commentaries on all parts of Torah. Upon publishing a particularly difficult work, *HaAmek She'eilah,* the Netziv invited his family and students to celebrate, where he told this story:

> When I was a child, I didn't pay attention in school. One evening, I overheard my parents talking. "Naftali will never become a Torah scholar," my father said. "Let's arrange for him to become an apprentice shoemaker."
>
> I was shocked! I ran to my parents and begged for a chance to prove that I'm a good student. Since that day, I've been immersed in Torah study – culminating in the commentary that we celebrate today.

The Netziv paused to reflect on the magnitude of the moment, then shared:

> Imagine if I hadn't overheard my parents' conversation. I'd have ended up as a shoemaker – and a pretty good one, besides! At the

end of my life, I'd get to Heaven and be asked the existential question: "Naftali, how did you maximize your life?" I'd proudly show
them a pair of my beautiful shoes – noting the exquisite design,
quality leather and fine workmanship.

Then I'd be asked: "But Naftali, where is the bookshelf filled with
your scholarly writings? Where are your ten thousand students?"

A variant of this story could be told about Kalman Packouz. A
natural-born leader, full of creativity, pragmatism, courage and
idealism, Kalman was on track to become a successful attorney –
and a pretty good one, besides.

That version of Kalman would get to Heaven and be asked,
"Where are your dozens of children and grandchildren? Where are
the thousands of people you personally touched with generosity,
compassion and kindness? Where are your hundreds of thousands
of weekly *Shabbat Shalom* readers? Where is the first Aish HaTorah
branch that you built? Where are the one million written words in
your books and articles? Where is your appearance on the *Today
Show* to promote Jewish marriage? Where are the millions of people
inspired by your Western Wall camera? And what about the fifteen
million dollars you raised to fund Jewish educational programs?"

Fortunately, that scenario never played out. Because in 1973 in
Jerusalem, this talented young man met Rabbi Noah Weinberg and
became inspired by the power of Torah. It changed the trajectory of
his life. Kalman became one of Aish HaTorah's six original students
and Rav Noah's lifetime partner in the monumental mission to
promote Torah values and reconnect Jews to their heritage.

What makes this story even more profound is that Kalman was a
"regular" person, with shortcomings like all of us. Yet, with determination and commitment, Kalman molded himself into a paragon
Torah ambassador – wise, warm, compassionate, generous and
joyful. This combination of outstanding traits became known affectionately as "Kalman's Way."

The title *Thumbs Up!* refers to Kalman's perpetual optimism and love of life. It is poetic justice that this humble person, whom Rav Noah described as the epitome of loyalty, became the subject of a book. Up there, I imagine Kalman having a good chuckle.

PERSONAL CONNECTION

I wrote this book with a perpetual smile on my face, reliving the myriad ways that Kalman influenced me during our thirty-year friendship.

Though I was a decade younger, Kalman and I followed similar life paths – secular American Jews in our twenties who caught fire and joined Rav Noah's "Torah Revolution." As a yeshiva student in Jerusalem in the late 1980s, I was a frequent Shabbos guest in the Packouz home. I saw up-close how Torah life manifests in a happy, loving family.

Kalman's exceptional integrity and compassion reminded me of my own father, of blessed memory. I recall as a child riding with my father through a classic Buffalo, New York storm. He'd pull up to a bus stop, roll down the passenger-side window and (in an era when people were more trusting) offer rides to drenched and frozen strangers. Kalman could surely relate.

Throughout the years, whether in Jerusalem, Miami or even Poland, Kalman and I spent many hours together, talking about life and our shared passion for Jewish education. Kalman was the consummate friend and colleague who took personal interest in my success. Sometimes, when deep in thought, I can still hear his voice ringing in my head – calm, warm and encouraging.

When Rabbi Yitzchak Zweig asked me to write this book, I sensed Divine orchestration. This was a superb opportunity to both tell Kalman's story and to apply my twenty years of experience as Rav Noah's ghostwriter.

Kalman "collaborated" in writing this book, in the sense that he left a written archive of over a million words on all topics of Judaism and self-growth – a treasure chest from which I drew.

A word about the spelling of Rav Noah's name. "People unfamiliar with Hebrew might mispronounce 'Noach' as rhyming with 'roach,'" Rav Noah told his students. "So I prefer to spell Noah without a 'c'." Given Kalman's insistence in following this directive, we defer.

All the stories and anecdotes are true. Name changes are marked with an asterisk *.

This year marks the fifty-year anniversary of Kalman's first meeting with Rav Noah in Jerusalem. My hope is that his story will inspire a new generation to take a deeper look at Torah – and apply their talents and passion to helping the Jewish people.

During his lifetime, thousands of people – of all ages and affiliations – loved Kalman. With this book, we hope you fall in love with him, too.

Shraga Simmons
September 2023 / Tishrei 5784
תהא שנת פריצת דרך
Moshav Matityahu

Beyond Portland

June 1972. Ken (Kalman) Packouz – smart, personable and creative – has the whole world before him. He's just graduated with a psychology degree from University of Washington in Seattle, taken the LSATs and applied to law school.

Yet these are tumultuous times. In the wake of the Summer of Love, Vietnam War protests and the emerging Watergate scandal, the foundations of society are shaking. At age twenty-two, Ken is not ready to jump straight to law school. The Vietnam draft lottery places his birthday – May 15 – far down the list, reinforcing his determination to take a gap year off. "Law school can wait a year," Ken tells family and friends.

Ken returns to his hometown of Portland, Oregon and devotes the next six months to the Jewish youth group, BBYO (B'nai B'rith Youth Organization). In high school, Ken was elected "Aleph Gadol" – President of the Pacific Northwest Region. Now, with maturity, wisdom and a finger on the pulse, he traverses the country advising BBYO.

Ken's sights soon shift to the second half of his gap year: a global travel adventure to explore if there's more to life than being a lawyer.

1

On January 1, 1973, Ken and Phil Tobin, friends since first grade, fill their backpacks with essential gear, $2,500 cash each and a return ticket. They plan to travel all of Europe until the money runs out.

The intrepid pair spends their first month in England and Scotland – exploring museums and castles. Next, they planned to cross the English Channel by hovercraft to France.

One morning at breakfast, Ken approaches Phil with some news.

"Don't be angry," Ken says. "I know we're supposed to travel together, but it's cold in Europe and I'd enjoy a warmer climate. Israel is close by and I've always wanted to go."

"It's your money and your time," Phil replies. "I love you now and I'll love you always. Go and enjoy."

"Thanks for understanding," Ken says. "I'll be back in two months."

CHAPTER ONE

Looking Deeper

UNDERWATER WORLD

Ken flew to Tel Aviv and after a few days of Mediterranean sun and sand caught a bus to Israel's southernmost city, Eilat. As the bus traversed the long, flat stretches of Negev desert, Ken observed the green agricultural patches in stark contrast to the barren brown sand. *It's amazing how the desert blooms,* Ken marveled, making a mental note to find out more.

In Eilat, Ken rented snorkeling equipment at Coral Beach, the Red Sea scuba diving mecca famous for pristine tropical waters. Submerged, Ken was treated to an explosion of luminescent red and blue corals, perched atop meadows of sea grass, populated by schools of jellyfish, stingrays, angelfish, sea snakes and sea turtles. *Now I know why I came to Israel!* he thought.

That evening at the youth hostel lounge, Ken felt relaxed and content. As the sunset shimmered off the sea, he reflected on the monolithic expanse of water, concealing a vast underwater world. *External appearances can deceive,* Ken noted. *In life, always look deeper, beneath the surface.*

DESERT KIBBUTZ

After one week in Eilat, Ken was ready for the next chapter in his Israel adventure. He approached the tourist information desk in a hotel lobby. *"Boker tov!"* Ken said with a wave of the hand and a smile, enjoying his novice command of Hebrew. "I'm looking for an authentic experience to connect with the local atmosphere and vibe."

"How about volunteering on a communal-living kibbutz?" the agent suggested.

"Great! I grew up as a Reform Jew. Do you have something with that flavor?"

"There are good options in northern Israel."

Ken's thoughts turned to the impressive desert agriculture he'd seen from the bus. "Perhaps something in the Negev?"

"Kibbutz Urim is in the Negev."

"Perfect!" Ken enthused.

Turns out, not so perfect. Ken was assigned a tedious task in the kibbutz knife factory. For the creative and curious Ken, this would not last long.

TESTING THE WATERS

One of the few people that Ken knew in Israel was Ron Balshine, his best friend since high school. Ron had become Jewishly observant and was studying at the yeshiva of Rabbi Chaim Brovender in Jerusalem. With a three-day break from the kibbutz coming up, Ken suggested getting together.

"Come stay with me at yeshiva," Ron said. "You can have an authentic Jewish experience and try some classes."

The idea interested Ken who, unlike many of his childhood friends, had not been alienated by Hebrew school. He'd even won the coveted John F. Kennedy Award as the top Hebrew school student at Portland's Temple Beth Israel.

A few days later, Ken met up with Ron in Jerusalem. The yeshiva was in mid-session, and the curriculum – not designed for walk-ins – made it difficult to click with the flow of study. Yet this taste of Torah intrigued Ken – revealing more beneath the surface and planting a seed.

Ken headed back to the kibbutz to ponder his next move.

SHEMA YISROEL

Meanwhile in Jerusalem, Rabbi Noah Weinberg had recently opened a Torah study program for English-speaking young men with little Jewish background. Rav Noah hailed from an illustrious rabbinic family and, Manhattan born-and-bred, was well-familiar with Western mentality. In America, Rav Noah observed a growing disconnect from Torah and – recognizing the threat to Jewish continuity – pledged to one day do something about it.

Rav Noah moved to Israel, got married and started a family. Then in 1967, Israel's miraculous lightning-quick victory in the Six Day War awakened the dormant religious identity of Jews around the world.

> At the newly liberated Western Wall, Israeli soldiers were overcome with emotion, praying and crying.
>
> When one non-religious soldier began crying, his friend asked, "Why are you so emotional? What is your connection to this Wall?"
>
> "I'm crying," the first replied, "because I don't know why to cry."

Rav Noah recognized that this newfound spiritual yearning – combined with the idealistic, free-spirit Sixties energy – presented a rare opportunity to create a *ba'al teshuva* (return to Judaism) movement. With determination, Rav Noah launched various Torah study programs in Israel – though for various reasons, each had failed.

In 1973, Rav Noah tried again, this time launching a yeshiva named Shema Yisroel, strategically located within walking distance of Jerusalem's tourist spots. Rav Noah would hang around the Central Bus Station and the Western Wall, engaging with young backpackers and encouraging them to take a fresh look at Jewish values. "Come to Shema Yisroel for one day," he'd say. "You'll learn ancient Jewish wisdom for happiness, relationships, spirituality and success."

TIMELY SUGGESTION

In Jerusalem, Ron Balshine heard about Rav Noah's new yeshiva and had a flash of inspiration. Slipping an *asimon* (token) into the pay phone, Ron called Ken's kibbutz. "There's a new yeshiva that combines Torah study with practical life wisdom and personal development," Ron told Ken. "It could be perfect for you."

At the next kibbutz break, Ken phoned Rav Noah to inquire about the yeshiva… unaware that his life was about to be irrevocably altered.

"I teach a class every morning at nine o'clock," Rav Noah said. "Come by at eleven and we'll talk."

That Sunday morning, Ken arrived at Jerusalem's Central Bus Station, folded street map in hand. Ken headed down Jaffa Road, then over to Malchei Yisrael Street and the religious Geula neighborhood. Like a curious anthropologist, Ken snapped a photo of men in long black coats and women in colorful head coverings – unlike anything he'd seen in Portland or Seattle.

Ken then passed through Kikar Shabbos, admiring the historic Zion Orphanage. Thoughts of needy youngsters triggered a childhood memory:

Eleven-year-old Ken is sitting at the kitchen table, enjoying an afternoon snack. He spots the *Portland Oregonian* newspaper, where a starving baby with a bloated stomach stares out from the front page.

Ken sighs, pain mixed with confusion. *"God" and "good" are the same word. If God is good, how could this happen?*

Applying his 160-IQ logic, young Ken surmises two possibilities: *Either there is no God and life "just happens." Or there is a God and life is meaningful.*

This leads to two more possibilities: *Either life is one big sitcom, with God creating episodes for entertainment, or God is absolute goodness, and everything — even the challenges — has intrinsic purpose and meaning.*

At the kitchen table, young Ken continues to ponder:

Why do bad people prosper and good people suffer? If God is good, there must be ultimate justice. Yet justice isn't always apparent. So there must be some great equalizer — where good people receive ultimate reward and evil people receive their just desserts.

Young Ken makes solving this riddle a personal quest. At Hebrew school, he asks every teacher, "Do Jews believe in the afterlife?"

Ken's authenticity, warmth and sincerity make his inquisitive approach endearing. The variety of answers (none of which is "Yes") include: "No, the afterlife is a Christian idea"; "There is if you want there to be"; and "People live on in the name they leave behind."

In response to these answers, Ken would ask a follow-up question: "How do you know?"

Time and again, Ken received the same, unsatisfying answer: "It's my opinion, as valid as any other."

Ken's thirst to understand remains unquenched, and he eventually concludes there are no answers to be had.

MEETING RAV NOAH

In Jerusalem, Ken wound his way through the Bukharan shuk abuzz with craftsmen, eventually arriving at the address he'd written down: *Novardok building. 14 Shimshon Polanski Street.*

Ken admired the large, three-story institutional building, nestled between apartment blocks. Climbing two flights of stairs to the top floor, he entered the yeshiva study hall and immediately identified Rav Noah as the large, bearded man in his early forties – engaging a backpacker in conversation.

"On a kibbutz, you experience socialism," Rav Noah was telling the young man. "Why not give equal time to Judaism?"

"I make a meaningful contribution to Israeli society by picking oranges," the young man said.

"That contribution could be made by someone else," Rav Noah countered. "In yeshiva, you'll discover your unique contribution to the Jewish people and to humanity. Torah is a living, breathing document – the lifeblood of our nation. We're the 'People of the Book.' But have you read the book?"

The backpacker shrugged, curiosity aroused. "So what is Torah exactly? A history book? A collection of laws? A code of ethics?"

This was the opening that Rav Noah was waiting for. "Torah study is different from other academic subjects. Torah literally means 'instruction.' The Almighty gave us *Torat Chaim* – 'instructions for living' – the owner's manual for life. The purpose of Torah study is not merely to acquire new information, but to live with that awareness. We invest years learning how to 'make a living' – but do we learn how to 'live'? Do you want meaning and purpose; to fulfill your potential; to build a healthy, ethical society; to have a successful marriage and raise well-adjusted children? Then study the Almighty's instructions for living!"

The backpacker played devil's advocate, "I can be street-smart and learn through trial and error."

"Life is too short to stumble on unnecessary mistakes," Rav Noah said. "The wise person learns from others. Whether you aspire to become a rabbi, a CEO, an academic or an athlete, by studying Torah you can acquire life-changing wisdom."

Ken watched the conversation unfold, impressed with Rav Noah's combination of charisma and humility. *But,* he thought, *the real test is the "afterlife question" that I've had since Hebrew school.*

With determination, Ken sauntered up to Rav Noah and bluntly declared, "Rabbi, do Jews believe in the afterlife?"

"Of course we do!" Rav Noah said with a joyous smile. "The afterlife is a fundamental Jewish belief, one of Maimonides' Thirteen Principles of Faith. The afterlife is where we experience ultimate justice, based on our ethical choices. Without an afterlife, there is no way to understand God as good and just."

Ken was shocked – a Jew espousing belief in the afterlife!

Ken nearly forgot his follow-up question, but quickly recovered. "What's your evidence?"

Rav Noah opened the Chumash (Five Books of Moses) and pointed to a few allusions in the text.

"Why is the afterlife only alluded to?" Ken asked.

"Because the goal of life is to attain pleasure in *this* world," Rav Noah said. "The afterlife is a consequence, an eternal reflection, of what we create during this lifetime."

This makes sense, Ken thought. *And whether this rabbi is right or wrong, at least he has a source and not just an opinion.*

Skeptical by nature, Ken spotted another rabbi and, to avoid collusion, quickly sidled over to ask the same question: "Do Jews believe in the afterlife?"

"Of course!" the rabbi said. "This world is the entrance hall to the eternal afterlife."

Ken stopped to reflect on the moment. He'd long intuited the idea of an eternal afterlife. Now, after years of seeking answers and striking out, he was experiencing the emotional-intellectual equivalent of a grand slam home run.

PLEASURE PRINCIPLE

Rav Noah caught up with Ken and asked, "So, are you ready to learn Jewish wisdom?"

"Sure," Ken said. "How do I acquire wisdom?"

"That's precisely the question!" Rav Noah said with a joyous clap of his hands. "The beginning of wisdom is to desire it. Let's start with the fundamentals: What is the purpose of life?"

"To be happy?" Ken surmised.

"The first human was placed in the Garden of Eden – literally the 'garden of pleasure,'" Rav Noah explained. "The Almighty created this marvelous world for one purpose: for us to attain maximum pleasure."

"I'm pretty good at getting pleasure," Ken said. "Why do I need Torah?"

"Not all pleasures are created equal," Rav Noah said. "Despite the many physical and material pleasures that Western culture promotes, nothing quite seems to satisfy. There are higher pleasures of love, meaning, creativity and transcendence. Don't settle for lower-level pleasures. Become a pleasure connoisseur!"

For Ken, this was a paradigm shift. He'd always assumed that Western culture had a monopoly on pleasure, with Judaism antiquated, out-of-touch and full of restrictions like "no driving on Shabbos or eating at McDonald's."

Standing there, Ken had an epiphany: *My Jewish education ended at my bar mitzvah. I have a thirteen-year-old's view of Judaism.*

Rav Noah's voice broke Ken's thoughts. "I teach a class called '48 Ways to Wisdom.' Join us tomorrow at nine a.m. The topic is love. Do you know the definition of love? Give it some thought."

Ken walked outside, hit by a cool gust of Jerusalem air. *Meaningful and inspiring Jewish wisdom? Is this for real?*

Skeptical but energized, Ken checked into a Jerusalem youth hostel for a good night's sleep.

KALMAN'S WAY: TEN ESSENTIALS

- **Kindness.** Nice guys finish first.

- **Growth.** Life is a process of self-improvement.

- **Effort.** Forgo temporal comfort for the sake of future gains.

- **Respect.** Every person is an entire world.

- **Curiosity.** Be awed by our intricate, spectacular world.

- **Honesty.** Say what you mean, and mean what you say.

- **Perseverance.** Hard work is always an advantage.

- **Compassion.** No man is an island.

- **Commitment.** Employ discipline, goal-setting and follow-through.

- **Gratitude.** Recognize that life is full of gifts that we inherited for free.

CHAPTER TWO

Jerusalem: Decision Point

DEFINE YOUR TERMS

Monday morning, 9 a.m. at Shema Yisroel. A young back-packer was telling Rav Noah, "This is my first visit to Israel, and I'm disappointed with this so-called 'Holy Land.' I've been everywhere – from Jerusalem to Masada, from the Golan to the Negev – and haven't found spirituality anywhere!"

Rav Noah waved his hand as if engaging in deep philosophy. "Tell me, my friend, are you a *bavoostik*?"

"Ummm, what's a *bavoostik*?" the backpacker said.

"Just answer the question. Are you a *bavoostik*?"

"How can I answer if I don't know what I'm talking about?"

"Precisely!" Rabbi Weinberg said. "And how do you define 'spirituality'? Incense, yoga, organic food and meditation on a mountaintop – with visions of colorful fairies chanting prophecy?"

Rav Noah and the backpacker shared a laugh, then Rav Noah told a story:

A man is walking through the forest. He sees a tree painted with a target – and an arrow in the bullseye. The man continues walking, amazed to encounter tree after tree with arrows dead-center.

Eventually, the man comes across a boy with a bow and arrow, and asks, "Do you know who shot these arrows?"

"Yes," the boy replies. "I did."

"Amazing! What is your secret formula for hitting bullseye every time?"

"Simple," the boy says. "First shoot the arrow, then paint the target."

Rav Noah got serious and said, "My friend, if you're serious about spirituality, you'll need an objective definition. Otherwise, you're just stumbling along, never sure whether you hit or miss."

FOCUS ON VIRTUES

A few minutes after nine o'clock, Rav Noah's class began:

"The Mishnah in *Pirkei Avos* lists '48 Ways to Wisdom,' practical tools for successful living. We study one 'way' every day. Way number 32 is 'Love Humanity.' So let's define our terms: What is love?"

"Affection," one student said.

"Attachment," said another.

"Romance," suggested a third.

Rav Noah nodded approvingly. "Love can include all these. The Torah instructs us: 'Love your neighbor as yourself.' Yet how is it possible to mandate an emotion? The answer is that love isn't something that 'just happens.' Love is a choice – to focus not on flaws, but on others' virtues. The more positive qualities you can identify in others, the more you'll experience the pleasure of love."

A student's hand went up. "What about a difficult person? How do you love someone like that?"

"It is realistic to love everyone," Rav Noah replied, "because every human has intrinsic virtue: created in the image of God, and possessing intelligence, vitality and potential. Associate people with their virtues, and the love will come."

After some lively back-and-forth discussion, Rav Noah suggested, "Make a list of virtues. Think of the people you love, and analyze why it's so. Start with obvious virtues, then work your way toward more difficult ones. Finally, prioritize the list: Which virtues are most important? Do this and you'll have more love in your life."

———⋙⋅◆⋅⋘———

After the class, Ken approached Rav Noah. "Thank you, Rabbi. I didn't realize Judaism had so much to say about life."

"Tell me something," Rav Noah said. "Would you rather be happy or rich?"

"Happy."

"Eskimos have a dozen words to describe different types of snow. Judaism has a dozen words to describe aspects of joy. Ken, stay in yeshiva for a week and we'll teach you the secret of happiness."

Ken tried playing devil's advocate: "What if a person chooses to be miserable. Isn't that their prerogative?"

"No," Rav Noah said firmly. "Happiness is an obligation. We all live in this world together, and we must be careful not to cause damage. Wearing a sour face is a form of public damage."

Ken nodded, then said, "I'd like to take the rest of the day to explore Jerusalem and think about things."

Ken headed downtown, his thoughts swirling. *On one hand, if Torah is authentic Divine wisdom, there is nothing more important than this. On the other hand, I was planning to return to Europe.*

That evening, Ken was back at 14 Polanski Street to check into the dorms – for one week.

WHAT ARE YOU LIVING FOR?

Ken was up bright and early for his first full day of yeshiva. Rav Noah arrived and began teaching the opening lines of Rabbi Moshe Chaim Luzzato's *Mesilas Yesharim (Path of the Righteous)*:

> The foundation of piety, and the root of complete service, is to clarify and make real: What is one's obligation in this world? With a lifetime of toil, where should a person direct their vision and aspirations?

Rav Noah explained, "Be clear on your life goal. Be sure that whatever you invest in, is the ultimate in living. Otherwise, you could be a billionaire and miserable. In the American Revolution, Patrick Henry famously said, 'Give me liberty or give me death.' Judaism says, 'Clarity or death!' Know what you're willing to sacrifice for. Until then, you haven't begun to truly live."

Rav Noah then shared a story:

> Alfred Nobel was a wealthy Swedish industrialist, the inventor of dynamite and a leading global producer of explosives.
>
> When Alfred's brother died, the newspaper mistakenly published an obituary of Alfred instead. Under the headline, "The Merchant of Death is Dead," Alfred's "obituary" described his lifetime legacy as "finding ways to kill more people faster than ever before."
>
> For Alfred Nobel, this was a wake-up call. He dedicated the rest of his life to rewarding those who make a positive impact on humanity – establishing the Nobel Prize.

Rav Noah continued:

> What do you want the newspaper to write about you? No obituary ever glorified the size of a person's house or bank account.

Beyond the blessings of health, career, family and friends, happiness depends on having goals and ambition. What are you living for? What accomplishment would you be proud to have written on your tombstone?

Once you clarify this, you'll leap out of bed each morning with energy to fulfill that goal – no alarm clock necessary.

———⊰•◆•⊱———

That evening in the dorm, Ken spent time with the other students, among them Rhodes Scholars and Ivy Leaguers, engaging in passionate debate and probing the existential question: "What am I living for?"

As the hour drew late, one student suggested postponing further discussion until the following day. "What?!" another protested. "We can't sleep now! What if we don't wake up? We'll never know what we're living for!"

WHY PRAY?

The next morning, before prayers, Rav Noah shared some insights. "Have you ever prayed?" he asked.

Almost every hand went up.

"Was your prayer answered?"

The hands stayed up.

Rav Noah continued, "Even those who claim not to believe in God, in the same breath say that they pray. Yet why do we pray in the first place? We can't 'bribe' God, who already has everything. It must be that God loves us. Our Father in Heaven has all the resources and power imaginable – and wants to give us everything."

A student asked, "Why is it sometimes difficult to feel God's presence?"

"We're distracted, overwhelmed by culture and media, trained to not take God seriously," Rav Noah said. "We say in *Aleynu* at the end of the prayer service: 'Know this today, and place it in your heart.' It's a far distance from head to heart – from intellect to emotions. Speaking sincerely to God in prayer is a way to connect with your emotions.

"If you haven't prayed in years and feel it's too late to start, or you feel like a hypocrite – don't worry. God wants a personal relationship with each of us. He could have made robots, but instead He wants us to choose the relationship."

A student asked, "I don't understand the whole idea of prayer. If God can get us out of a tough situation, why put us there in the first place?"

Rav Noah gestured skyward. "If we're not paying attention, the Almighty needs to wake us up. I recently met a backpacker who said, 'Rabbi, I don't need to study Torah, because God and I are very close. He does miracles for me!' I asked him to please share a miracle, and he told me this story:

> One day, I was riding my motorcycle on a winding mountain road. A truck came around a curve and swerved into my lane, heading straight at me. My only choice was to veer off the cliff. I flew a hundred feet in the air, with nothing but jagged rocks below. "God! Help!" I screamed.
>
> A moment later, my bike landed between two rocks, which cushioned me like a shock absorber. I was tossed off the bike and landed gently in a hedge of bushes. I walked away without a scratch. It was a total miracle! So you see – God and I are very close."

Rav Noah paused for dramatic effect, then continued, "I asked the young man, 'Tell me, my friend, Who do you think pushed you off that cliff?' God is not Superman, waiting till you stumble, then swooping in to save you. The Almighty controls every aspect of life, both the problems and the solutions. Why would God toss someone in the air and catch him at the last moment? To send a message: Wake up and start living!"

⟹⋗⟸

At breakfast, Ken sat with the other students, all secular American Jews like himself, who'd gone exploring the world and ended up studying Torah in Jerusalem. Ken noticed a student mutter some words before taking a bite of food.

"What were you saying?" Ken asked with a mix of curiosity and skepticism.

"A blessing," the student replied, happy to share his newfound Jewish enlightenment. "Life is all about awareness and appreciation. Beyond the instinctive, animalistic response to hunger, blessings add a spiritual dimension – showing gratitude to God as the Source of all good. We are not merely 'living to eat' – to survive physically, but 'eating to live' – to pursue higher consciousness."

RECOGNIZING TRUTH

It was time again for "48 Ways to Wisdom." Rav Noah began, "We all want to do the right thing. Nobody wakes up in the morning and says, 'I plan to do evil today.' Even terrorists and dictators claim to be heroically saving the world – with 'evidence' to support their false ideas."

A student asked, "If everyone claims to be good, how do we know what is objectively good?"

Rav Noah explained, "The Talmud says that while in our mother's womb, the Almighty sends an angel to teach us wisdom for living. Then, just before we're born, the angel taps us under the nose – forming that indentation – and we forget everything we learned."

"What's the point of the angel teaching us, if we need to relearn it all?" a student asked.

"To give us the joy of discovery," Rav Noah explained. "Buried within our subconscious lies the knowledge of everything we need to know: the purpose of life, how to love and how to reach our potential. Truth and wisdom are right under our nose!

"Did you ever hear an idea for the first time, and it resonated as true? That's tapping into your internal compass. Education is not about forcing your opinion or convincing others. It's about helping people rediscover what they intuitively know."

"Things aren't always black and white," a student said. "One person's terrorist is another's freedom fighter."

"That's why it's important to define your terms," Rav Noah said. "Terrorism is premeditated, politically motivated, violent intimidation of civilians. A freedom fighter supports the cause of freedom – both mine and yours – and does not attack civilians. But a terrorist wants to wipe out the other side completely."

"If everyone claims to be good, what is the litmus test to identify the bad guy?" a student asked.

"Look at their methods. Do they forcibly control others with intimidation and threats? Or is their impact achieved through inspiration and rational ideas? Do they welcome constructive criticism? Do they empower others to achieve their potential? And are the long-term results pleasant and peaceful?"

<hr />

On a break between classes, Ken overheard Rav Noah speaking with a backpacker who'd dropped by. "I'm an atheist!" the young man proclaimed defiantly.

"Fabulous!" Rav Noah said. "I've always wanted to meet a genuine atheist. Please share your evidence that there is no God."

"Umm," the young man hesitated. "I'm really agnostic."

"Oh, I'm disappointed," Rav Noah said. "I was hoping to meet a real atheist. But agnostic is second-best. So please share your evidence that we cannot determine the existence of God."

The fellow lowered his eyes – and his bravado. "I guess I never looked into it that much."

"In that case," Rav Noah said, "stay for the next class. We'll discuss the rational basis for the belief in God."

FIVE-FINGER CLARITY

Rav Noah explained, "Maimonides begins his epic four-teen-volume *Mishneh Torah*: 'The foundation of wisdom is to know there is a First Being, Who caused everything to be. Nothing exists independent of God. If God did not exist, nothing else could exist.' The Almighty did not create the universe and then go on vaca-tion. God is the ongoing Sustainer and Supervisor – guiding every moment of our lives."

"Isn't this all just a matter of faith?" a student asked.

"Notice that Maimonides doesn't say to 'have faith' in God's existence – but rather 'to know,'" Rav Noah said. "The first of the Ten Commandments is: 'Know there is a God.'"

A student asked for clarification: "What exactly is the difference between knowledge and faith?"

"Faith is an emotional leap, an unsupported wish that some-thing is true," Rav Noah explained. "Knowledge is a rational belief, based on facts. We are to investigate the evidence for God's exis-tence. The more evidence, the stronger the knowledge. This is life's most important question, from which all else flows."

"How can we be certain that *anything* is true?" a student asked.

Rav Noah opened his palm wide and held it up for all to see. "Do you have five fingers on your hand?"

"Yes," the student said.

"Are you certain?"

"Yes."

"That's called 'five-finger clarity.' Judaism says to strive for 'five-finger clarity' in everything you know. What does the evidence suggest? Know what you know! If it's true, move forward with confidence. That's five-finger clarity."

"You're talking about evidence," a student said, "but I thought Jewish belief is based on tradition."

Rav Noah clarified: "Some religions say to have 'blind faith,' to 'just believe' and not ask questions. Judaism says to combine tradition with rational investigation. The first blessing of the *Amidah* refers to *Elokeinu* – our 'personal God,' as well as *Elokei Avoseinu* – the collective 'God of our ancestors.' Independent investigation plus tradition is the best of both worlds. One complements the other."

Ken's Hebrew school misconceptions were being shattered.

"What is the basis to know that God exists?" a student asked.

"Go back to the very beginning," Rav Noah explained. "Something cannot be created from nothing. Logic says that the universe had an infinite 'First Cause' that designed the world and brought it all into existence. We call this 'God.'"

"You claim that our physical world is purposeful," a student said. "But maybe it's all an accident."

"Look at DNA, with a perfectly ordered structure and ability to replicate itself," Rav Noah said. "Sophisticated design indicates Designer. The prophet declares, 'Open your eyes and see who created all this' [Isaiah 40:26]. In the Midrash, Rabbi Akiva explains that just as a garment indicates a weaver, and a house indicates a builder, so too the universe indicates a Creator. The beauty and precision of our universe declare God's perfect Oneness."

A student challenged the premise: "Maybe the world came into existence through random accident, by a gazillion-to-one odds. The proof is that it happened!"

Rav Noah replied, "You wouldn't claim that a complex machine had no engineer to design or manufacture it. Or that ink spilled onto paper and produced a brilliant manuscript. Yet when it comes to the universe, you're willing to bet a gazillion-to-one?"

———✦———

As the leader of his high school debate team in Portland, Ken was familiar with the science of epistemology (knowledge, logic and evidence). Though he still had many questions about Torah, he could not dismiss its position as irrational.

Additionally, Ken had never met someone with Rav Noah's combination of qualities: scholarly, personable, humble, sensible, sincere and funny.

That evening, Ken wrote to his parents in Portland:

Dear Mom and Dad,

I've taken a break from the kibbutz to spend a few days in Jerusalem studying at a yeshiva. This has been eye-opening and exhilarating. I'm meeting idealistic young men. We study philosophy, history and spirituality – and practical life wisdom for being a good person.

I'm fascinated with the Torah's sophisticated view of human nature. And I'm empowered by the idea that each person has a unique role in the grand eternal plan.

I'll write more next week.

All my love,

Ken

INDEPENDENT THINKING

"To be an educated Jew, study the text," Rav Noah said. "The Five Books of Moses is the primary source of Jewish history, ethics, national mission and relationship with God."

A student challenged, "Isn't religion an escape from the real world, a way to avoid thinking?"

"You've heard of 'talmudic hair-splitting'?" Rav Noah said. "The premise of Jewish study is to probe and challenge. There is no such thing as 'rabbinic infallibility.' Don't blindly accept others' beliefs as your own. Seek the truth. Ask questions until you're satisfied – emotionally and intellectually.

"In Western society, parents bronze a child's first shoes. In Judaism, we bronze a child's first question. Remember the 'Four Questions' at the Passover Seder? Jewish wisdom is built on questions. That's why the best answer to a question is often another question."

"I'm all for independent thinking," a student said. "What's the process to get there?"

"Let's look at Genesis, chapter 12," Rav Noah said. "God told Abraham, '*Lech lecha* – Go to yourself, from your land, from your birthplace and from your parents' home – to the land that I will show you.' Abraham was told: Don't accept something just because you were raised with the idea or because it's popular in your culture. Work it through yourself."

A hand went up. "Are you saying to automatically cast aside everything we learned growing up?"

"No," Rav Noah explained. "I'm saying: Don't live as an accident of birth. During the U.S. Civil War, nearly everyone north of the Mason-Dixon Line was against slavery, and nearly everyone south of the line was pro-slavery. Did all the pro-slavery people somehow gravitate like a magnet to the South? Of course not.

"We are all products of society. In Soviet Russia, many people carry around the *Communist Manifesto*. In Haiti, many people visit a voodoo doctor. In Jerusalem, many people wear tzitzis.

"That's why it's so important to ask yourself: What are my most passionate social, political and spiritual beliefs? Why are these important to me? And what is the origin of these beliefs?"

TOOLS TO CONNECT

Ken's "experimental week" in yeshiva was a heady one. He participated in the regular class schedule and – to avoid getting "swept away" – took frequent breaks to process the material. One evening, Ken was relaxing in the yeshiva's expansive front yard, pondering the day's events, when Rav Noah approached.

"How's it going?" Rav Noah asked with a pat on the back. "Are you enjoying Torah study?"

"I love the practical wisdom," Ken said with a smile. "But something is bothering me. Why does Judaism have so many rules about what you can eat and all the other restrictions?"

Rav Noah explained, "Every musician, athlete and artist knows that boundaries are essential to the creative endeavor. In basketball, dribbling and staying in bounds provide context for the game. Similarly, Torah's 613 mitzvahs are the Divinely ordained framework for a successful life."

Ken was confused. "I thought there were only Ten Commandments, not 613. Why so many?"

"The word mitzvah (מִצְוָה) is rooted in the word *tzavta* (צַוְתָּא) – a connective bond," Rav Noah said. "Every mitzvah is a connection-point to the transcendent dimension. Mitzvahs are not about rote habit and trying to rack up as many points as possible. The goal of every mitzvah is to connect with God."

"So where should a person start?" Ken asked.

"You can start anywhere. Judaism isn't all-or-nothing," Rav Noah explained. "But there are six constant mitzvahs – such as 'Know God' and 'Love God' – which apply to every waking moment. These constant mitzvahs are states of mind that gauge our God-awareness."

As they talked, Rav Noah intermittently pointed and snapped his fingers.

"What are you doing, Rabbi?" Ken asked.

"I'm reviewing the six constant mitzvahs. Each landmark represents a different mitzvah. That lamppost is 'love of God.' That storefront is 'awe of God.' The finger-snapping focuses my attention and reinforces my constant connection with the Almighty."

STANDING AT SINAI

The next day, Rav Noah's class on Maimonides discussed the Sinai experience.

"How do we know that Torah is true?" a student asked. "Can an intelligent person really believe that God spoke to the Jewish people at Mount Sinai?"

Rav Noah had heard this question before, yet replied with a fiery energy as if for the first time. "Thousands of religions begin with the claim that God spoke to one person or to a chosen few. Those claims are impossible to verify. By definition, belief in those religions is a matter of faith."

"That's always bothered me about religion in general," a student said.

Rav Noah nodded. "I agree. Yet there is one exception, in a category all its own: The Jewish experience of 'national revelation.' Three thousand years ago, the entire Jewish nation of three million people stood together and heard God speaking at Sinai."

"Rabbi, that feels like ancient history," a student said.

"It's not so long ago," Rav Noah replied. "There are only 120 generations from Sinai till today."

"Maybe over the years, the text was corrupted," a student challenged.

"The accuracy of our text has been carefully preserved," Rav Noah said. "For a Torah scroll to be kosher, every letter must be perfect. That is the Torah's built-in security system for an accurate and unbroken chain of transmission."

"Maybe Mount Sinai was one big conspiracy theory," a student surmised.

"That would mean the entire Jewish nation was in on it," Rav Noah said. "That's highly improbable, given the difficulty of getting even two Jews to agree on anything!"

Ken nodded. From his experience with organizations, he knew this too well.

"Think of it this way," Rav Noah continued. "Why has no other religion ever made a claim of national revelation? Christianity and Islam both sought to replace Judaism as the authentic monotheistic religion. Yet they built their religions on the back of the Jewish experience at Sinai. Why not simply start from scratch?

"The answer is that national revelation cannot be faked. A person might be uncertain about what *someone else* experienced, but they'll never be falsely convinced of their *own* experience."

These words hit Ken like a lightning bolt of logic. But Rav Noah wasn't finished.

"Look at Deuteronomy 4:33," he said, opening a Chumash. "The verse says, 'Has a people ever heard the voice of God, speaking from amidst the fire, as you have heard, and survived?' Three thousand years ago, Torah had the audacity to predict that throughout the course of human history, no other religion will ever make a claim of national revelation.

"That prediction has proven one hundred percent true."

⇒◆⇐

Ken went for a walk and headed to the southern end of the Old City. There, the historic site of King David's palace sat buried beneath millennia of rubble, its historical secrets to be excavated and revealed in ensuing decades. Ken followed the path of the Pilgrim Road, used in Temple times by those ascending to Jerusalem. He waded through the ancient pools of Shiloach, then down the Kidron Valley to the tomb of King David's son, Avshalom.

Ken took a deep breath and pondered his place in Jewish destiny. He thought of the generations of Jews who courageously clung to the Torah way of life. He thought of his grandfather who'd immigrated to Portland in 1898 from a shtetl in Latvia, then became a founding member of Kesser Israel, today a stronghold of Torah Judaism in the Pacific Northwest.

If the purpose of my trip abroad was to gain perspective and reevaluate my value system, Ken thought, *this has been a very rewarding few days.*

CELEBRATING SHABBOS

On Thursday, as Ken's first week in yeshiva drew to a close, conversations buzzed about the coming highlight of the week: Shabbos. "It's like Thanksgiving dinner every week!" one student raved.

Ken was invited to experience his first Shabbos at the home of Rav Noah. Yet aside from an address written on scrap paper – 13 *Imrei Bina, Kiryat Sanz* – Ken didn't know what to expect when stepping into the Weinberg home that Friday evening.

He was immediately struck by the wall-to-wall Jewish books and the intoxicating scent of fresh-baked challah. In the corner of the living room, a cluster of flickering silver candlesticks took his breath away.

"Why so many candles?" he asked Rebbetzin Weinberg.

"One for each member of the family," she explained, "because every individual is unique and precious."

Ken made himself comfortable on the couch, and soon Rav Noah and some students returned from shul. Ken noticed how Rav Noah's first priority was taking his wife aside for a moment of private conversation.

The mood at the Shabbos table was energetic and festive, with robust singing and scrumptious food befitting a royal banquet. Rav Noah made his children the center of attention – entertaining them with stories, questions, treats and show-and-tell of their school-work.

Ken took the opportunity to ask, "Why on Shabbos is there no driving, cooking or writing?"

"The Almighty empowers us to improve the world," Rav Noah said. "Yet we shouldn't mistakenly think we control our destiny. So once every seven days we cease all creative activity and declare, 'I don't run the world.' On Shabbos, we regard our work as 'complete' – not speaking or, ideally, even thinking about it. We relax and connect with family, community, the Almighty and our spiritual self. Shabbos is the simple joy of being."

Between the courses of gefilte fish and chicken soup, Rav Noah engaged the students with a Torah question:

> The Jews are slaves in Egypt, suffering horrific conditions. The verse says, "They groaned because of the work, and their outcry reached God" (Exodus 2:23). Immediately after, the Almighty appears to Moses at the Burning Bush (3:2) with instructions to take the Jews out of Egypt (3:10).
>
> This is an urgent situation of saving lives. Yet instead of heading straight to Egypt, Moses goes to his father-in-law, Yisro, requesting permission to leave (4:18). In doing so, Moses effectively delayed the Jewish people's redemption. What was Moses thinking?
>
> Argue it out. That's Jewish entertainment!

The students presented various theories, which Rav Noah probed and analyzed in a masterful display of logic. Toward the end of the meal, Rav Noah presented his own resolution:

From here we see the power of gratitude. When he arrived in Midian as a refugee, Moses was welcomed into Yisro's home and married Yisro's daughter. Moses understood that before leaving Midian, proper behavior – *derech eretz* – called for gratitude and respect toward Yisro. The Almighty agreed, because only after Moses visited Yisro did God issue the final directive: "Go to Egypt" (4:19).

The lesson for us: Do the right thing, every step of the way. We'll never lose out.

The hour drew late and the meal ended.

"Thank you so much," Ken said. "I truly enjoyed it."

Rav Noah winked. "Now you know why every Jew should experience an authentic Shabbos at least once!"

Ken walked slowly back to the yeshiva, drinking in the sights and sounds of Shabbos in the Holy City. The atmosphere was otherworldly, with everything shut down for twenty-four hours: no stores, restaurants or public transportation. Strolling past a synagogue, Ken overheard the sounds of singing and peeked inside to glimpse a Friday night chassidic gathering (*tisch*). Outside, from the holy to the mundane: One of Jerusalem's infamous cats, descended from the British Mandate era, nibbled at trash from a recently concluded Shabbos meal.

Back at the dorm, Ken lay in bed, hands behind his head. He breathed deeply and pondered: *How incredible to be here in Jerusalem… experiencing Shabbos as we have for thousands of years.*

CHOOSE LIFE

Saturday evening, Jerusalem sprang back to life. Stores and restaurants opened again, buses were running – and it was time for Ken to head back to the kibbutz. The week at yeshiva had been a real eye-opener. Ken's creative juices were energized by the practical wisdom; he was inspired by Rav Noah's combination of joy, humility, idealism and humor; and he found the other students to be idealistic, curious and intellectually honest in seeking answers to life's great questions.

In considering his immediate plans, Ken thought of a class Rav Noah had given earlier that week:

> The Torah says (Deuteronomy 30:19), "I place before you life and death. Choose life!" What does it mean to "choose life"? And what might it mean, as the verse implies, to "choose death"?
>
> The Torah is not speaking of biological life and death, but rather of spiritual connection. "Death" is when we limit ourselves to satisfying the needs of the body: food, sleep, comfort and indulgence. "Life" is when we choose higher, long-term pleasures of the soul – love, meaning, impact, transcendence. "Choose life" means to put the soul in control.
>
> The choice between life or death, between reality or escape, is a choice we make every moment. These two forces are in constant battle. If the body wins, the soul is debased. But if the soul wins, the body becomes a partner in the higher choice.

Ken was at a crossroads and wanted to make a mature, responsible decision. His plan to return to the U.S. in June 1973 was still a ways off, so he decided to stay for one month at yeshiva and immerse himself in Torah study, figuring: *At least I'll be educated. That much I owe to myself and my future family.*

Ken wrapped things up at the kibbutz and enrolled in Shema Yisroel's "Jewish literacy track" – covering the Chumash, the 613 mitzvot, "48 Ways" and various sections of Maimonides.

Ken threw himself into the rhyme and rhythm of Jewish life – prayers, Shabbos, kashrut. To help master the Torah text, Rav Noah taught memory devices and a mental filing system. The more Ken learned, the more things made sense.

One month turned into two, and two months into three.

THE JOYFUL QUADRIPLEGIC

Rav Noah was speaking about handling life's challenges. "We don't control life's circumstances. We can only control our response. Happiness is an attitude. The Talmud says to bless God for the bad, just as we bless for the good."

"That's not realistic," a student challenged. "Anyone who is happy all the time has probably never faced true challenge."

"It's all a matter of focus and appreciation," Rav Noah said, illustrating with a story:

> The Maggid of Mezeritch was asked, "How is it possible to accept suffering with equanimity?"
>
> The Maggid replied, "To answer your question, go see Zusha. He will explain."
>
> Zusha lived in the poor section of town, at the end of a muddy path. There, the visitor found him in a tiny hut, beset by pain and poverty.
>
> "Welcome!" Zusha said. "How can I help you?"
>
> "Please explain how to remain positive in the face of adversity," the visitor said.
>
> "There must be some mistake," Zusha said with surprise. "You shouldn't be asking me. I've never experienced suffering in my life!"

Rav Noah concluded, "No matter how challenging our circumstances, we can rise above it. Be grateful and rejoice in your portion – Zusha on his level, you on yours."

⟜◆⟝

A few days later, one of the yeshiva students approached Ken. "I'm spending this Shabbos at the home of a friend, Avraham Cordish. Would you like to join me?"

"Sure," Ken replied. "Who is he?"

"It's quite a story," the student said. "A few years ago, Avraham was an all-America soccer player and PhD student at the University of Michigan. He was shot in an attempted robbery that left him permanently paralyzed from the neck down. Avraham became a *ba'al teshuva* and is now married and living in Jerusalem."

That Shabbos, Ken had an experience like no other. He sat with Avraham for hours, deep in conversation about the meaning of life.

"After being shot, I lay for weeks in the hospital, immobilized, staring at the ceiling," Avraham said. "Hour after hour, I pondered: *Since I'll never move my limbs again, what is the purpose of life?* I concluded there must be a dimension beyond mere physical existence. That led me to Torah."

Ken had barely digested this idea, when Avraham shared more, "Lying in the hospital, I realized that being shot was a wake-up call to change my life for the better. In that regard, being shot was a good thing. So I accept that everything, even life's challenges, are positive steps in my journey."

Saturday evening, Ken said goodbye, greatly inspired by Avraham's courage, vitality and optimism. On the bus ride back, Kalman told his friend: "Avraham is a regular guy who responded valiantly to life's circumstances and transformed into a holy person. Despite constant pain, hardship and physical confinement, his perspective on life is far clearer than that of most people."

Ken took these lessons to heart and doubled down on developing a positive outlook. "You can focus on the past," he'd say, "but there's no future in it."

EXTENDED TRIP

June 1973. Upon completing the yeshiva's three-month introductory program, Ken arranged to meet with Ron Balshine, his old friend from the Pacific Northwest, at a Jerusalem hamburger stand.

"I've got a problem," Ken said as he heaped condiments onto his burger. "I feel that Shema Yisroel is the place for me. I've never met someone like Rav Noah, full of wisdom and joy, and a mission to empower others to serve the greater good. I want to keep studying Torah."

"That's great!" Ron said. "So what's the problem?"

"I promised my parents that I'd come back for law school."

"But that's not till September," Ron said. "Why leave now?"

"In theory, that's true," Ken said. "But getting my parents on board won't be simple."

Not simple, indeed. At the time, the only way to make an international call from Israel was at the main post office. Even more challenging was the emotional turmoil (at times, hysteria) experienced by some parents upon hearing the news that their child wanted to stay in yeshiva.

Ken headed to the post office on Jaffa Road and placed the call. "I'm extending my stay in Israel for a few months," he told his parents. "This gives me more time at yeshiva, with plenty of time to be at law school in September."

Ken's parents were concerned. They knew nothing about Rabbi Weinberg, Shema Yisroel or even much about Torah itself. Ken was a perennial straight-A student, destined to succeed at any chosen field – and they surely didn't want their upwardly mobile future lawyer becoming religious.

Ken assured them that he was in a good place and growing immensely as a person.

"Okay," they reluctantly agreed. "But no more extensions!"

WALK IN GOD'S WAYS

In the classroom, Rav Noah was teaching Genesis chapter 18: "Abraham is sitting at the entrance to his tent, recuperating from circumcision, when God comes to visit. In the middle of this transcendent experience, Abraham sees three strangers passing by and runs to greet them."

With masterful timing, Rav Noah let the room fall silent, as the weight of the scene sank in.

"Deep down, every human yearns to reach beyond self, to connect with the Source of all existence," Rav Noah said. "Artists think they have it, but God is the real aesthetic experience. Nothing finite, nothing bound in this world can compare.

"Imagine I told you that in the next room, you can speak for an entire hour to the Creator of our universe. Even an atheist admits that talking to God would be the ultimate experience. So why does Abraham leave the conversation with God in order to help some strangers?"

Curious silence.

"Abraham understood that the world is built on kindness. God, Who by definition has no lack, created everything as a pure act of love. The world is one big hospitality inn, a manifestation of the Almighty's absolute love and kindness.

"We are created in the image of God, and our greatest virtue is to 'be like God.' Life is not about 'serving yourself,' but helping others to whatever degree possible. Emulate the Almighty, the ultimate Giver, and become a living, breathing reflection of the Divine!"

Rav Noah leaned forward to deliver the punch line. "Though he was having a direct transcendent experience, Abraham ran to help the strangers because he understood: More important than talking to God is to be like God. By helping others, Abraham was not interrupting the Divine conversation, but deepening it."

⟫•⟪

That night, Ken stayed up late at the yeshiva, composing a list of character traits he hoped to master: Compassion. Generosity. Patience. Optimism. Loyalty. Integrity.

At 3 a.m., Ken decided to call it a night. He walked back to the nearby dorm, deep in thought, enjoying the rarified air of a peaceful Jerusalem night. Suddenly, he spotted Randy, a college student who'd been checking out the yeshiva.

"Shalom!" Ken said with a smile. "Where are you headed at this late hour?"

"I don't know," Randy replied. "I'm enjoying the classes, but I'm not ready for a lifestyle change. I'm moving on."

"Everything is closed at this hour," Ken said. "Why don't you come to my dorm and get a good night's sleep? Then we'll enjoy breakfast and you can be on your way."

Randy was tired and couldn't argue with the offer.

The next morning, Ken helped Randy organize his things. As they walked to breakfast, Ken suggested: "Before you leave, maybe we should stop for a minute to see Rabbi Weinberg."

Randy agreed and, whatever conversation transpired in that room, it changed the course of history. Today, "Reuven" is approaching his fiftieth wedding anniversary, with eleven children and dozens of grandchildren.

Rabbi Baruch Taub, the founding rabbi of the Bayit of Toronto, the largest Orthodox synagogue in North America, reports, "Every day, I study Torah with Reuven. Over the years, he has become an expert in Talmud and Jewish law. Kalman's share of this merit is infinite."

Reuven reflects, "Kalman was genuinely concerned for my welfare, sensing that I was tired and hungry. That act of kindness transformed generations. And I'm still mystified that he was up at 3 a.m."

HEBREW NAME

Day after day at Shema Yisroel, Ken pondered the implications of following the Torah path, in particular the challenges of adopting a lifestyle not shared by his family and friends back home. After six months in yeshiva, he was convinced that Torah is the best path to personal pleasure and the fulfillment of Jewish destiny. He was further convinced that Providence had called upon him to take responsibility for promoting Jewish values. It was a decision that – though it could always be revisited – required wholehearted commitment.

One day, Ken was speaking with a friend at yeshiva. "There's something on my mind," he said. "Everyone knows me as 'Ken.' But I want to raise a Jewish family and maybe live in Israel. So I was thinking to start using my Hebrew name. When I was eight days old, at my bris milah, I was named Kalman, after my great-grandfather. At my bar mitzvah, I was called up to the Torah as Kalman. And God willing, Kalman will be written on my *ketubah*. So I'm thinking to switch from Ken to Kalman. What do you think"?

"Go for it," the friend said. "What's your hesitation?"

"I like the name Kalman," he explained. "But it's unusual. Combined with my unusual last name, I wonder if it's too much."

"Look at it this way," the friend said. "As the only Kalman Packouz on the planet, you're bound to make a unique contribution to the world!"

From that day forward, Ken was Kalman.

DEFERMENT DECISION

By August, it was time to place another difficult call home.

With his parents on the line, Kalman spoke with trepidation. "I've decided to defer law school for a year, to continue my studies and explore how this impacts my life direction."

"You're brainwashed by Rabbi Weinberg!" his parents cried.

Kalman tried to persuade them, but the prospect of their brilliant, talented son waylaying his legal career clashed with their vision and was too much to bear.

Kalman, shattered, went to see Rav Noah.

"It is a great mitzvah to honor your parents," Rav Noah said. "Do whatever you can to alleviate their concerns."

Kalman flew to Portland for a visit and to provide reassurance. That trip proved immensely challenging, due to Kalman's internal conflict of not wanting to disappoint his parents, yet wanting to pursue what his mind, heart and soul told him was the right thing.

"You gave me the gift of life," Kalman told his parents, "and taught me to use my intelligence to find the best path."

"But not this path!" they said.

"You instilled in me many positive Jewish values. I want those values for my life. With today's unstable world, anchoring those values in Jewish tradition will help me pass them on to my children."

Kalman's parents were unwilling to accept this. They sent him to speak with Rabbi Emanuel Rose of Beth Israel, who asked Kalman about his transition from Reform to Orthodox.

"I was taught in Hebrew school that Reform Judaism is about doing Jewish things that one finds meaningful," Kalman explained. "I find all of Judaism meaningful. I guess that makes me the ultimate Reform Jew!"

Frustrated at Kalman's new direction, his parents declared, "We cannot condone that Torah cult!"

Kalman swallowed hard and tried to remain calm. "With all due respect, that's an unfair characterization. Cults try to separate adherents from their family, whereas the Torah says, 'Honor your parents.' That's why I came to see you!

"Second, cults offer an emotional high that cannot withstand intellectual scrutiny. Torah is all about asking questions and using rational evidence to discover the truth.

"Third, cults are all about shutting off your mind and depending on a leader. Torah empowers you to think independently and take personal responsibility.

"Fourth and finally, you raised me to be a proud Jew. If Judaism is a cult, then it's the cult of our ancestors!"

No logic could sway Kalman's parents. They remained adamantly opposed, and even attempted to put Kalman in a mental institution for "deprogramming."

During that trip, far from Rav Noah and the Jerusalem environs, Kalman had time to reassess his perspective. He spent hours of reflection walking the local beaches, forests and mountains. He found peace of mind in the Oregon Caves – his high school stomping grounds, where he served as a tour guide – exploring the miles of solid marble underground pathways.

It was here, back among these wonders of nature, that Kalman forged a deeper connection to God and reaffirmed his commitment to Torah.

SPIRITUAL ACCOUNTING

In September 1973, Kalman returned to Israel, with renewed eagerness to embrace the Torah path. He was glad to be back in Jerusalem, where he most tangibly felt the Jewish people's mission and the possibility of achieving it. The yeshiva – indeed, all of Israel – was gearing up for the High Holidays, and Rav Noah spoke about the sounding of the shofar:

"Rosh Hashanah is when opportunities are set for the coming year. The shofar blast is like an alarm clock, shouting, 'Awaken from your slumber! Evaluate your deeds!' This is a time of introspection and accountability – a reality check to become the best we can be.

"Ask yourself: *What am I living for? What are my lifetime goals? What do I want life to look like ten years from now? If I knew I only had one year to live, how would I spend my time?"*

"What's the best way to ensure we're on target?" a student asked.

"Numbers 21:27 speaks of the 'rulers' who conquer their lower inclination by practicing *cheshbon hanefesh* – a daily self-assessment," Rav Noah replied. "Every CEO understands the need for defined goals and a concrete plan of action. Just as a business regularly reviews its ledgers, so too we have a daily system to assess 'gain versus cost.' Don't just dream about goals. Make a plan to ensure that your actions are consistent with those goals. Do this consistently and become great."

Kalman took *cheshbon hanefesh* seriously. Each night before going to bed, he spent five minutes asking himself:

• What is the most meaningful goal to live for?
• What is my special contribution to advance that goal?
• What did I do today toward my goal?
• What more could I do tomorrow?"

Using a notebook, Kalman faithfully conducted this self-assessment – night after night – for the next forty-six years.

YOM KIPPUR WAR

For the High Holidays, Rav Noah and the students prayed at the legendary Mirrer Yeshiva in Jerusalem. Kalman knew this would be different from his experience in Portland, yet he could not have imagined what awaited on Saturday, October 6, 1973 – Yom Kippur, the holiest day of the Jewish year.

At 2 p.m., on a short break before afternoon prayers, Kalman was walking through Jerusalem's Beit Yisrael neighborhood. Suddenly, the silence of the holy day was shattered by the wail of air raid sirens. Word quickly emerged that in the south, one hundred thousand Egyptian forces had overrun a few hundred Israeli soldiers – then crossed the Suez Canal into the Israeli-controlled Sinai Peninsula. Simultaneously, Syrian forces had invaded the Golan Heights in the north.

All of Israel was thrust into a state of emergency. Soldiers were mobilized; hospitals were emptied of all but critically ill patients; and all trucks and planes were requisitioned.

That afternoon in Jerusalem, Kalman saw a military jeep turn onto the street. A courier carrying mobilization orders entered a synagogue and ascended the podium. He called on the congregation for silence, then read out the names of IDF reservists. By Divine providence, men throughout Israel were easily located in their neighborhood synagogues. Plus, with no vehicular traffic on Yom Kippur, the roads were totally clear, enabling reservists and tanks to mobilize quickly and efficiently. Kalman watched in dread and amazement as men in prayer shawls drove their cars – something strictly forbidden on Yom Kippur, except in life-threatening situations.

Kalman shuddered as he recalled the heartrending *U'nesaneh Tokef* prayer he'd chanted just a few hours earlier: "On Yom Kippur it is sealed... who shall live and who shall die... who by fire and who by sword..."

Aside from a few Vietnam veterans, Kalman and the other yeshiva students had never experienced war so closely. The ensuing days were harrowing, with the students locked down under a full travel ban. Communication was largely cut off, with bits and pieces of news filtering through the grapevine and transistor radios. The sense of anxiety was exacerbated by reports of heavy Israeli losses and retreat. In the north, Syrian troops had conquered the strategic Mount Hermon, raising the specter that the Galilee region, and even all of Israel, could be overrun.

Kalman and the other students volunteered to assist however they could. In the morning, a truck would stop in front of the yeshiva and take them to the old Jerusalem train station, where they'd work to unload sacks of flour, potatoes and sugar. They'd return to yeshiva in the evening and – with all of Jerusalem on wartime blackout – study Torah by candlelight.

One week into the war, things were looking bleak until – to Kalman's pride and delight – the United States agreed to a massive airlift, sending hundreds of cargo planes and tons of materiel to Israel.

The tide turned. In some of history's largest tank battles ever, the Syrians were pushed out of the Golan Heights. In the south, Israeli troops crossed the Suez Canal and surrounded the Egyptian Third Army.

Three weeks after the war began, a cease-fire was reached. At a heavy cost of lives, Israel had not only prevailed, but strengthened its position. Kalman breathed a deep sigh of relief, feeling fortunate to have contributed to this critical time in Jewish history.

KALMAN'S WAY: CHECKLIST FOR GREATNESS

- **Integrity.** Be transparent. Align actions with values. No gain is worthwhile if it comes at ethical expense.

- **Priorities.** Define your mission and set clear, achievable goals.

- **Kindness.** Let your motto be: "Share and care."

- **Objectivity**. Have a system to check that your actions are free of bias.

- **Accountability**. Ensure that you are organized and taking timely, strategic action.

- **Patience**. Take pleasure in your achievements, calm in the knowledge that everything is a process.

- **Loyalty.** When necessary, stand up to defend family, friends and colleagues – even at personal risk.

- **Awareness.** Don't treat problems as obstacles to avoid, but as opportunities to improve.

- **Persistence.** Stay focused on the goal. Maximize your time and avoid distractions.

- **Commitment.** Employ discipline, goal-setting and follow-through.

- **Loyalty.** Be a caring and faithful friend. When necessary, stand up to defend others – even at personal risk.

CHAPTER THREE

Aish HaTorah: Fresh Start

TEN LEADERS

Rav Noah's Thursday evening *mussar schmooze* was a pep-talk on personal ethics:

"Imagine this scene during the Yom Kippur War. A mother peers out the window, with tears in her eyes, as troops and tanks amass at the border, threatening to invade. It's all hands on deck. She peers into the eyes of her beloved eighteen-year-old and – with heartfelt blessings – sends him off to war, to put his life on the line protecting freedom."

"I served in Vietnam," one student said, "and the ethics of war aren't so clear."

"That's why it's critical to understand what you're defending," Rav Noah said. "I once met an Israeli man who'd raised a large family and built a successful business. I asked him, 'What were the best times of your life?' He told me that in 1947, he joined a group that fought for Israeli independence. He carried a gun, which was illegal under British occupation. He told me, 'Had I been caught,

I'd be hanged. Every day, I faced death. But I was truly alive. Those were the best years of my life.' "

Rav Noah let the scene sink in. "People are willing to die to be good. Even more importantly, find out what you're willing to die for. Then proactively and passionately live for it. That's being truly alive!"

Kalman loved the idealism and the confidence, conjuring up images of George Washington crossing the Delaware.

"Fighting for the Jewish people is our most noble endeavor," Rav Noah thundered. "Give me ten leaders! Ten talented, idealistic, passionate young people. We'll create a revolution, bring back the Jewish people and change the world!"

Kalman humbly turned to look behind him, certain that Rav Noah was talking to the other students.

Intrigued, Kalman asked: "What is your definition of a leader?"

"Unlike a follower who waits to be told what to do, a leader identifies the problem and commits to fixing it," Rav Noah said. "There is no such thing as, 'It's not my problem,' or, 'I can't.' A leader takes responsibility for all aspects of the mission and doesn't stop till the job is done. That's how Abraham and Moses both answered the Almighty's call: *Hineini* – 'I am here to serve.'"

Kalman walked out of the session with his head ringing. He'd completed one year in yeshiva and was certain that his calling in life was as a rabbi, not a lawyer. He pondered:

> *I was fortunate to have discovered Torah study and fall in love with being Jewish. I want every Jew to have this same opportunity. Am I serious about emulating Rav Noah as a Torah teacher, lover of the Jewish people and servant of the Almighty? Am I ready to do whatever it takes to be one of the "ten leaders"?*

By March 1974, Kalman signed up for life and strove to be a lieutenant to Rav Noah the general.

"The day I first visited yeshiva," Kalman asked Rav Noah, "why did you tell me to come at eleven o'clock, rather than invite me to sit in on the '48 Ways' class at nine o'clock?"

Rav Noah laughed heartily. "It usually requires great effort to recruit a new student. When you called, and I didn't have to convince you to check out yeshiva, I suspected you were either crazy or a missionary!"

SHIFTING SANDS

By the spring of 1974, the yeshiva's name, Shema Yisroel, had been changed to Ohr Somayach. More significantly, the partners who Rav Noah had originally brought in now opposed his leadership. They sought a more traditional yeshiva, whereas Rav Noah was looking to build a manpower training center to transform the Jewish world.

Visions clashed and it soon became obvious that Rav Noah was no longer welcome. He'd need to find a new home and start over again.

"Rebbe, why is this happening? It's so awful!" Kalman said.

Rav Noah offered perspective. "It looks bad now. But the Torah says, *'Banim atem la'Hashem Elokeichem* – You are children of the Almighty.' A loving parent wants what's best for the child and will do everything to help them succeed. So too, God – with every resource at His disposal and Who loves us more than any parent loves a child – arranges to provide us with maximum blessing."

Kalman was incredulous. "Are you saying there's an upside to this?" he asked.

Rav Noah recognized the teachable moment. "Everyone falls down on occasion. Yet we shouldn't confuse 'falling' with 'failing.' King Solomon says that 'The tzaddik falls seven times – and gets up.' When we encounter obstacles and overcome them, it toughens us to move forward. I've started many organizations and yeshivas, and gained a lot from 'falling seven times.' Starting over is the Almighty's way of advancing the mission to the next level. I am confident that we'll emerge better than ever. My only regret is the lost time in the process."

Kalman was distressed to learn that even high-level Torah Jews can engage in a dispute they are unable to resolve. He discussed the matter with a rabbi, who explained, "There are seventy facets to Torah. Every individual is a diverse mix of personality and experience. We cannot say whose perspective is right or wrong. In fact, both can be correct."

During this time, the yeshiva students were lobbied by both sides – either to join Rav Noah's new institution, or to remain in Ohr Somayach. Kalman was clear where his loyalty lay, yet he was invited to meet with a prominent rabbi who tried to influence his decision.

"Rav Noah is a dreamer and will never be able to sustain an institution," the rabbi argued. "His plan for a revolution will never work. He'll push you to expand your horizons – but who knows if that's best for you."

After listening respectfully to the rabbi's plea, Kalman spoke. "I'm relatively new to the Torah world, so I can't argue with your assessment. But given that Rav Noah started this yeshiva and recruited the other rabbis to join, wouldn't logic say to support Rav Noah?"

The next day, Kalman related the conversation to Rav Noah, who beamed with pride at this display of loyalty and courage.

Years later, Kalman reflected, "Bringing that joy to Rav Noah was a highlight of my life."

FIRE OF TORAH

In the summer of 1974, Kalman went back to visit family and friends in Oregon – while Rav Noah strategized his next move.

Rebbetzin Weinberg suggested opening a new yeshiva in the Old City of Jerusalem. This was just seven years after the Six Day War and, with most of the Jewish Quarter having been destroyed by Jordanians, the area was under heavy reconstruction, with the unpaved alleyways populated by donkey carts hauling construction materials.

Rav Noah secured a ground-floor apartment at the corner of Misgav Ladach and Chayei Olam streets, near the top of the steps leading to the Western Wall. With millions of people visiting the Wall, this location was perfect for drop-in classes.

On Rosh Chodesh Elul 5734 (August 19, 1974), the new yeshiva – Aish HaTorah – opened its doors. That week, Kalman flew back to Israel, headed straight to Jerusalem's Old City, and was inducted as one of Aish's first six students.

The yeshiva's Crusader-era apartment had majestic stone arches and artistic masonry. Yet accommodations were rustic, especially by American standards. The living room served as both a study hall and dining hall. The two bedrooms served as offices. In the evening, strategically placed mattresses turned the apartment into a dormitory. In the winter, the ceiling leaked, and a system of heated bricks was a primitive attempt to cut the chill.

Yet the yeshiva was on fire, with fresh energy and excitement, a stone's throw from the holiest spot on Earth. That Thursday, Rav Noah stood before the six students and explained why he chose the name, Aish HaTorah:

> In talmudic times, Rebbe Akiva was a forty-year-old shepherd who could not even read the *alef-beis*. One day, he sat by a stream and noticed that a constant drip of water, day after day, had carved a hole in a rock. Rebbe Akiva concluded, "If something as soft as water can carve into solid rock, how much more can the fire of Torah – *Aish HaTorah* – make an indelible impression on my soft heart."

Rebbe Akiva went on to become the greatest sage of his generation, with 24,000 students.

Rav Noah asked, "Besides mentioning Aish HaTorah, what is the message of this story?"

A student spoke up: "Like us, Rebbe Akiva began learning only later in life. This story shows that it's never too late to start."

"Correct," Rav Noah said. "Yet there's an even deeper theme. Rebbe Akiva had despaired of becoming great, and the water on the rock was an epiphany. To the naked eye, each drop appeared to have no impact. Yet over time, those drops caused a transformation. Rebbe Akiva concluded: In spiritual growth, every drop of effort combines to create a breakthrough."

Rav Noah then spoke to the six students as if addressing a crowd of thousands: "This same idea applies to our mission to teach Torah wisdom. This week, with the founding of Aish HaTorah, we begin a process that – drop after drop, with our combined dedication and the Almighty's help – will bring about a revolution!"

SPIRITUAL JOY

One of Aish HaTorah's first teachers was Rabbi Zelig Pliskin, who taught daily classes in *parasha*, mitzvahs, Talmud and – during Rav Noah's travels abroad for fundraising – "48 Ways to Wisdom."

Rabbi Pliskin introduced Kalman to his first taste of Talmud. As a pragmatist, Kalman found Talmud study a bit too theoretical, yet he respected the rigorous intellectual process. One fellow student explained, "My law firm encouraged me to attend yeshiva for a year, because Talmud study sharpens your logical thinking and gives you an edge in problem-solving."

That Sukkos, Rabbi Pliskin hosted Kalman for the holiday and explained, "Sukkos is known as the 'holiday of joy.' We leave our regular home, with its comforts and conveniences, and dwell in this temporary sukkah."

Kalman was puzzled. "Yet if Sukkos is a time to rejoice, why should we sit in a frail hut that seemingly disturbs our happiness?"

Rabbi Pliskin explained, "When we recognize that material possessions are temporary, and that life's greatest pleasures are in the spiritual realm, that is a tremendous source of joy."

Kalman became enamored with Rabbi Pliskin's combination of humility, joy and infectious zest for life – and launched a lifelong friendship.

POWER OF SPEECH

In 1975, Rabbi Pliskin, whose father had studied with the saintly Chofetz Chaim in Poland, published the first of his twenty-seven books: *Guard Your Tongue*, exploring the prohibition of *lashon hara* – gossip or other negative speech that arouses animosity and may cause physical, psychological or financial harm. Rabbi Pliskin taught:

> Speech and communication are humanity's most potent tool. God desires that people live together in peace and unity. *Lashon hara* causes division and separation, destroys friendships and careers, and causes pain even at great distance.
>
> Harming someone with words is considered worse than harming them financially, because damage from words once spoken cannot be erased. As King Solomon says, "Life and death are in the power of the tongue."

Rabbi Pliskin then outlined the basic rules of clean speech:

- Promote others' well-being. When in doubt, don't speak out.
- Don't pull people down. Focus on the positive.
- Humor is great, but not at others' expense.

- Be kind to yourself. Don't self-deprecate.
- Think before you speak – especially if you're angry, hurt or jealous.
- Don't listen to gossip. If you can't change the conversation, politely leave.
- If you hear damaging information, don't accept it as true without investigating.
- Always give others the benefit of the doubt.

Kalman was blown away by the degree of care that Judaism places on speaking with positive, uplifting words. "What is the litmus test of ethical speech?" he asked.

"Simple," Rabbi Pliskin explained. "Does it raise people up, or put them down?"

Kalman walked down to the Western Wall, where teams of archeologists were busy uncovering antiquities from Temple times. Suddenly it dawned on Kalman: *My Hebrew school de-emphasized the ritual aspects of Judaism, in favor of ethical values like kindness and justice. Yet clean speech is an entire category of ethical behavior that was never mentioned!*

From that day forward, Kalman made it his business not to speak *lashon hara*. In the event he found himself in a conversation with someone speaking negatively, he had a technique to stop it without causing tension or embarrassment – a "vest pocket" question, specifically a non-sequitur, to pull out and change the topic. Kalman would ask: "Who was the only pitcher to ever throw two consecutive no-hitters?"

People would look quizzically and respond, "Who cares?" or, "I hate baseball" or, "It's football season!" Yet on Kalman's scorecard, it was a win-win – because the conversation invariably made a 180-degree turn in a less toxic direction. (The answer: Johnny Vander Meer of the 1938 Cincinnati Reds.)

FIRST RESPONDER

Rav Noah had a special knack for assigning each yeshiva student the role most suited to their personality and skill set. Kalman was a natural leader with a warm, personable style, who understood people and truly sought their good. His assignment: Big Brother, to welcome new students and provide a stable, supportive presence during their acclimation to Torah life.

In this role, Kalman would show new students to their room, familiarize them with the yeshiva premises and schedule, and provide a map for navigating the maze of Jewish Quarter alleyways. In addition, Kalman patiently taught new students the basics of morning prayers and how to put on tefillin.

When Tom Meyer, a journalist with the *Detroit News*, first came to Aish HaTorah in 1975, he was led to an Old City apartment that served as a dormitory. Tom was assigned a comfortable room, where he put down his things, then went to explore his new abode. In the living room, he noticed one bed tucked into a corner, with a sheet serving as a makeshift divider. The small space afforded little privacy or comfort, yet Tom observed that someone was using it as a bedroom.

"Whoever sleeps there must be low on the totem pole," Tom remarked.

"That's Kalman Packouz's bed," came the reply.

Tom was taken aback, as it contradicted his paradigm of viewing life from the perspective of self-interest.

Later that day, Tom caught up with Kalman. "You've been in yeshiva for two years," Tom said, annoyed at having his assumptions shaken. "So why are you sleeping in a corner, rather than in the nice room I was assigned?"

Kalman's response impacted Tom's life forever. "If you'd been assigned an uncomfortable space, you might not stay in yeshiva. I prefer the inconvenience, so you can study Torah."

IF YOU KNOW *ALEF*

On Saturday evenings, after the conclusion of Shabbos, Rav Noah conducted outreach training sessions at his home, as a way to develop the yeshiva students into leaders.

"If you ever had the opportunity to save a life, you know how precious that is," Rav Noah said. "Even greater is to connect someone with meaning and purpose. God loves every human and never gives up on one of His children. The Talmud says: *Kol Yisrael areivim zeh ba'zeh* – every Jew is responsible for one another. We're all in this together, and that's why it's important to reach out to others. A 'chance meeting' in a bus or bank might be that person's only opportunity to connect."

Kalman, the pragmatic-idealist, spoke up, "But Rebbe, we haven't studied enough to teach!"

Rav Noah rejected the premise: "A man named Eliyahu Essas lives in the Soviet Union, where it is illegal to study Torah. A few years ago, he had no Torah teacher and didn't know how to read *alef-beis*. So he obtained underground books, hid from the KGB and taught himself.

"Today, Essas is one of the few Torah teachers out of five million Soviet Jews. When people come to study with him – always in secret – he says, 'My time is in great demand. I will teach you on condition that you teach others."

Rav Noah concluded, "When fires are infrequent, a single company of firefighters is sufficient. Yet when spiritual and social 'fires' are common, every community requires volunteers. So don't sell yourself short. Everyone who knows even a small amount of Torah can share it according to their ability. With one piece of wisdom, you can make an impact. If you know *alef*, teach *alef*!"

———⇒◆⇐———

Kalman could not shake the image of Soviet Jews hovering in a cellar, studying Torah in secret. This strengthened his appreciation for Torah – "the tree of life for all who grasp it."

Soon after, a non-religious young man, a recent graduate of Yale University, came to study Torah in Jerusalem. Kalman was assigned to welcome him and help with whatever was needed.

"How did you wind up at yeshiva?" Kalman asked.

"In college, I majored in the Russian language and went to study as an exchange student in Moscow," he explained. "A few months ago, I heard about a celebration for the Jewish holiday of Simchat Torah. I went and saw tens of thousands of Jews dancing in front of Moscow's Great Synagogue. *Nobody* dances in the streets in Moscow! Yet these Jews, under the eyes of the KGB, were full of joy.

"I connected with some Russian refuseniks who were teaching Torah illegally. I attended a class and noticed that the teacher seemed quite novice. I asked, 'How long have you been studying Torah?' He replied, 'I've attended classes a few time a week, for six months. Torah is so precious that I'm risking my life to study. My teacher is risking his life to teach me. I'm willing to risk my life to pass it on.'"

The young Yale grad looked at Kalman and said, "The power of that message is what brought me to study Torah in Jerusalem."

ATHEIST'S PRAYER

In the summer of 1975, an American student named Jeff, prior to entering Harvard Business School, was in Norway visiting his non-Jewish fiancée. Having never been to Israel, Jeff decided to visit.

Standing at the Western Wall in jeans and a cardboard kippah, Jeff felt a spiritual spark and was moved to utter what could be called an "atheist's prayer":

God, I don't believe in you. But maybe I'm making a mistake. So if you're there, God, please make an introduction.

Suddenly, Jeff felt a tap on the shoulder. Startled, he whirled around and shouted, "What the *blankety-blank-dash-bang* do you want?!"

"Would you like to learn about God?" the seemingly omnipresent Rabbi Meir Schuster asked.

Before Jeff could answer, and still shocked by the serendipity of events, he was hauled up the stairs of the Jewish Quarter and into the Aish HaTorah study hall, then handed off to the designated first responder, Kalman Packouz.

For the next few days, Kalman took Jeff under his wing, sitting together at meals and touring Jerusalem. Kalman sensed that Jeff would enjoy Torah study and persuaded him to postpone the next leg of his trip to Greece. Due largely to Kalman's care and persistence, Jeff spent the next two months at yeshiva, where he became Torah observant.

During this time, Jeff noticed a young religious woman in the Old City of Jerusalem and uttered a prayer, *May God help me find a wife like this.*

Upon returning to Boston to begin MBA studies, who did Jeff meet at Shabbos services? Yes, that same young woman he'd admired in Jerusalem. Jeff approached her, introduced himself and said, "I saw you in Jerusalem."

"Yes, I know," she replied. "I saw you, too.'"

They were married one year later.

BNEI BRAK BONDING

In those early days of Aish HaTorah, Kalman filled a key role as Rav Noah's right-hand administrator and problem-solver. At the time, Kalman bought a secondhand Subaru station wagon, both for the convenience and as a way to serve the cause. "However the car can be helpful," Kalman told Rav Noah, "it will be my privilege."

"As a matter of fact," Rav Noah said, "every Thursday, I travel to Bnei Brak to speak with the leader of the generation, Rabbi Elazar Shach, about issues confronting the Jewish people. Riding together will give us the opportunity to talk."

Kalman was thrilled with the suggestion. In those pre-cellphone days, this afforded Kalman hours of uninterrupted, private time to ask questions and probe the depth of Rav Noah's teachings.

That Thursday, while driving to Bnei Brak, Kalman inquired about the reason for the weekly meetings.

"Aish HaTorah is breaking new ground in Jewish education," Rav Noah explained. "Sticking your head out of the crowd always invites criticism. Some well-intentioned people might complain to Rav Shach. At these weekly meetings, I discuss our approach and get Rav Shach's guidance and advice. This will hopefully preempt any complaints about us."

In Bnei Brak, Kalman was awed by the grand Ponevezh Yeshiva, its ornate sixteenth-century 22-carat gold Ark representing the pinnacle of Torah scholarship. Kalman was even more impressed by how Rav Shach sat humbly on a wooden bench, eschewing all trappings of honor. Kalman was further gratified to see Rav Noah humble himself before a more prominent rabbi. Most impressive of all was Rav Shach standing in honor when Rav Noah – whom he called the "*mumcheh* (expert) in Jewish outreach" – entered the room.

The two rabbis met privately, while Kalman went to explore the yeshiva. An hour later, Rav Noah emerged and they drove back to Jerusalem. Week after week, Kalman was the designated driver for these visits to Bnei Brak – cementing his lifelong partnership with Rav Noah.

Over the decades, one of the only times Kalman heard Rav Noah get angry was when someone spoke disrespectfully about

Rav Shach. "Torah tradition is all we have," Rav Noah rebuked. "Tearing that down is uprooting the Jewish people's most valued asset. You are free to disagree on issues, but to personally attack a humble, sincere bearer of our tradition, is to assault the very essence of our nation."

LOYAL FAMILY

Kalman considered Aish HaTorah his "spiritual family." The students – raised by the same spiritual guide, under the same roof and devoted to common cause – were a band of brothers.

Rav Noah regarded team loyalty as a cardinal value. He explained, "Exodus 1:8 says that 'a new king arose over Egypt who did not know Joseph.' In truth, the king knew very well that Joseph had built the Egyptian economy – yet was unwilling to acknowledge it. Torah stands for the opposite: gratitude and loyalty. That's why God's description of Moses' outstanding trait is 'faithful' [*ish ne'eman*, Numbers 12:7]."

This emphasis on loyalty was manifest in Rav Noah's organizational approach, where he routinely forgave failures as part of the entrepreneurial process. On the personal side, Rav Noah modeled loyalty by flying internationally to visit students in need of spiritual and emotional guidance.

——◆——

Kalman personified loyalty to God, the Jewish people and Rav Noah's mission. Yet his loyalty was not a matter of switching off his brain and following blindly. Rather, it was driven by the belief that Judaism is humanity's most precious asset and provides the richest life possible. Kalman also knew that hitching his wagon to Rav Noah, a once-in-a-generation visionary, provided the best opportunity to impact the Jewish people.

"Rav Noah leads the way," Kalman said. "I'm just hanging onto his coattails."

On one occassion, at the Aish international meetings, Rav Noah was asked to go around the room and sum up each person in one word. When it came to Kalman, Rav Noah conferred the accolade: "Loyalty."

INTERNAL OPPOSITION

With the memories still fresh of Rav Noah's dismissal from the previous yeshiva he'd founded, Aish HaTorah students were on guard against any internal opposition.

One morning in yeshiva, there were rumblings of rebellion against Rav Noah. "We can do better!" the rebels vowed. Rav Noah was upset to hear about this and discussed it with Kalman.

"'We can do better' is actually a backhanded compliment," Kalman said, trying to ease the mood. "At the beginning of any groundbreaking initiative, people say, 'You're crazy, it can't be done.' When you've had some success, they say, 'We knew it all along.' Genuine success is when they say, 'We can do better.'"

Rav Noah loved this quote and repeated it over the years when encountering naysayers.

—————◆—————

On another occasion, an Aish HaTorah staffer was agitating against Rav Noah. To garner support, the agitator approached the esteemed Rabbi Chaim Walkin, Aish HaTorah's first advanced-level Talmud instructor.

"Rav Noah is introducing new methodologies," the agitator said. "This is inappropriate and must be stopped."

Rabbi Walkin listened with great concern. "I suggest speaking about this with Rav Shach. Let's you and I go see him this after-noon."

And so it was. That afternoon the two traveled to Bnei Brak, where the agitator told Rav Shach his complaints against Rav Noah.

"This is very troublesome and urgent," Rav Shach said. "I will call Rabbi Weinberg right now, while you're sitting here."

Rav Shach picked up the phone and dialed the yeshiva.

"Good afternoon, Aish HaTorah," the secretary said. "How may I help you?"

"I'd like to speak with Rabbi Weinberg."

"Who may I say is calling?"

"Luzer Shach." (Yiddish for Elazar)

Rav Noah stood up in respect for the great sage and took the call. "In what merit am I privileged to receive this call?" Rav Noah asked.

"I'm here with Rabbi So-and-so. He told me everything that's going on at your yeshiva, and how he's stirring a rebellion against you."

Rav Noah waited for the other shoe to drop.

Rav Shach continued, "We're calling to say that he is very sorry and promises not to make trouble again."

Later that day, Rav Noah related the incident to Kalman, who was giddy with joy. They agreed: Every hour and every mile, back and forth to Bnei Brak, was well worth it.

SAVING SIX MILLION

By 1977, Aish HaTorah was making inroads in the Jewish world as a hub of high-profile activity. That year, Israel's most famous entertainer and movie star, Uri Zohar, set off an uproar by becoming a *ba'al teshuva*. Zohar was enamored with Rav Noah's teachings, and they spent many hours studying together.

Zohar used his star status to get Rav Noah meetings with Israeli Prime Ministers Yitzhak Rabin and Yitzhak Shamir. On one occasion, cabinet minister David Levy visited Aish HaTorah for the bris of Zohar's son. Zohar joked that they were forbidden to be there, as the building was the subject of a legal battle between Aish HaTorah and the Israeli government. Levy responded that the building would remain Aish HaTorah's. And so it was.

―――――――

That same year, Rav Noah celebrated the birth of his son Yehuda. For the bris, Rav Shach came to Aish HaTorah – a visit that caused great excitement. Rav Shach was thrilled to see the fruits of Rav Noah's work, guided in no small part by their weekly meetings in Bnei Brak. Rav Shach inquired of the assembled, "Who here is a *ba'al teshuva?*" To his surprise, nearly everyone raised his hand.

Inspired, Rav Shach rose to speak, as the crowd fell silent in rapt attention. "Today there is a battle against assimilation," he declared. "If one person could kill six million Jews, one person can save six million."

Those words touched Kalman's core. He now understood the "power of one": Just as every person has the potential to destroy the planet, we have equal power to elevate all humanity.

―――――――

Also in 1977, Kalman's yeshiva friend Chaim (Mike) Willis was thrown into the global spotlight when the "counterculture bible," *Rolling Stone* magazine, published a 20,000-word piece entitled, "Next Year in Jerusalem," chronicling Chaim's spiritual journey at Aish HaTorah. The article was authored by Chaim's progressive-activist sister, Ellen Willis, who visited Jerusalem and wrote:

> Mike's premises were not only far more sophisticated than I had thought; they were the basis of a formidably comprehensive, coherent world view. All along Mike had been asking me questions I couldn't answer. How did I explain the creation of the world?

How did I explain the strange history of the Jews – their unremitting persecution and unlikely survival, their conspicuous role in world affairs? How did I explain the Torah itself, with its extraordinary verbal intricacy…

There began to be moments – usually early in the morning, before I forced myself to get up and face the day – when I was more inclined than not to believe that it was all true, that I was only resisting because I couldn't stand the pain of admitting how wrong I was. What about the prophecies… and the way modern history seemed almost a conspiracy to drive the Jews back to Israel.

Though intellectually and emotionally swayed, Chaim's sister ultimately chose not to become Torah-observant. From this, Kalman learned a key lesson in Jewish education: religious observance and belief in God is a personal choice. Nothing can be imposed on anyone. People act when they are ready, each at their own pace and level.

The *Rolling Stone* article carried enormous credibility, and its honest reflection had profound impact on spiritual seekers worldwide. Indeed, young Jews visiting the Far East were often told by Buddhist monks to read the *Rolling Stone* article and check out their own heritage in Jerusalem.

By the late-1970s, word was getting out about a Torah revolution in Jerusalem.

GIVING & RECEIVING

Kalman was meeting with Rav Noah when they were interrupted by a student excited to share good news. "Rebbe, did you hear that Shmuel is engaged?"

"That's wonderful!" Rav Noah responded. "Thank you so much for telling me."

A few minutes later, another student came to share the same news. A minute after that, a third student did the same. Each time, Rav Noah responded with equal enthusiasm, "Wonderful! Thank you so much for telling me."

Kalman was startled by Rav Noah's response, given that most people would be upset at the intrusion, or deflate the messenger's enthusiasm by saying, "I already heard."

When the stream of students petered out, Kalman asked, "Rebbe, why did you do that?"

Rav Noah explained, "Each student wanted to share good news. It's my job to accept it graciously, whether I need it or not."

Kalman was amazed at Rav Noah's patience and sensitivity, and asked for the source of this idea.

"In Genesis chapter 18, Abraham feeds the angels disguised as people," Rav Noah explained. "But angels don't eat! They only *appeared* to benefit from the food. Abraham desperately wanted to give, and accepting the food was their way of 'giving him the opportunity to give' – even if they didn't need it."

This lesson resonated deeply with Kalman. As a young man, he'd saved up money to buy someone an expensive gift. He looked forward to the recipient's joy upon receiving the gift, and anticipated their appreciation for his thoughtfulness. Yet upon giving the gift, the response was different than Kalman expected.

"You shouldn't have spent so much money," the recipient said. "Especially because I'll never use this."

The recipient then thrust the gift back into Kalman's hand, saying, "Take it back and get a refund."

Kalman felt rejected, disrespected and deflated.

The recipient then added, "You want me to be honest, right?"

Kalman wanted to say, "Actually, I'd prefer to see your face light up, as you graciously accept the gift with the same expression of love with which it was given. Then, after I leave, you could either give it away, take it back to the store, or toss it in the trash."

Yet Kalman didn't say any of that. Instead, he bit his tongue.

Now, years later, hearing the story of Abraham and the angels, Kalman understood that his intuition was correct: Whenever someone cares enough to give, our task is to receive it graciously – and make them feel like a million bucks.

FINDING THE ONE

Rav Noah was speaking with the students about love and relationships. "Why get married?" he asked.

"For companionship," one student offered.

"For convenience," said another.

"For a tax break," suggested a third.

Rav Noah shook his head. "Marriage is a holy bond that unites two halves of a whole. Marriage is the commitment that two people make to pursue common life goals together. Marriage is where we master the art of giving."

——➤➥——

At age twenty-seven, Kalman felt ready to get married. He set out in search of a lifetime partner, going on dozens of *shidduch* dates. None of those dates panned out. Yet Kalman was undeterred, given Rav Noah's similar path years earlier to finding a match. "The search for a soulmate is like seeking a lost item," Kalman said. "I shall keep looking!"

Before long, Kalman had exhausted the pool of young American women in Israel and was in need of new prospects. He visited the Midrasha women's seminary and spoke with a staff member about a potential English-speaking match.

Shoshana Kramer, age nineteen, had moved with her family from the U.S. to Israel a few years earlier. Though raised observant, Shoshana always hoped to marry a *ba'al teshuva*. "I grew up doing mitzvot, without thinking much about God," she says. "I sensed that *ba'alei teshuva* have a certain 'fire' of living with the reality of God."

One day, the seminary staffer was speaking with a friend. "I met a bright and charming *ba'al teshuva* named Kalman Packouz," she said enthusiastically. Shoshana's friend overheard the conversation and immediately dialed the Kramer home. "I heard about a *ba'al teshuva* guy who sounds terrific," she told Shoshana. "Just don't laugh at his name!"

At the time, the *teshuva* movement was still new, and the idea of dating a *ba'al teshuva* was atypical. But Shoshana's father, who'd become *ba'al teshuva* at a young age, appreciated the potential upside.

At the time, one of the Kramer's neighbors, Rabbi Moshe Lazerus, was teaching at Aish HaTorah. Shoshana's father dialed the Aish office and got Rabbi Lazerus on the phone. "Bottom line," Shoshana's father said, "would you let your daughter marry Kalman Packouz?"

"Absolutely," Rabbi Lazerus replied. "I respect your family for its sincerity and integrity, and Kalman excels at these same qualities." (Providentially, Kalman happened to be standing nearby… but Rabbi Lazerus didn't let on.)

Later that day, Rabbi Lazerus spoke with Kalman and encouraged him to give it a try.

Following their first date, Kalman returned to the yeshiva and told his friends, "I met the perfect woman. But I don't expect she'll go out with me again."

Kalman knew that Shoshana was sharp and that he'd need to present a cogent life mission and vision. On their second date, he spoke about his dream of working to revitalize the Jewish people by educating adult Jews about the beauty and wisdom of their heritage.

Shoshana was attracted to Kalman's idealism and joyful spirit. "Kalman always maintained that *ba'al teshuva* freshness," she says.

"He was a real person. Real with his strengths and his weaknesses. Real with God. Real with everything."

On their third date, they spoke about family backgrounds. Shoshana has four brothers, and Kalman asked her to write down their names. She was impressed, assuming that he wished to remember their names. Kalman had another motive, however. He'd studied graphology in high school and considered handwriting analysis a good way to reveal undetected issues.

This method proved particularly popular among Aish HaTorah students, all thousands of miles away from home and transitioning to a new lifestyle. Whenever a *shidduch* showed potential, students would have a graphologist analyze the handwriting (a legitimate method discussed in traditional Torah sources, albeit with a margin of error).

The graphology report came back positive. After just four dates, Kalman and Shoshana were engaged – leaving some friends and family surprised, given their eight-year age difference and diverse religious backgrounds.

Subsequently, in the name of transparency, Kalman told Shoshana about the handwriting analysis – hoping she wouldn't be upset. "I'm also interested in graphology," she said. "We're on the same page with that."

Following the engagement, Kalman encouraged other students who were having trouble finding their match, saying, "The long search was totally worth it!"

WEDDING DAY

As Kalman's wedding day approached, Rav Noah offered words of advice. "A happy wife makes a happy life. Every day when you come home, devote at least the first fifteen minutes to your spouse. Ask three questions: What did you do today? How are you feeling? What are you thinking about?"

After a six-month engagement, the wedding day finally arrived. Kalman ran errands in Jerusalem, accompanied by Gedalia Zweig, a *shomer* (guardian) to ensure that no harm befalls the groom. Kalman's head was in the clouds, and at one point he absent-mindedly stepped off the sidewalk and into the busy traffic of Malchei Yisrael Street. At that moment, a motorbike came whizzing by. Gedalia instinctively grabbed Kalman's arm and pulled him back – as the motorbike barely missed crashing into Kalman.

Kalman was shaken by the close call. Fortuitously, a moment later, they bumped into Rebbetzin Weinberg, who was thrilled to hear of the pre-wedding miracle.

That evening at Jerusalem's Central Hotel (now Prima Palace), four hundred guests joined the wedding celebration. Following Jerusalem custom, the live music consisted of only a singer and drummer. Yet the lively spirit carried the night. Kalman was euphoric, envisioning the warm and loving Jewish home that Shoshana and he would build together.

Kalman's parents flew in from Portland. Though they opposed him becoming *ba'al teshuva*, they enjoyed meeting his friends and classmates. Kalman's father commented with pride, "It is difficult to find a more dedicated Jew than Kalman."

Kalman's parents loved the experience of their first traditional Jewish wedding – which they'd only previously seen in *Fiddler on the Roof*. On the airplane home, the in-flight movie was, appropriately, *Fiddler on the Roof*.

KALMAN'S WAY: KINDNESS

- Treat others with dignity and respect.

- Greet people joyfully and cheer up anyone who is sad.

- Judge others favorably.

- Offer constructive criticism.

- Speak out against injustice.

- Assist others in earning a livelihood.

- Proffer good advice, wisdom and mentorship.

- Be respectful of other opinions, even if you disagree.

- Take joy in, and pray for, others' success.

- Alleviate others' pain and discomfort.

- Respect people's privacy.

- Love kindness. Happiness comes from doing what you love. A master of kindness is a master of joy.

- Every situation has its reason. Continually ask people, "What can I do for you?"

- Ask yourself, "If I were this person, what would I want others to do for me?"

- Everyone needs encouragement. Ask yourself, "What encouraging words can I say?"

- You have a unique set of skills, knowledge and resources. Ask yourself, "In what unique way can I help others?"

- When other people act with kindness, ask yourself, "What can I learn from this to be more kind?"

CHAPTER FOUR

Promoting Jewish Identity

CUT FLOWER

Kalman and Rav Noah were on their weekly trip to Bnei Brak. "Rebbe, the Jewish community seems to barely focus on young adult education," Kalman said. "What makes you different?

Rav Noah became pensive and explained, "I was sixteen when my father passed away. I didn't want my mother, a widow, to bear the burden of support. So during yeshiva vacations, I became a salesman, traveling by train across the United States – to Texas, Colorado, California.

"The Jews I met had pride in their heritage, but little connection to Torah. I knew that Jewish pride can't be based on good feelings alone. Like a cut flower, Judaism severed from its source loses vitality. That's why today's generation is hard-pressed to answer the question: *Why be Jewish?* Do you think the alternatives – Buddhism, Christianity, Transcendental Meditation – are more enlightening than our Torah? Jews don't leave Judaism out of disenchantment, but due to ignorance… drifting away without a fight."

For Kalman, this reality hit home when a Jewish high school friend became a born-again Christian. Kalman was both heartbroken and dumbfounded that someone so bright would choose a life path without giving Judaism a fair hearing. "Be intellectually honest," Kalman had implored his friend. "Compare Jewish and Christian theology. We are the original, with direct connection to God, no intermediary necessary. Discover the beauty of being Jewish!"

"What can we do to reverse this trend?" Kalman asked Rav Noah.

"Teach *Toras Chaim* – relevant Jewish wisdom. Every Jew deserves a chance to explore their heritage in an atmosphere of open questioning and mutual respect. Minimally, we need to ensure that Jews marry Jewish – because intermarriage is often the first step of the Jewish line becoming lost forever.

"The situation is urgent, and those who understand what's at stake can prevent this calamity. The Torah teaches: 'Do not stand idly by your brother's blood.' If someone is drowning and you can help – jump in!"

Kalman flashed back to March 13, 1964, a date seared in his thirteen-year-old consciousness. That day, Kitty Genovese was murdered in New York City. As the murder took place, police were summoned to the scene, but did not respond. More shockingly, apparently no bystanders came to her aid as the murderer tried once – then returned again – to kill her.

The American public was horrified. Young Kalman was horrified. He resolved never to rely on others to take action when someone needs help.

That evening, Kalman gathered some fellow students to brainstorm a campaign to encourage people to take a closer look at Torah. The result was a poster depicting a bagel and cream cheese, with the caption, "Is this the culmination of 3,500 years of Jewish heritage?"

FAMILY CRISIS

For Kalman, the crisis of assimilation ceased to be theoretical in 1975, when word arrived that his younger brother was engaged to a non-Jewish woman. Kalman was distraught. "Rebbe, what should I do?" he asked Rav Noah.

"In America today, the broader Jewish community still appreciates the importance of Jews marrying Jews," Rav Noah said. "So make the case to your brother. He may not like it, but being a brother is not a popularity contest. You have an obligation to share your concerns. Never with anger, always with love."

For Kalman, it was unimaginable that his brother would be cut off from the beauty, wisdom and joy of Jewish life. So he wrote letters that harnessed evidence from sociology, history, philosophy and science to support the relevance and veracity of Torah.

After a few weeks without headway, Kalman placed an international call.

"If you love me, you'll respect my decision," his brother said.

"Actually, it's because I love you and care about you, that I can't in good conscience stand by," Kalman said. "Being Jewish is not a mere preference of style or taste. As the role models of ethical monotheism, the Jewish people have a special mission. It's our core identity!"

Kalman's brother objected to the premise. "Opposing this marriage is racist."

"Let's define our terms," Kalman said, trying to stay calm. "'Racism' is the belief in someone's inherent value based on race. Yet there are Chinese Jews, Moroccan Jews, Ethiopian Jews, Russian Jews, Eskimo Jews and Indian Jews. Anyone can become Jewish by converting, and is equally accepted as every other Jew. Nobody could construe Judaism as racist."

"But my fiancé has no interest in converting," Kalman's brother said. "So your opposition is hostile toward non-Jews."

"I love every human being, and I'm all for tolerance and multi-culturalism," Kalman said. "But utopian society isn't a monolithic melting pot as popularly theorized. Humanity is not a single instrument that's part-trumpet, part-violin, part-piano. Rather it's a symphony that produces great music when each instrument harmonizes with the others. The Jewish people, with our long and treasured history, value our contribution to civilization. And we want to preserve that heritage for generations to come. "

Despite Kalman's best efforts, nothing seemed to work.

BROTHER TO BROTHER

The next day, Kalman spoke with Rav Noah. "I'm not getting through to my brother," Kalman said. "He seems so far away and disinterested. I'm not even sure there's a spark there to ignite."

"It may seem like he doesn't care, but deep down he really does," Rav Noah said, sharing a story:

> Toward the end of World War II, as the Nazi slaughter of Euro-pean Jews intensified, Jewish agents operating out of Switzerland arranged an audacious deal with Nazi leader Heinrich Himmler to purchase the freedom of 300,000 Jews. The price? Five million dollars – less than $17 per person.
>
> In February 1945, as a sign of good faith, Himmler released 1,210 Jews from Theresienstadt. The rescue funds were to come from a U.S.-based emergency committee. Yet a U.S. wartime law prohib-ited transferring assets to the enemy. For the rescue plan to work, a special license was required – approved by President Roosevelt himself.
>
> Rabbi Aaron Kotler and Irving Bunim, a community activist, traveled to Washington to meet with U.S. Treasury Secretary Henry Morgenthau and explain the urgent situation. Morgenthau, whose

lifestyle bore little evidence of Jewish identity, opposed the plan. Politely but firmly, he declined to help.

With 300,000 Jewish lives at stake, Rabbi Kotler stood up, pointed at Morgenthau and spoke forcefully in Yiddish: "One Jewish life is worth more than all the positions in Washington! If you don't help rescue fellow Jews, your position is worth nothing!"

Morgenthau asked Bunim to translate. Clearing his throat, he diplomatically said, "Rabbi Kotler understands that, due to political considerations, you cannot force the issue. Yet given the mitigating circumstances, perhaps something might be worked out."

A look of relief came across Morgenthau's face, indicating to Rabbi Kotler that his urgent message had not been accurately conveyed. "No!" the rabbi shouted at Bunim in Yiddish. "Tell him exactly what I said!"

Bunim looked at Morgenthau, then spoke slowly and deliberately. "Rabbi Kotler thinks you may be unwilling to help, fearing this would threaten your cabinet position. Rabbi Kotler says that one Jewish life is worth more than any position."

Morgenthau put his head on his desk to ponder the gravity of the moment. After a few long minutes, he looked up and stood to address Rabbi Kotler directly. "I am a Jew," he said with dignity and emotion. "I am willing to give up my position – and if necessary, even my life – for the Jewish people."

The rescue plan unfortunately never came to fruition. Yet that day in Washington, a rabbi's urgent plea ignited an eternal and indestructible Jewish spark.

Kalman nodded with understanding, and his thoughts turned to his seventeen-year-old self back in Portland. "I remember the weeks leading up to the Six Day War. Arab leaders were promising to 'throw Israel into the sea.' Jews came out of the woodwork to donate their jewelry and homes to the United Jewish Appeal and the Israeli Emergency Fund. Jews by the name of O'Reilly,

Smith and Brown – Jews who had changed their names to assim-
ilate – suddenly realized how deeply they care about the Jewish
people."

Rav Noah spoke encouragingly. "Don't give up on your brother.
If you can make one more effort, now is the time."

———⊰◦⊱———

Kalman flew to the States for a face-to-face conversation with his
brother.

"We love each other," his brother said matter-of-factly.

"Romantic love alone is not enough to sustain a marriage, and
when romantic love dissipates, it can expose some harsh realities,"
Kalman said. change sentence to: "When a couple shares a common
heritage, it cements the bond with a foundation of shared goals and
ideals."

"I've dated Jewish women," change to: his brother said. "But
they don't interest me."

"Your Jewish soul has a Jewish soulmate," Kalman said. "You
deserve it all and can have it all. Why settle for less?"

His brother looked stoic. "I don't much care about being Jewish.
I hated Hebrew school."

"I'm not surprised," Kalman said sympathetically. "It's impossible to appreciate the riches of Judaism with a grade-school
education. Come spend a week at yeshiva. Experience an authentic
Shabbos. Explore why generations of Jews heroically went through
fire and water to preserve their Jewish identity and pass that torch
to us. How did the Jewish nation – scattered, persecuted and few in
number – have such an outsized influence? This is what you'll learn
at yeshiva."

"No, thanks," Kalman's brother said. "I don't see any good
coming from it."

Kalman's frustration began to show. "Why not? Are you afraid
you'll discover the deep riches of Judaism and the joy of a vibrant

Jewish home? No one will threaten, hypnotize or force you into anything. Everyone makes their own choices in life, and I will always love you, no matter what. Yet please don't make a lifetime commitment while leaving this fundamental aspect of life unexplored."

Kalman's brother was unmoved.

There was nothing left to say.

PARTNER IN CREATION

On the flight back to Israel, Kalman was disappointed and distressed at how his brother's future was playing out. He wondered how to channel that pain in a positive direction... and his thoughts drifted back to the study hall in Jerusalem:

"Adam, the first human, was created alone, to teach that every person is an 'entire world,'" Rav Noah says, waving his hand in a gestured arc. "That's why everyone should say: *Bishvili nivra ha'olam* – 'the entire world was created for me.' This doesn't mean we should eat as many hamburgers as possible! Rather, 'the world was created for me' is a call to *Tikkun Olam* – world repairs.

"If someone spills ink on the floor and asks you to clean it up, you might refuse by saying, 'I didn't make the mess.' But if you're walking down the street and someone is bleeding – even if you're not a trained medic – you'll stop to help. Nobody says, 'Since I didn't cause the problem, why should I do anything about it?' Everyone agrees: If you know how to eliminate poverty, cure cancer or bring world peace, you'll step up – even if it means canceling your vacation. To the best of your ability, you are responsible to fix the world..

"*Mesilas Yesharim* instructs us to ask, 'What is my obligation in this world? With all life's toils, where should I direct my gaze and aspiration?' Ultimately, this is what we yearn for. If you could press a button and immediately solve the word's problems, you'd want that privilege."

"Why am I more responsible than everyone else?" a student asks.

"You're not," Rav Noah says. "We are each responsible according to our ability. Yet even if others avoid their obligation, that doesn't let you off the hook."

Rav Noah continues, "Genesis 9:9 describes Noah as 'righteous, perfect in his generations.' Yet although Noah was righteous, the prophet Isaiah (54:9) calls it 'Noah's Flood.' That's because prior to the Flood, Noah didn't even attempt to remedy the situation. Instead, he locked himself in the Ark and thought he could escape society's problems. For this lack of responsibility, 'Noah's Flood' is associated with his name."

"That's for Noah," a student says. "But what about me?"

"Everything on Earth – the beauty, as well as the problems – was created for you, an opportunity to engage in something meaningful beyond yourself. Whenever you encounter a problem, ask: *What is the message for me? How can I make a difference? Why is this part of my path to perfection?*

"Awareness of a problem signals a special opportunity – regardless of your position, resources or abilities. Don't wait for someone else to make things happen. Strategize. Organize. Find creative solutions. You are the answer. With the Almighty's help, you will change the world."

"Aren't there others more qualified to do the job?" a student asks.

"Only if someone else is available and steps up," Rav Noah replies. "The Torah describes how Moses, the greatest leader of all time, sees an Egyptian beating a Jewish slave. Moses turns both ways and, seeing no person, strikes down the Egyptian. What does it mean that Moses 'turned both ways and saw no person'? Moses checked to see if anyone else was available or more capable of dealing with the problem. Only then did Moses take action. As the Mishnah says, 'In a place where no one is taking responsibility, strive to be that person.'"

In an airplane high above the Atlantic Ocean, Kalman thought of ways to channel his pain in a positive direction.

TAKING ACTION

In the end, Kalman's brother went ahead with the wedding, and Rav Noah's dire predictions of rampant assimilation were coming true. Kalman went to Rav Noah. "Rebbe, what should I do?" he asked in despair.

"Before I answer, I want you to think about it," Rav Noah said, employing one of his favorite methods of empowering others. "Work it through yourself. Reach some independent conclusions. Then come back and tell me what you worked out and why. Then I'll share my opinion."

That evening, Kalman was distracted from his studies and headed down to the Western Wall to think. Rav Noah's words rang in his ears: "When something bothers you, it's a signal to take responsibility. Let the pain awaken you to bring more goodness to the world."

At the time, few books were available for teaching Jewish tradition to secular Jews. Standing at the Wall, Kalman pondered: *The more information people have, the better decision they'll make. If only there was a user-friendly book in English to explain the importance of Jewish identity, Jewish marriage and building a Jewish home.*

Kalman mentally began to outline such a book. As the evening wore on, sadness and frustration transformed into inspiration and creativity.

The next morning, Kalman went to Rav Noah and presented his idea: a practical guide that presents the case for marrying Jewish and helps parents raise proud Jewish children.

Rav Noah listened intently. "It's an excellent idea. The world needs such a book. The Almighty put you in this situation because you have the passion, talent and motivation to write this book. In a place where no one is taking responsibility, strive to be that person!"

Kalman did not anticipate such a ringing endorsement. "It feels like a huge undertaking," he said.

"Regardless of the magnitude of the task, we can only try," Rav Noah said. "As the Mishnah says, 'It is not your duty to finish the task, nor are you free to neglect it.'

"Don't worry about ultimate success or failure. Success is not a matter of intelligence, talent, resources or lineage. It's about caring and taking responsibility. If you want it badly enough, cry for it. When you commit to taking responsibility, the Almighty – the ultimate Resource – will help you achieve it."

"How do I know this will even make an impact?" Kalman asked.

Rav Noah threw up his hands. "Does the Almighty want you to be happy and succeed? Does the Almighty want you to know the entire Torah? Does the Almighty want you to impact every Jew?"

Kalman knew the only answer: "Yes."

Rav Noah continued: "Greatness means taking risks and trying new things. Make the commitment and don't look back. When people say to a young idealist, 'You'll grow up,' what they really mean is, 'You'll give up.' Don't grow up by giving up. Undertake the project and I'll put up half the money."

That vote of confidence was hard to ignore. That evening, Kalman wrote a letter to his maternal grandfather, Grandpa Light, who'd always proudly supported Kalman's Jewish studies. Kalman described the book project and – in his first-ever fundraising effort – successfully secured the remaining funds.

Kalman got straight to work, using every spare moment to research issues relating to dating and marriage: religious and cultural differences, parenting challenges, in-laws and divorce statistics.

Kalman plugged away, day after day, on his Smith Corona typewriter in a corner of the Aish HaTorah office. Yet the finish line remained elusive, and Kalman realized the need for single-minded, focused time to complete the project. So he packed up the typewriter and traveled to the northern Israeli town of Tzfat, nestled on a quiet hillside and known for its fresh air and spiritual vibe.

After a few weeks of drafts and rewrites, the manuscript was ready.

TRAILBLAZING PUBLICATION

In 1976, Kalman published one of the first-ever "Torah outreach" books in English. The book explained the Jewish perspective on marriage, presented tried-and-true advice for avoiding pitfalls, and included a lengthy questionnaire to ask oneself before committing to marriage.

Kalman's book hit the market with the credibility of Jewish leaders behind it. The Chief Rabbi of the British Commonwealth, Lord Immanuel Jakobovits, contributed two articles for inclusion in the book. In a written approbation, Rav Noah described the book as "excellently done, with cogent arguments, effective suggestions and positive approaches… an effective tool to help thousands of parents in their time of need."

In that pre-Amazon era, pallets of books were delivered to the Aish HaTorah offices. Kalman spent countless hours packing up books for synagogues, universities, libraries and English-speaking influencers around the world – then lugging the packages to the Old City post office.

The book became a bestseller in Jewish publishing, with 6,000 copies sold. The *Jewish Press* called it "a must for anyone who cares about the survival of the Jewish people and wants to do something about it."

From start to finish, the book was a labor of love, Kalman's humble contribution to remedy a painful situation he'd encountered first-hand. And as Aish HaTorah's first foray into mass-media educational products, the book became the organization's calling card to the broader Jewish world.

This was Kalman's first groundbreaking endeavor – yet far from his last.

JEWISH HOME

Kalman was not the only yeshiva student to encounter assimilation, and so became the go-to expert for dispensing advice. "The best prevention is through exposure to Jewish communities, and a powerful, Torah-based educational experience," Kalman would advise. "Otherwise, you're not addressing the core issue, and the pattern is bound to repeat."

Indeed, one yeshiva student told Kalman, "Remember how my sister was planning to marry outside our faith, and you helped me write a letter to try convincing her otherwise? Well, it worked!"

"Wonderful!" Kalman said. "I'm so happy to hear."

"Yeah," the student said. "But I need your help again..."

As a popular and well-traveled rabbi, Kalman was frequently asked to share wisdom for choosing the right spouse. He'd say, "Many people go by gut feeling alone. The challenge is to distinguish between a burning heart – and heartburn."

Tourists visiting Jerusalem often asked to meet with Kalman to discuss issues relating to Jewish dating and marriage. "We're expecting our first child in a few months," the young couple asked. "What advice do you have?"

Kalman replied with an illustration: "When a trauma victim regains consciousness, the first question the doctor asks is, 'What's your name?' Throughout the ages, one thing that has kept Jews connected is our Jewish names. Tragically, many Jews today don't even know their Hebrew name."

Kalman continued, "That's why it's important to give your child a meaningful Jewish name, in memory of an ancestor who was a loyal, faithful Jew. This forges a strong connection-point to our heritage."

Kalman then added, "Also, get acquainted with your own Hebrew name, and know who you're named after!"

On another occasion, Kalman met for coffee with parents seeking advice. "How do we maximize the odds that our daughter will marry Jewish?" they asked.

Kalman explained, "For children, more relevant than the question of 'Why marry Jewish' is the question of 'Why be Jewish in the first place?' The best answer – 'Because I love it!' – depends on how you, as parents, transmit a compelling case for Judaism."

"How do we do that?" they asked.

"By studying Torah," Kalman said. "That will infuse Jewish values into your consciousness, reaffirm our historical mission and strengthen your connection with the Almighty. It's a sociological fact: Where Torah is studied and observed, Jewish identity remains strong."

"Our daughter is seven years old," they said. "So we have time."

Kalman shook his head in disagreement. "This issue doesn't begin when a teenager starts to date. Parental influence needs to happen much earlier, before the die is cast. Because good luck confronting a teenager!"

"That makes sense," they said. "What's an appropriate message for her age?"

Kalman beamed a broad smile, animated by a childhood memory. "One thing I learned in Hebrew school is that Judaism is AWOL – A Way Of Life. Parents convey to children three things: example, example, example. The best sermons are lived, not preached. If you love Judaism and model those values at home, your child's life will be built on a similar foundation. Send your child to a Jewish school. Live in a Jewish neighborhood. Join a synagogue. Say the Shema. Speak Hebrew. Visit Israel."

"That sounds like a lot," they said. "What if we had to pick one thing?"

Kalman thought of his own love of Judaism. "Build a warm Jewish home. Create positive memories of Shabbos candles, Kiddush and the Passover Seder. Fill your home with Jewish books, Jewish music and Jewish observance. Begin small by picking one non-kosher food you don't bring into the house – just because you're Jewish."

ETERNAL IMPACT

Michael* was a Jewish student at the University of Waterloo in Ontario, Canada. As was common on campus, he was dating a non-Jewish woman, Susan.* As the relationship progressed, the topic of marriage periodically came up. "Is it a problem that I'm not Jewish?" Susan would ask, to which Michael would invariably respond, "No problem at all!"

Susan sensed there was more to say about this topic, so she began researching Judaism at the university library. One day, while browsing the stacks, a book about Jewish marriage by Rabbi Kalman Packouz caught her eye. She picked it off the shelf, flipped it open, and read in black-on-white:

"Marriage is a contract before God. Deuteronomy 7:3 instructs Jews to marry Jewish."

Susan was shocked! She stood for a long while in the library aisle, devouring page after page, transfixed by the book's clear and unapologetic approach.

Susan checked the book out of the library and brought it to Michael. "Look here!" she shouted, waving the book at him. "How can you claim that intermarriage is no problem?"

This marked the beginning of Michael's own Jewish journey. He began attending local classes and opened his eyes to the beauty of Torah. In time, Michael visited the Old City of Jerusalem, where he personally thanked Kalman for being the emissary that turned his life in a Jewish direction.

The end of the story? Michael became an ordained rabbi and dedicated his life to furthering Jewish education and community-building.

Today, Michael reflects, "I'm extremely grateful for my beautiful Jewish family and the many Jewish souls I've managed to impact. It's all a combination of Kalman's groundbreaking book, a brave and honest young woman, and the One above Who orchestrates events."

ADVISING PARENTS

In his research and discussions, Kalman discovered that young Jews who'd intermarried, then gotten divorced, frequently expressed a similar sentiment: "I wish that my parents, and others who cared about me, would have been more forceful in expressing their concerns."

In Jerusalem, Kalman met for coffee with a set of distraught parents.

"Our son is planning to marry a non-Jewish woman," they said. "We feel this is a mistake. In the meantime, he's given us an ultimatum: 'Either accept my fiancée, or I won't have anything to do with you.' We don't want to alienate him. What should we do?"

Kalman felt their distress, and replied with confidence and compassion, "First, understand what not to do. This is not a guilt-trip of 'If you really love us, you won't marry this person,' or

'Grandma will be upset.' Guilt is not an effective motivator, and 3,300 years of Jewish destiny is surely driven by far more powerful forces."

"Okay, so what's the best approach?"

"Ask your son to spend one week in Jerusalem, studying and experiencing Judaism. At least have him set aside one hour a week to study Jewish wisdom. This has proven effective."

"Unfortunately, we didn't raise our son to appreciate Judaism," they said. "Isn't it hypocritical to make a big deal about it now?"

Kalman reassured them. "My experience shows that you can say, 'We didn't previously realize how important it is that you marry Jewish. But we realize it now. So let's discuss this together.'"

<hr />

One couple, whom Kalman advised, reports:

> We taught our children to marry Jewish and to celebrate Jewish traditions. Our daughter dated Jewish men, and upon graduating from college got a job at a multimedia company, where she met a nice young man.
>
> A few months later, our daughter wanted us to meet the "love of her life." We wanted to be thrilled for her, and indeed this young man was bright, educated, successful and had many Jewish friends. But he was not Jewish.
>
> We tried to dissuade her from dating him, but every "argument" proved unsuccessful. Then someone suggested Rabbi Packouz's marriage book which, having sold so many copies, was out of print. So Rabbi Packouz did us the kindness of snail-mailing (pre-digital days) a photocopied manuscript of the book.
>
> Using the advice in the book, we had long and loving discussions with our daughter. Periodically, Rabbi Packouz followed up to offer assistance.

Ultimately, our daughter decided that she wanted a fully Jewish home, and a few years later she married a wonderful Jewish man. Our beloved grandchildren are now continuing our family's Jewish tradition – thanks to the care and expertise of Rabbi Packouz.

KALMAN'S WAY: DATING CHECKLIST

Kalman's "Dating Checklist" became a popular tool to help people evaluate prospective marriage partners:

(1) Kindness. Two people, each looking for self-gratification, is a recipe for disaster. A successful marriage is based on expanding beyond "self" to include another's needs. That fuses "two into one."

(2) Loyalty. A marriage partner is someone you can trust and rely on, with a pledge to be there through thick and thin – forever. Without that commitment, if your spouse upsets you, or you think someone else can please you more, the marriage will likely break down.

(3) Honesty. Honesty means an authentic, transparent and truthful representation of who you are. Lack of honesty, when discovered, creates suspicion and doubt that makes trust and intimacy difficult to achieve. "Honesty" means open communication and no hidden secrets.

(4) Respect. Ask yourself: Does this person have good character? What of their qualities do I respect? Do I seek to emulate this person? Will I be happy if my children turn out like this person?

(5) Expectations. Don't marry "potential," expecting the other person to change. If you aren't happy with someone's personality and habits, don't get married. You'll both end up frustrated and resentful. Ask yourself: Can I accept this person exactly as they are – and be happy for decades down the road?

(6) Chemistry. The Talmud says that an important prerequisite for getting married is physical chemistry.

(7) Goals. Beyond chemistry and common interests, it's important to share the deeper connection of common life goals, priorities and values. A soul-mate is a goal-mate. Get clarity on what you are living for, then find a partner who has independently arrived at the same conclusion.

(8) Jewish. The Jewish people are an extended family with millennia-deep roots. Before considering intermarriage, ask yourself these questions relating to Jewish identity:

- Do I believe in God? What is my definition of God?

- How will I react if my partner becomes more involved in their religion?

- How will my partner react if I become more involved in Judaism?

- Is it important for me to observe the Jewish holidays? How does my potential spouse feel about this?

- Does my potential spouse plan to observe any non-Jewish holidays? How do I feel about this?

- Does my potential spouse want religious symbols in our home? How do I feel about this?

- If I have a son, will I want him circumcised? How does my potential spouse feel about this?

- If my potential spouse is Christian, will they insist on baptism? How do I feel about this?

- If our marriage dissolves, would my potential spouse continue to raise our children as Jewish, or would they switch to another religion?

- What is my emotional response to anti-Semitism, the Holocaust, and terror attacks in Israel? How does my potential spouse relate to these same topics?

- Do I feel a special connection to Israel, Judaism's ancestral homeland? Does my potential spouse share this feeling?

CHAPTER FIVE

Trailblazing in St. Louis

ABRAHAM'S MISSION

After getting married, Kalman continued to study at yeshiva, absorbing wisdom in preparation for a future of teaching and inspiring others.

At a Saturday evening outreach training session, Rav Noah explained, "Abraham is considered the first Jew — not only due to his deep understanding of God, but because he went out and shared that knowledge with others. Today, too, the world is thirsting for ethical clarity and we need to present Torah in creative and innovative ways."

A student asked, "Didn't mingling with the masses compromise Abraham's own spiritual level?"

Rav Noah shook his head. "The Chasam Sofer, the great nineteenth- century Hungarian rabbi, writes that had Abraham chosen to live in seclusion, spending his time in peaceful meditation and study, he would have risen to the highest spiritual level. Yet Abraham understood that connecting others to God is even more important than one's own self-development. This propelled him to even greater heights."

"What if it's not my personality," a student said, "and I'd rather be doing something else?"

"Personally, I'd rather be sitting in a corner, studying Torah all day," Rav Noah said. "But the Jewish people are facing a crisis. To fulfill the needs of the generation, we need to do whatever is necessary – even overcome our nature. Look at Rabbi Meir Schuster – though incredibly shy, every day he manages to convince dozens of strangers to attend a Torah class."

Rav Noah concluded, "Today, with so many Jews disconnected from their heritage, fixing this is a tremendous *kiddush Hashem* – sanctification of God's Name. This goes beyond any other 'good deed.' This is the entire purpose of creation."

FIRST BRANCH

In 1978, newlyweds Kalman and Shoshana flew to New York to begin a two-month cross-country road trip, culminating with a visit to Kalman's parents in Portland. Midway, they spent Shabbos in St. Louis at the home of Kenneth Spetner, a successful life insurance salesman who was active in Jewish community projects.

Spetner asked Kalman about his future plans.

"When you love something, you want to share it with others," Kalman said. "I love God and Torah, and it hurts me that so many people are missing out. My life goal is to share this amazing pleasure."

Throughout Shabbos, Kalman's maturity and presence made a strong impression, and Spetner's wheels churned with ideas about how to bring that energy to St. Louis.

On Sunday, he phoned Rav Noah in Jerusalem. "After spending time with your student," Spetner said, "I'm convinced that a Torah outreach program in St. Louis can help stem the tide of assimilation. What resources can you provide?"

North American expansion had long been on Rav Noah's radar, but at this stage he had little to offer. "We have Kalman's marriage book, and we can occasionally provide a guest lecture from Jerusalem," he said.

Spetner presented an offer that Rav Noah couldn't refuse. "I want to open an Aish HaTorah branch in St. Louis. Send me two of your best guys, and I'll arrange the first year of seed money."

Rav Noah's antenna shot up, sensing a breakthrough on the horizon. He understood that a local branch in North America would confer a triple-advantage: not only impacting one city, but also directing students to the Jerusalem yeshiva and – crucially – serving as a source of partners for the global mission.

Rav Noah's immediate concern was manpower. He had initially looked to the Orthodox community to become "Torah ambassadors," to reach out and study with other Jews. But the *ba'al teshuva* movement was just beginning, and few observant Jews were convinced that *kiruv* (Torah outreach) could succeed.

The manpower solution, Rav Noah discovered, was in-house. He'd recently launched pop-up outreach programs in Tel Aviv and Tzfat, led by the inimitable Rabbi Sammy Kassin and staffed with newly minted *ba'alei teshuva* who proved to be exceptional Torah ambassadors. Having seen both sides and made the choice to follow the Torah path, *ba'alei teshuva* are intimately familiar with secular culture and mentality, speak the same language, relate to the same experiences, and – with enthusiasm, urgency and dedication – present Jewish wisdom in a language that is meaningful and accessible. Most of all, *ba'alei teshuva* are uniquely qualified to guide people through a transition process toward observance.

Rav Noah was confident that two of his students could succeed in St. Louis. "Absolutely," he told Spetner on the phone. "You have a deal."

ALL HANDS ON DECK

Upon Kalman's return from America, Rav Noah called together his married students. "It's time for the next phase of our mission. A unique opportunity has come up for our first major foray outside of Israel. We will be establishing a Torah outreach program in St. Louis, on campus and in the community, to teach Jewish wisdom and guide spiritual journeys.

"I'm looking for two good men to blaze the trail. This requires talent as both a teacher and fundraiser. Your wife must be on board to host Shabbos guests. And to inspire the students, you must be a personal role model."

Rav Noah then conveyed the gravity of the moment. "Most of all, this requires the courage and creativity to go where none have gone before. The Almighty's plan for the Jewish people and humanity will ultimately be fulfilled. The only question is what role each of us will play. If this project succeeds, it will set a precedent for decades to come."

Kalman did a double take. He'd been studying in yeshiva for five years and was eager to dive into front-line outreach. As his mind raced, his thoughts were broken by a student's question. "Rebbe, that's a huge responsibility. We're young and inexperienced. What realistic chance do we have to succeed?"

Rav Noah replied with a parable: "A parent and child are walking along a riverbank. Suddenly, the child falls into the water and is drowning. But the parent is unable to swim and can't save the child. An EMT arrives on the scene and is willing to help – but needs a rope. If the parent has a rope, will they give it to save the child? Of course!"

Rav Noah continued, "The Almighty's children are drifting away. Are you worried about a lack of talent, skill and experience? Take the problem seriously and the Almighty will provide the means. Ask not what you can do for your Creator. Rather, ask what you will allow your Creator to do for you."

———✦———

Later that day, Kalman went to speak with Rav Noah. "Rebbe, I'm thinking about St. Louis. But perhaps others could do a better job?"

Rav Noah affectionately jabbed a finger at Kalman. "Kalman, you're a lucky one who found his way back to Torah. What about the thousands of Jews in St. Louis who dropped out after Hebrew school and remain disconnected? Today, Jewish leadership is scarce and the situation is critical. Anyone willing to tackle the problem has special Divine assistance. Kalman, you're a natural leader – creative, independent, dedicated, reliable. Become an outreach entrepreneur and transform the Jewish people!"

Eager to innovate, and with the courage to pioneer, Kalman went home that evening to present the idea to Shoshana. For her, it would mean moving away from family and friends. Yet she recognized this as best for Kalman, for their family and for the Jewish people. She gave the thumbs up.

The next day, Kalman was back in Rav Noah's office. "I'll go to St. Louis."

Rav Noah was delighted. "I was hoping to hear this, Kalman. You're my first choice. This will prepare you to independently teach, fundraise and carry forth the mission. I've devised a six-month rabbinic ordination program. Meanwhile, we'll work together to devise a game plan."

The other student to accept the challenge was Rabbi Chaim Willis, whose wife Shelley was originally from St. Louis.

THE GATEWAY

Rav Noah called Kalman and Chaim into his office to discuss plans. "Running a branch requires a division of responsibilities: one of you as the primary teacher, and the other as the primary fundraiser. I can say from experience that fundraising is the more difficult, and more noble, position."

Kalman realized that Chaim was the obvious candidate for teaching. Two years earlier, *Rolling Stone* magazine had published a lengthy article chronicling Chaim's spiritual journey, making him somewhat of a celebrity, with street cred that would prove helpful in interacting with young adults.

Kalman asked, "What's the upside of being the fundraiser?"

Rav Noah answered with a story:

> A man involved in community service came to the Chofetz Chaim and complained, "I don't like my job. I'd rather be sitting all day in a quiet study hall."
>
> The Chofetz Chaim thought for a moment. "Which shoes sell for a higher price: factory-produced or handmade?"
>
> Not sure where this was going, the man answered, "Handmade shoes are more expensive."
>
> "So a shoemaker is wealthier than a factory owner?"
>
> "Of course not. The factory owner is wealthier, since he sells a large quantity of shoes."
>
> The Chofetz Chaim explained, "The Talmud says, 'Greater than doing a mitzvah, is helping others do a mitzvah.' With community service, you gain exponential dividends beyond what you could achieve alone. Do you really want to forfeit all that wealth?"

Kalman got the message. Though he had minimal fundraising experience, he enjoyed a good challenge, and neither intimidation nor fear of rejection ever stopped him from doing the right thing.

In a place where nobody is taking responsibility, strive to be that person, Kalman thought to himself. "Sure," he said, breaking the silence. "I'll be the fundraiser."

"This will be good for you," Rav Noah assured. "It will help you reach your potential. It's all a matter of believing that anything is possible."

Rav Noah thought for a moment, then chuckled, "Kalman, this reminds me of my favorite joke."

Mendel lives on one side of town and works on the other side. In-between is a gloomy, foreboding cemetery. Every day, back and forth, Mendel takes the long way around the cemetery.

One evening, Mendel is tired and saves time by cutting through the cemetery. In the pitch-dark, moonless night, with haunting sounds of owls and dogs, Mendel doubts the wisdom of taking this shortcut.

Suddenly, Mendel trips and falls into an open grave – six feet deep – hitting the bottom with a bang. He frantically tries to climb out, but the walls are sheer, and the dirt crumbles in his hands.

After an hour of futile effort, Mendel is resigned to fate. *I'll wait here and be rescued tomorrow at the funeral. At least I'll have a good story to share.* He curls up in a corner and goes to sleep.

Meanwhile, another man is taking a shortcut through the cemetery when, lo and behold, he stumbles into that same grave – with a thud and a yelp.

Mendel wakes up, startled. In the pitch dark, he sees the shape of someone frantically trying to dig out – with no idea that Mendel is there.

I tried unsuccessfully for an hour, Mendel thinks. *Let me save this person some time, and perhaps we can find a solution together.*

Mendel reaches over, taps the man's shoulder and gently says, "I'm sorry, but there's no way out."

The second man – in total shock – jumps out of the grave!

"Isn't that hilarious?" Rav Noah said with a hearty laugh.

Kalman felt no inclination to smile, much less laugh. "Rebbe, what's so funny about this joke?"

Rav Noah's eyes twinkled. "The irony is that Mendel could have also gotten out. Beneath the surface, we have a huge reservoir of untapped potential. Yet we underestimate ourselves and doubt whether we have what it takes to become great. We have the potential to succeed beyond our wildest dreams, yet we don't use it. Isn't that an amazing irony?"

Kalman nodded. From that day forward, this became his favorite joke, too.

FRONT LINES

In the spring of 1979, six years after first walking into Shema Yisroel, Kalman received rabbinical ordination. He was gratified that his original plans for a law career had morphed into rabbinics – what he called "a Judaism lawyer with advanced degrees in social work and education."

In May 1979, Kalman and Shoshana packed their bags and, with their first infant in tow, headed off to St. Louis, gateway to the West. Decades before the proliferation of outreach kollels and campus programs, and with no previous model upon which to rely, the Packouz and Willis families became trailblazers – equipped with idealism, enthusiasm and a burning desire to share the beauty and wisdom of Torah.

The families moved into a small apartment complex, populated primarily by young Orthodox families and within walking distance of the synagogue. (Those humble apartments, forty years old in 1980, are still standing today.)

Kalman and Chaim immediately got to work reaching out to students at Washington University in St. Louis. They set up tables on the campus quad and asked passersby, "Are you Jewish?" Those who responded, "Yes," were engaged in conversation and offered one-on-one Torah study.

To establish commonality, Kalman joked with Washington University students about being an "almost-alumni," having graduated from the University of Washington in Seattle.

———◈———

One morning, Kalman was hanging out on the quad, recruiting for a class. "Excuse me, are you Jewish?" he asked.

"Yes."

"Tell me," Kalman said, "would you rather be rich or happy?"

"Happy!" the student replied.

"What's the key to happiness?"

The student's face went blank.

Kalman waited a few beats, then said, "True happiness doesn't depend on wealth, fame or adventure. The ancient Jewish secret of happiness is: Appreciate what you already have. Let's meet at the Student Union and learn about gratitude."

———◈———

Kalman came to St. Louis with expectations of attracting large numbers of students, figuring that the typical student lifestyle – unmarried, unencumbered by a job and with lots of free time – was conducive to growth and change.

Kalman discovered, however, that most students were less receptive than those roaming the Western Wall thousands of miles away. "University students are dependent on their parents for money, and under pressure to get good grades," Kalman bemoaned. "It's hard to get past preconceived notions, cultural bias and selective cognition – no matter how intellectually honest someone claims to be. As Winston Churchill said, 'People occasionally stumble over the truth, but most pick themselves up and hurry off as if nothing happened.'"

One day, Kalman stopped a student on campus. "Excuse me, are you Jewish?"

"Yes, but I'm not interested in Judaism. I don't believe in religion or absolute morality."

Kalman tried an approach he'd heard from Rav Noah. "Are you sure there are no absolutes?"

"Yes," the student replied emphatically.

"Are you *really* sure?" Kalman asked again.

"Yes!"

Kalman raised one eyebrow and asked, "Are you *absolutely* sure?"

———◆———

Kalman set up a table at the student center and a young woman approached. "Hi, Rabbi," she said. "I'm interested in converting to Judaism."

That's an interesting introduction, Kalman thought. "Judaism teaches that every righteous person, Jewish or not, has a portion in the eternal afterlife," he told her. "Why do you want to convert?"

"I'm dating a Jewish fellow and we're serious about getting married," she said. "I was brought up Catholic and I'm wondering if it's better that we share the same religion."

Kalman spent a few minutes speaking with the young woman, citing research that marriages with fewer religious and cultural differences are more likely to succeed.

The young woman thanked Kalman sincerely, then walked away.

The next day, a large young man, with wild hair and a head-band, came storming into the Student Union. He pounded angrily on Kalman's table and yelled, "Stop talking to my girlfriend!"

As dozens of students watched the spectacle unfold, Kalman kept his cool, mindful of the Jewish teaching "not to pacify someone in their moment of anger."

When the tirade had petered out, Kalman said, "If you'd like to know why I spoke with your friend, and what was said, let's sit and talk about it."

The young man turned and left in a huff. Kalman never heard from either of them again, yet later found out they'd broken up. His conclusion: "When it comes to the idea of Jews marrying Jews, you never know who will be most receptive."

EFFORT & RESULT

Rav Noah was in constant contact with Kalman and Chaim, troubleshooting and dispensing advice. A few months after opening the branch, he visited St. Louis to strategize with the rabbis and meet with students.

"My *tach'sheet* (jewel)!" Rav Noah greeted Kalman joyfully. "Do you know how much the Almighty loves you?"

"Yes, of course," Kalman said. "Yet I'm frustrated by the level of success. We came here to transform the city, but we're progressing in baby steps. More often than not, my nuggets of wisdom fail to penetrate, like water off the back of a duck. How do we get a breakthrough?"

"Don't be disappointed," Rav Noah said. "Dreams don't come true overnight. It's a process. Everything in its time. As long as you're moving in the right direction, enjoy the journey. There is great pleasure in conquering challenges and reaching the mountaintop. As the Sages say: 'More pain, more gain.'"

"I'm not even certain we'll succeed," Kalman said.

Rav Noah stroked his beard. "Kalman, which is more accurate to say: 'I can' or 'I can't'? When you say 'I can't,' that implies the Almighty doesn't have the power to help. On the other hand, 'I can' means that with God on your side, every problem is manageable. The truth is that without Divine help, we can't even lift a finger. So ask for help. One person, together with the Almighty, is a majority."

"But there's so much frustration and struggle," Kalman said. "And we've even endured setbacks."

"In the Almighty's eyes, success is measured by effort, not results," Rav Noah explained. "The Torah speaks harshly about a missionary *(meisis)* who attempts to draw others away from Judaism. A person is considered a *meisis* even if their words have no impact, and even if the effort was completely unsuccessful.

"All the more so, the converse is true. Undertaking to bring Jews closer to Judaism is a precious accomplishment – even if completely unsuccessful," Rav Noah said. "We only need to try our best. The outcome is not in our control. We make the effort, but success is from Above. Either way, reward is guaranteed."

"Isn't there a direct correlation between effort and result?" Kalman asked.

"Not always," Rav Noah said. "My grandfather lived in Tiberias in the late nineteenth century, a time of extreme poverty in Israel. His family had no money and was in danger of starving. So he told a friend, 'Let's walk down to the *shuk* (marketplace) and see what opportunity presents itself.' They went to the market and walked from one end to the other. Yet nothing happened and they headed back."

Rav Noah continued, "When my grandfather arrived home, an Arab was waiting there with sacks of wheat, and explained, 'I have to leave in a hurry and need someone I can trust. Take this wheat, sell it and keep the profit. Whenever I return, just give me the wholesale price.' My grandfather took the deal."

Kalman was listening with rapt attention as Rav Noah delivered the punchline: "My grandfather told his friend, 'You probably think going to the *shuk* accomplished nothing. That's not true. We showed the Almighty that we're serious. For that reason, our efforts bore fruit.'"

Rav Noah told Kalman, "You only need to try. The Mishnah says, 'It is not our duty to complete the task, yet neither are we free to neglect it.'"

The next day, Kalman told Rav Noah, "I appreciate our conversation. You've said this message before, but only now it penetrated. Don't you get impatient repeating the same thing over and over?"

"No, it's fun." Rav Noah laughed. "I imagine it like a video game, where my goal is to figure out different ways to get you in touch with your own greatness."

LOCAL POLITICS

As fundraiser, Kalman was responsible for the salaries, rent and programming costs. At the outset, Kalman gave himself a $12,000 annual salary and – with characteristic humility – set Chaim's salary at $15,000.

Kalman's mettle was put to an early test. Fundraising by nature is challenging, but this situation was exacerbated by local Jewish politics and territorial issues. Other rabbis were suspicious of the "new guys in town" who might threaten their turf.

Kalman called Rav Noah for advice.

"Assure the other rabbis that you're not competition," Rav Noah said. "Explain that you're there to serve the existing community, with no intent of starting a new shul, school or kashrut supervision. Make it clear that you seek to widen the circle, to attract more Torah students and supplement the good work the community is already doing."

Kalman's diplomatic skills were tested in the cauldron of Jewish community politics. At the time, St. Louis had the reputation of not taking kindly to Orthodox rabbis. Kalman and Chaim became the target of a sustained attack from one non-Orthodox rabbi who did everything possible to keep them off the university campus.

Kalman made a concerted effort to build a personal relationship with this rabbi, and the attacks abated.

During that first year, another challenge manifested when the Orthodox community split into two factions. Everyone lined up on one side or the other, but Kalman communicated clearly that Aish HaTorah took a fully neutral position. They survived, thanks to Kalman's deft ability to steer clear of disputes and maintain broad-based community connections.

With courage and resilience, and buoyed by incremental progress, the team plowed forward. When asked by a St. Louis newspaper how to rate their success, Kalman replied, "We are one hundred percent successful. Every Jew we encounter gains a more positive feeling about Judaism than previously."

Meanwhile, Kalman worked hard to cultivate new donors. The seed funding – paid partially by the Jewish Agency for Israel – was only for one year and by no means secure. With a keen focus on developing partners who appreciate the mission, Kalman succeeded in doubling the branch's budget in the second year.

Above all, Kalman and Chaim proved it was possible to inspire and influence young Jews outside the immersive Jerusalem experience. Kalman's parents visited St. Louis, pleased to meet many parents who were grateful for Kalman's guidance in helping their children become committed members of the Jewish community.

With this success in establishing a viable, independently functioning outreach branch, Rav Noah sent a steady stream of yeshiva students from Jerusalem to train in St. Louis as front-line "rabbinic interns." Additionally, Shalom Schwartz and Yehuda Appel, founders of Aish Toronto and Aish Cleveland respectively, visited St. Louis for a firsthand look at on-the-ground operations. They followed Kalman around, taking notes and asking questions – then returned home to apply the St. Louis model to their own local branch.

As such, Kalman's efforts impacted not only St. Louis, but ultimately the entire Jewish people.

CARING FRIEND

Beyond the fundraising, Kalman taught weekly Torah classes for university students and young professionals. Based on Maimonides' "Thirteen Principles of Faith" and Rav Noah's "48 Ways to Wisdom," the topics included Jewish perspectives on dating and marriage, happiness, success and the afterlife. Kalman's goal was to create a welcoming, inclusive, low-pressure space where Jews can learn at their own pace.

Steven Finer, one of Kalman's students in St. Louis, recalls, "I was running a successful business, and one night I looked up and, with tears in my eyes, said, *Is making money all that there is? Where is the meaning in life?*

"I was looking for answers but there was nowhere to turn. The local Orthodox shul didn't offer a regular schedule of classes and programs – certainly not at the entry-level. A friend suggested that I check out a new group in town, Aish HaTorah: two young rabbis from Israel who, like me, were American, in their late twenties and from a secular background."

Steven got information about a class that Kalman taught Tuesday and Thursday evenings at Hillel House across from Washington University. He recalls, "The class was a mixture of college students and young professionals from different walks of life. We didn't know each other previously, yet we had the common bond of coming from a Jewish home, intent on marrying a Jewish spouse and interested in learning more about being Jewish. I was one of the more 'observant' Jews at my high school, but I couldn't name the Ten Commandments. Someone once asked me to explain what it means to be a Jew. I remember kicking the ground with my shoe because I didn't know."

Kalman was a master educator whose presentation was always clear and captivating:

> "Life presents a basic dichotomy between physical and spiritual," Kalman explained. "Throughout human history, various approaches have tried to resolve this. Some cultures take an ascetic approach, where physical pleasure is a necessary evil best avoided, and where holy people engage in celibacy and isolation."
>
> "I know what you mean," a student said. "I just spent a month in India, meditating on a mountaintop – all day, every day."
>
> Kalman continued, "At the opposite extreme is the hedonist, who worships physical and material pleasure as an end unto itself. The hedonist takes the decadent view: 'Eat, drink and be merry, for tomorrow we may die.'"
>
> "Western society definitely leans that way," a student noted.
>
> Kalman nodded and continued. "Judaism offers a third option, the 'golden middle path' that neither retreats from materialism nor becomes consumed by it. We use the physical world as a portal to transcendent pleasures. On Shabbos, we have delicious meals and wear nice clothes. We raise the cup of wine – not to get drunk, but to say Kiddush and sanctify the day. In this way, we uplift and elevate the mundane world for a higher purpose."

Students from that time insist that Kalman's character made the biggest impression. Steven Finer describes: "One evening during a rainstorm, I arrived at class and found Rabbi Packouz waiting in the lobby, reading a book. He looked up and said, 'Nobody else showed up, but I waited because I knew you'd come.' That spoke volumes about Rabbi Packouz's dedication to me as a person. I wasn't just some statistic on a list. He was a caring friend."

The Packouz home became a meeting place for young adults to celebrate Shabbos and holidays, giving students a firsthand look at how Torah life functions. Kalman discovered that Shoshana's spectacular feasts were typically more persuasive than his erudite words of wisdom.

One student recalls, "Shoshana was extremely gracious, lovely, smart and accomplished. The meal was fantastic, but it wasn't just the tasty food. An expensive restaurant will satisfy your palate. But what impressed me was how Kalman and Shoshana, who barely knew me, opened their house. It became my home away from home. They helped me get on the right path, without asking anything in return. And my story is one among many."

———⟫◆⟪———

A highlight of Aish HaTorah's programming was when Rav Yaakov Weinberg – a highly esteemed rosh yeshiva and Rav Noah's older brother – came twice to give guest lectures in St. Louis. The first time, he was billed as the "man who can answer all your questions." Rav Yaakov was not pleased by that description, and in response to the evening's first question, replied dryly, "I don't know."

Kalman and Chaim also encouraged students to experience a few weeks of touring and study in Israel. Many returned to St. Louis eager to embark on a path of Torah observance. During this time, St. Louis students Mike Berger, Andy Mensch, Yehoshua Baron and Sender Axelbaum all went to study at Aish HaTorah in Jerusalem and became rabbis.

David Kinberg was the number-two ranked racquetball player in his age category in the United States. A student at Washington University, he had plans for medical school. Yet after attending Aish HaTorah classes in St. Louis, he tried out yeshiva in Jerusalem. He liked it and became a rabbi.

COURAGE ON THE TRAIN

Rav Noah told a story that occurred in the 1930s, when he was a toddler:

> My father sent my seventeen-year-old sister Chava to Krakow, Poland, to study at Sarah Schenirer's original Bais Yaakov Seminary. After a two-week ocean voyage, she arrived in Germany and boarded a train to Krakow. On the train, someone vomited. The conductor came to check it out. He accused a certain man of being the guilty party and began beating him.
>
> My sister was a teenager, who spoke no Polish and was barely five feet tall. Yet she was determined to fight the injustice. With great courage, she marched up to the conductor and said sternly – in English: "I've been here the entire time. This is not the man who vomited. Now take your hands off him!"

This story resonated with Kalman, who was generally calm and soft-spoken – yet could not tolerate injustice.

<hr/>

On a visit to New York City in 1980, Kalman was riding the D train from Brooklyn to Manhattan. In those days, the subways were a grimy, graffiti-filled, underground danger zone. At one stop, a young bully entered the subway car, his boombox blaring at full blast. The passengers cautiously minded their own business, eyes lowered and buried in newspapers.

Suddenly, a little old lady shouted, "Turn off that noise!" Everyone dug deeper into their newspapers.

Boombox Bully smiled wickedly at the old lady and said, "If you want to stop the music, come turn it off yourself."

The old lady got up, shuffled over to the boombox and – with an outstretched finger – flipped the switch.

The bully became enraged and cocked his fist to punch her.

Kalman watched the scene unfold and instinctively jumped up between the two combatants. "Don't hit her!" Kalman shouted as he blocked the man's arm. Boombox Bully, a bit bewildered, glared back. Kalman flashed an uncertain smile and quickly sat back down.

Moments later, the boombox was back on, with the old lady yelling again, "Turn that off!" Again, the bully issued a challenge: "Turn it off yourself." Again, the woman sauntered over and the bully stood up to punch her. Again, Kalman stepped in to intercede.

"You're getting on my nerves!" the bully growled at Kalman. "Do you wanna fight?"

"No. Just please don't hit the old lady."

The subway train pulled into the next station and the bully got off, ending the confrontation. Kalman was gratified at having done the right thing. Then, his attention focused on the old lady just a few seats away. Kalman anticipated a comment along the lines of, "Thank you so much for saving my life – twice!" But she ignored him, without a word of appreciation.

Kalman was shocked at the ingratitude and began to stew. After a minute, he caught himself: *Fool! Am I any better? When the man backed down from punching me, the Almighty saved my life – twice! Have I thanked Him?*

Kalman's takeaway from this story: "When pointing a finger at others, remember that three fingers point back at yourself."

COMPUTER DATING

Kalman was an itinerant tinkerer and gadget-owner. He was also a master of ingenuity and creativity, constantly on the lookout for new ideas. He traced this predilection back to his great-uncle Joe Friedman (his mother's mother's brother), the legendary

"Patent King" who, back in the day, invented a process for 3-D films and a revolutionary fountain pen.

Friedman's creativity reached its zenith in the 1930s when, upon seeing his young daughter struggling to drink soda with a straw, had an epiphany. Friedman inserted a screw into the straw, then used dental floss to press the straw into the screw's threads. He then removed the screw and – voila! – the straw could now bend. Uncle Joe washed out the straw and, to his daughter's delight, the newfangled tube facilitated far more efficient drinking. Friedman patented the "Flex-Straw," which took off and changed the face of beverage consumption forever.

Kalman never met his great-uncle Joe, but he was greatly inspired by the family legend.

—————

One day, Kalman and Rav Noah were speaking about creativity. "Whether painting a gorgeous picture, composing a piece of music, or formulating a new idea," Rav Noah said, "the creative process echoes how God created the world from nothingness. Kalman, as a *ba'al teshuva*, you have the power to create in new and dynamic ways. The Talmud says, 'In a place where *ba'alei teshuva* stand, even the most righteous can't stand.' So tell me, besides your fundraising and teaching, what have you always been passionate about, that you could now apply to promoting the Jewish cause?"

"I have a longtime fascination with technology," Kalman said, which in 1980 was far ahead of the curve. In those days, PCs were almost non-existent and most computers – big and bulky – used punch cards.

"Okay," Rav Noah said. "Now imagine how technology can help create more Jewish education and awareness."

Kalman thought for a moment and said, "In St. Louis, I've found that many young Jews want a Jewish marriage partner, yet they have no effective way to meet appropriate candidates. Perhaps technology might help solve this problem."

Kalman spent the next few weeks brainstorming about how computers could replicate the traditional "matchmaking" method, where dates are pre-screened to increase compatibility. Kalman arrived at an idea completely ahead of its time: the Jewish Computer Dating Service.

Kalman hired a company to do the programming and, after a few months of tweaks and iterations, had a viable prototype ready for market.

The idea of Jewish computer dating was revolutionary, and Kalman went into publicity mode, sending press releases and countacting media outlets. The response was spectacular: Local news coverage touted the service as "Shadchan Made Modern," and "Yenta Becomes Honeywell" (a reference to an early PC manufacturer).

Kalman's project soon gained national attention, earning him an appearance on NBC's *Today Show*, at the time America's most popular morning show. One morning, a crew of cameras, lighting equipment, microphones and producers descended on the Packouz's living room in St. Louis to film Kalman demonstrating the dating service's basic functions.

Kalman then faced a hostile interviewer: "Rabbi Packouz, the Jewish Computer Dating Service that you've created promotes marriage between Jews. Yet in this day and age, America is moving away from discrimination. How do you answer those who say that your project is discriminatory?"

Kalman stayed calm and on message. "The matter is not one of discrimination, but rather preservation of the species. Allow me to share an analogy: A group in California is working to save the humpback whale. They believe if the humpback whale becomes extinct, the world and humanity will have lost something precious. That's how I feel about the survival of the Jewish people, who have surely done more for the world and humanity than the humpback whale."

The wave of publicity generated by the dating service boosted Kalman's outreach efforts in St. Louis. Plus, as Aish HaTorah's first national media exposure, it positioned the organization – at a critical time of expansion into other North American cities – as a leader in innovative Jewish education.

In the end, the Jewish Computer Dating Service was too far ahead of its time to succeed. People didn't yet appreciate the value of computer dating, thinking "that it's only for desperate losers who can't get a date in the real world."

Decades later, with the runaway success of Jewish dating websites and apps, Kalman's vision was vindicated.

MOVING UP

One spring day in 1982, Kalman was preparing marketing materials for a weekend seminar when the phone rang. It was Rav Noah calling from Jerusalem.

"Kalman, you've done an excellent job in St. Louis. You're an effective fundraiser in a challenging situation. You've proven that Torah stands up to scrutiny in the marketplace of ideas. And you've laid a solid foundation of partners and students. Now it's time to move to greater responsibility. Aish HaTorah is growing and our Jerusalem headquarters needs an Executive Director to oversee administrative operations and spearhead our international fundraising team. I need someone I can fully rely on – a strong leader who is loyally dedicated to the mission.

"Kalman, you're an ideal candidate: outstanding communication skills and a good listener; excellent judgment, problem-solving ability and decisiveness; wise and compassionate; responsible and dedicated; articulate and diplomatic; creative, dynamic and idealistic; and most of all, a team player.

"There are bigger fish to fry, Kalman. Please come back to Jerusalem to be my second-in-command."

Kalman was honored by the vote of confidence. Never one to shy away from responsibility, he understood this as an unparalleled opportunity to expand his horizons and impact the Jewish world – while helping to alleviate the constant financial pressures faced by Rav Noah.

As a huge bonus, Shoshana was thrilled to move back to Israel and reunite with her family and friends. She suggested purchasing an apartment near her parents in the Jerusalem neighborhood of Sanhedria Murchevet.

Kalman's response? A big thumbs-up.

Rabbi Dov Heller, Kalman's successor in St. Louis, recalls, "When I first came to the yeshiva in Jerusalem, I found it intimidating. I wasn't exactly sure what I was doing and why I was there. I felt lost and a bit anxious. Kalman was the first to befriend me. He greeted me with a warm smile and made me feel comfortable. We'd take walks and sit in the park. He was a friendly and comforting peer, a source of stability and normalcy. Kalman is one of the main reasons I stayed in yeshiva and became a rabbi."

When Dov took over the branch in St. Louis, Kalman was again there to assist. Dov recalls, "I was initially concerned about getting my bearings in an unfamiliar city and role. But if I could trust anyone to help, it was Kalman. He'd established an infrastructure and made everything as easy as possible. He showed me the lay of the land, briefed me on the Who's Who of students and donors, and prepped me on communal sensitivities."

After three years in St. Louis, Kalman and Shoshana packed up their house ("Pack-ouz") and headed back to Jerusalem, the center of the Jewish world, for their next impactful adventure.

KALMAN'S WAY: REACHING OUT

Kalman devised a playbook for reaching out and inspiring others about the beauty of Judaism:

- See the goodness in others and love them.

- Share interesting and inspirational books, articles and recordings that motivate people to learn more.

- Demonstrate the practical value that Torah brings to families, friends and community.

- Invite people to experience Shabbos and holidays, and connect them with other hosts.

- Learn from everyone. Ask questions and listen to people express their views.

- Be a friend. Call, send a gift or meet for coffee.

CHAPTER SIX

Jerusalem Leader

THE MISSION

On the flight back to Israel, Rav Noah's words rang in Kalman's ears: "We're not a Jewish outreach organization. We're an emergency rescue committee (*va'ad hatzalah*). We address any serious problem facing the Jewish people – not only the spiritual challenge of assimilation, but also physical threats: anti-Semitism, terror, and anti-Israel bias. As agents of the Almighty, we fight for justice and peace. We are humanity's hope!"

At age thirty-two and hitting his prime, Kalman sought to become one of Rav Noah's "Ten Leaders" taking responsibility for the Jewish people. Kalman dug deep to understand: *What is the purpose of my journey? What is my role in this Torah revolution? How can I best apply the skills and experiences I've developed in my lifetime?*

⊸•⊷

Kalman became the number-two face of the organization, with Rav Noah relying on Kalman's management, fundraising and interpersonal skills. Occupying the office adjacent to Rav Noah's, Kalman quickly settled into his role, pouring his energies into streamlining the administrative functions.

Each day, weather permitting, Kalman enjoyed a twenty-minute bike ride from his home in Sanhedria Murchevet to the Old City: down Shmuel HaNavi Street and past 14 Polanski Street, the location of his earliest yeshiva days at Shema Yisroel. For Kalman, this was coming full circle.

As Executive Director, Kalman hosted Aish HaTorah's annual International Meetings, where branch and program heads from around the world would descend on Jerusalem to brainstorm, strategize and share best practices. Kalman served as master of ceremonies for the three-day event, his words of inspiration and well-timed jokes arousing a spirit of camaraderie among the educators, supporters and students.

Rav Noah emphasized this sense of unity and brotherhood as crucial to the mission:

> The book of Genesis compares Noah's Flood with the Tower of Babel. The generation of the Flood was plagued by theft, abuse and infighting. The result was total destruction.
>
> In contrast, the generation of the Tower rebelled against God, yet were unified as "one nation and one language." On the basis of that positive trait, they were spared destruction and were merely scattered, no longer speaking the same language.
>
> Nothing can stand in the way of a unified group working toward a common cause. Divided, we are on our own. Unified, no goal is beyond our reach.

Kalman cherished this shared mission of brotherhood, and he faithfully attended Aish HaTorah events around the world. At the annual conference in America for students and partners, Kalman would position himself in the hotel lobby, as the unofficial "greeter" to welcome people. With his broad smile and signature "thumbs up," Kalman gave every attendee the feeling that their arrival was the highlight of the day.

With an eye for marketing and PR, Kalman produced various donor gifts – novelties like mouse pads and microfiber cloths that featured a gorgeous photo of the Western Wall. When Kalman thought to add Rav Noah's photo, Rav Noah told him, "Put your own photo. That way, when you call a donor, they'll feel the personal connection."

On one occasion, Kalman combined gratitude with humor to produce a mock "million-dollar banknote" with his smiling visage in the center and the tagline, "Thanks a million for supporting Aish HaTorah."

CONSTANT DEBT

Rav Noah's approach was to aggressively push the mission forward. As a result he was constantly in debt. One day in the office, Rav Noah let out a cheer and Kalman poked his head into the adjacent office. "Good news, Rebbe?"

"Yes, we just received a million-dollar donation."

"Wonderful!" Kalman said. "Now you can pay off the debts and spend more time in Jerusalem teaching."

Rav Noah had other ideas. "Do you think the Almighty sent this money so we'd take it easy? We'll use the money to start new programs – and I'll manage the debts."

⌐•⌐

Kalman was meeting with Rav Noah one day at the office, when the secretary brought in a special delivery letter. It was from a non-Jew, writing to say how much he enjoyed listening to an audio set of "48 Ways to Wisdom." He even had all the classes transcribed and turned into a book, printing copies for each of his children and grandchildren. As an expression of gratitude, he enclosed a check for $10,000.

Rav Noah shook his head in amazement, then looked at Kalman and said, "You never know the impact we're having."

⊰◦◦⊱

One day, Rav Noah asked Kalman to accompany him to an important meeting with a lawyer to discuss a sizeable sum of money owed to Aish HaTorah. That morning, Kalman had an upset stomach and, while waiting for the lawyer, realized that it was almost sunset and he hadn't yet put on tefillin that day.

When Rav Noah heard this, he immediately grabbed Kalman's hand and raced him to a nearby shul, where Kalman put on tefillin.

This taught Kalman a fundamental lesson: Financial considerations are secondary to serving God and helping others.

MEZUZAH SCROLLS

Rav Noah was teaching about the power of making Torah alive and real:

> Imagine a guy named Bob Johnson, owner of Johnson's Widgets, whose large factory operates at peak efficiency. Johnson is going on vacation, so he asks Jake the janitor to look after the factory while he's gone. Jake is skeptical about managing such a complex operation, but Johnson assures him, "It's all worked out to a science. I've posted a detailed set of instructions on the office wall."
>
> Johnson, confident that Jake will carefully follow the plan, enjoys a marvelous vacation. Yet he returns to find the factory in complete shambles: broken equipment, raw materials strewn across the floor, workers idle and the office area destroyed – with the written instructions smoldering on the wall.
>
> "What happened?" cries Johnson. "I gave you all the instructions!"
>
> Jake, with torn clothes and charcoal black face, says dejectedly, "I guess I forgot to read them."

Rav Noah raised his fist to drive home the message:

>   Torah is our "instructions for living" – with Divine wisdom for
>   actualizing our potential, building a great marriage, and finding
>   happiness and success. The mezuzah, the parchment of Torah
>   verses that we kiss as we pass through the doorway, is the "posted
>   instructions." Don't be like Jake in our story. Focus on the instruc-
>   tions. Study them. Live them!

⟹◈⟸

In the Old City of Jerusalem, Kalman had daily opportunities
to meet new people and share impromptu rabbinic teachings. One
time, a tourist stopped Kalman and asked, "Where can I buy a
mezuzah?"

Kalman escorted him to a nearby shop, where the man picked
out a few dozen beautiful mezuzah cases, then went to the
checkout to pay.

Kalman spoke up: "These cases are only to protect the scroll
inside."

"I don't need the scrolls," the man replied. "I'm not that religious."

Kalman responded gently, "We sometimes say, 'I'm not religious,' when we really mean, 'I'm not fully observant.' Everyone is
at least *somewhat* observant – helping the needy, honoring parents
and living ethically. Judaism is not 'all or nothing.' Imagine discov-
ering a diamond mine. You'll want to dig up every diamond. But
you wouldn't refuse to dig just because you can't have them all!
When it comes to Jewish knowledge and observance, each of us
is on a path, hopefully ascending. This is your opportunity to fill
these beautiful cases with kosher scrolls."

Inspired, the man did just that.

UNGRATEFUL BEGGAR

Kalman was headstrong, while at the same time extraordinarily humble and modest. He wrote:

> It's important to distinguish between pleasure and pride. Taking pride in one's achievements is not arrogance; it's a legitimate expression of self-respect. C.S. Lewis said, "Humility does not mean thinking less of yourself. It means thinking of yourself less."
>
> Arrogance is placing your self-importance above the welfare of others. Humility is admitting you are no better than others. This shows respect and honor – both to yourself and to others.

Friends report never hearing Kalman say a bad word about anyone. In fact, he'd constantly reframe situations to judge the other person favorably.

One day, Kalman and a friend were at the Western Wall when a beggar approached. Kalman reached into his pocket and gave a shekel.

"That's not enough!" the beggar yelled at Kalman.

Kalman's friend was taken aback, thinking: *Such chutzpah! We don't have to give you anything!*

Kalman, however, remained calm. Then – to his friend's shock – Kalman gave the beggar more money.

"I can't believe you did that!" the friend said after they'd walked away.

Kalman was committed to judging others favorably. "I figure he must really need the money. Otherwise, why would he behave like that?"

MISSIONARY TALE

The State of Israel, established in part to alleviate centuries of persecution against Jews, has little tolerance for missionaries who try to undermine Judaism. The Torah itself prescribes harsh punishment for missionaries. Rav Noah, whose lifetime goal was to bring Jews close to Judaism, aggressively opposed any attempt to do the opposite.

"The greatest gift you can give someone is to bring them close to God, which connects them with meaning and purpose," Rav Noah taught. "One of the great Jewish self-improvement guides, the eleventh century *Chovos HaLevavos*, writes, 'The reward for connecting people to the Almighty is completely immeasurable. Even someone who has scaled the heights of self-perfection, cannot compare to someone who teaches Torah and brings people close to God.'"

⸻◆⸻

Scott*, one of Aish HaTorah's recent arrivals, was hanging out in the Jewish Quarter's central square, when a missionary sat next to him and began proselytizing.

Scott, whose understanding of Judaism was still primitive, listened intently to biblical "proofs" of the Christian messiah. Scott was impressed and said with naïve sincerity, "You should share this information with Rabbi Weinberg. I'm not sure he's aware of this."

Scott brought the missionary to the Aish offices and sat in the waiting room. After a few minutes, Rav Noah came out to greet them. "Rabbi, this man has fascinating proofs about the Christian messiah," Scott said.

From the adjacent office, Kalman's antennae perked up. *Rav Noah meets a lot of people,* he thought, *but this one sounds really interesting.* And so it proved.

Rav Noah played a cool hand. "Tell me," he asked the missionary, "do you believe in every word of the New Testament?"

"Yes," the missionary replied. "Every word is absolutely true."

This was Rav Noah's cue. "How about Matthew 5:42 and Luke 6:30, which say, 'Give to someone who asks of you, and do not ask in return.' Do you believe this?"

"Of course. It's a binding obligation."

"Okay," said Rav Noah. "I'm asking you to give me your Bible."

The missionary protested, "This is my personal Bible, marked with notations. I carry it with me always!"

"Well, is it true or not: 'Give to someone who asks, and do not ask in return.' Do you believe or not believe?"

Reluctantly, the missionary handed his Bible to Rav Noah.

Kalman's eyes bulged as he watched the scene unfold.

Yet Rav Noah was not finished. "That's a nice shirt. Please give me your shirt."

The missionary did so. Rav Noah then continued until the man's watch, camera, shoes, pants and wallet full of traveler's checks were all neatly piled in a corner of the office.

Rav Noah pointed to the missionary wearing nothing but underwear and socks, and asked Scott, "What do you think of your genius friend now?"

"He's full of nonsense," Scott said, shaking his head in disbelief at his own gullibility... as the missionary made a beeline for the door.

The next morning, the missionary returned to the Aish HaTorah office – accompanied by a policeman.

"He's the one!" the missionary shouted, pointing at Rav Noah.

The policeman was fuming and confronted Rav Noah: "You took this tourist's clothes, money and everything else!"

Rav Noah turned to the missionary and calmly said, "You voluntarily gave me everything. I never threatened you."

Rav Noah then turned to the policeman and explained. "This man is a missionary, trying to convince one of our yeshiva students to believe in the Christian messiah."

The policeman, a traditional Moroccan Jew, became enraged. "Take your clothes and get out!" he shouted at the missionary. "And never come back here again!"

⟫•⟪

The epilogue to this story:

Scott attended classes for a few weeks, then suddenly disappeared. Rav Noah was concerned that he'd again been ensnared by missionaries. None of the other students knew of Scott's whereabouts.

Two years later, Rav Noah was lecturing in Chicago. Afterward, while speaking with some people in the audience, one man said, "I heard that you once stripped a missionary down to his underwear and socks. Is that true?"

"Where did you hear that story?" Rav Noah asked. "Do you know what ever happened to my former student?"

The man pointed the back of the room. "He's standing right there."

Rav Noah excused himself and darted toward Scott. "I can't believe it's you!" Rav Noah said with a bear hug. "How are you? Why did you disappear?"

"I'm sorry I didn't say goodbye," Scott said with some embarrassment. "I wanted to continue my trip around the world and was afraid that you'd talk me out of it. The entire time, your words echoed in my mind: 'If you don't know what you're living for, you're a zombie!' I returned to Chicago, got a job at a store and was promoted to store manager. If I stay another two years, I'll have enough money to return to Israel, get married, settle down and buy an apartment."

Rav Noah thought of the many people over the years who'd taken "a few years to save money" – then never returned to Jerusalem. "Come back now," Rav Noah advised. "You survived this long, but who knows what twists and turns await. Don't take any more chances."

Scott took Rav Noah's advice. He returned to Israel, got married, settled down and bought an apartment.

MATTER OF INTENT

In Jerusalem, Kalman was riding a public bus when he noticed that the grumpy driver was spreading misery to everyone on board. It was as if each passenger was an intrusion of noise and commotion, with the driver preferring to drive peacefully unencumbered.

Was it possible to change the driver's attitude? Kalman decided to try.

He approached the driver and said, "You're doing so many acts of kindness today!"

"Whaddya mean?" the driver grumbled. "I just do this for the money."

"Look at all the people you transport: a mother taking her child to the doctor; a man going to visit his elderly parents; a soldier going back to the base; a little girl going to school. Your day is packed with meaningful acts of kindness!"

"Hmm," the driver said, "I never thought of it that way. I like it!"

Feeling the momentum, Kalman pushed further. "Doing kindness is how we emulate the Almighty. Since you're already doing good deeds, you can shift focus and gain the added pleasure of emulating God. Why miss this opportunity?"

The driver thought for a moment, then threw up his hands (fortunately at a red light) and exclaimed, "You're absolutely right! Thank you!"

Kalman got off at the next stop, satisfied at having parlayed a mundane bus ride into a meaningful act of spreading Torah ideals – and changing one person's outlook on life.

ARMY RESERVES

During the 1980s, Kalman proudly served in the IDF Reserves. At age 35, he was sent to boot camp for three weeks to study army law and lore. Kalman learned how to disassemble and assemble M-16, Uzi and Galil rifles. He learned how to perform guard duty by scanning people's faces and mannerisms. And he polished his Hebrew.

"We were not what you'd call a crack army unit," Kalman recalled. "Since everyone in our group was a bit older, the IDF didn't make us do much exercise. They didn't want anyone dropping dead."

Kalman added wryly, "I'll never forget my fellow reservist who fired his Uzi at the target, while holding his forefinger in front of the barrel. He'll never forget that moment, either."

⟩◆⟨

In 1988, during the first Intifada, Kalman's unit was called up on emergency order and assigned to patrol the streets of Hebron. In the scorching Mideast heat, while lugging a heavy machine gun and gear during eighteen-hour shifts, Kalman recalled a teaching from Rabbi Zelig Pliskin: "In challenging circumstances, 'reframe' and perceive the situation differently. Rather than focus on the negative, find a positive spin. What can you gain or learn from this experience? Then integrate that clarity into your consciousness."

On the streets of Hebron, Kalman pondered the importance of protecting Judaism's oldest Jewish shrine and the second holiest site in Judaism, revered for 3,800 years as the place where Abraham purchased a cave to bury Sarah – making it the Jewish people's first claim to the land.

For Kalman, placing Hebron in context of Jewish national destiny provided a positive reframe during those long, grueling hours of patrol, as he repeated to himself, "Thank You, God, for giving me the merit to help protect the Jewish people."

During one stint in IDF reserve duty, Kalman was posted to a tank base and assigned to inventory nuts and bolts. He attacked the job energetically, in contrast to the unit's native Israelis who grumbled as they worked. "Hey, Packouz!" a fellow reservist called out. "Why are you so happy counting parts all day?"

Kalman relished the opportunity to share his mind frame. "First of all, I'm grateful not to be on eighteen-hour guard duty. Second, while we can't control the cards we're dealt in life, we can control how to play them. Since I'm here anyway, I might as well enjoy it."

One of the other reservists scoffed. "Packouz, that's Pollyana-ish. We're counting nuts and bolts, for goodness sake!"

Kalman replied, "It is said that 'For want of a nail, the kingdom was lost.' A seemingly minor issue can escalate into tragic consequences. If the IDF can't locate the right part to fix a tank, Israel could lose a war. So I view my work here as vital component of the whole."

In 1988, an incident in the Arab city of Halhul, near Hebron, prompted Kalman to counteract anti-Israel bias in the media. Bob Slater of *Time* magazine, the influential chairperson of the Foreign Press Association, had claimed that an IDF officer aimed a loaded gun at a photojournalist and shouted, "I'm going to kill you!"

Kalman, in uniform and on duty fifty feet away, witnessed the alleged incident. He wrote a letter setting the record straight, which was published in the *Jerusalem Post*:

> The photographer and his driver were given a direct order not to enter an area which would have been dangerous to their lives.

[The photographer] protested vigorously and exchanged heated words with our officer. The only time our officer raised his rifle was as a barrier to ward off a physical attack from the photographer. The rifle was extended parallel to the ground and was never at any time pointed at the photographer. Another officer had to physically restrain the photographer to prevent him from pursuing his attack.

RULES OF CONDUCT

As Executive Director of Aish HaTorah, Kalman made frequent fundraising trips abroad. Yet as a member of the IDF Reserves, he required documents granting permission to leave Israel.

One sunny morning, Kalman and another Aish student, IDF reservist (and Vietnam War veteran) Ben Karan drove to the ancient city of Jaffa on the Mediterranean coast. Winding their way through narrow cobblestone streets, they followed the signs to the IDF administrative office. Inside was a row of desks occupied by female soldiers. On the walls, were various pictures of women in immodest poses, which Kalman regarded as an affront to human dignity.

Rather than create a tense situation, Kalman first tried to ignore the distasteful decorations. Yet things got the best of him and he decided to take action.

Since Ben spoke fluent Hebrew, Kalman asked him to approach the ranking female officer and say:

We are certain that you and your colleagues are not responsible for the inappropriate pictures on the walls. However, according to page 147 of the *IDF Rules of Conduct* – chapter 6, sub-category C – it is forbidden to display anything not conducive to Jewish ethics.

If these pictures are not removed immediately, we will have no choice but to inform your commanding officer of the infraction.

Ben was skeptical about the wisdom of this strategy, yet agreed to speak with the officer. As he dutifully translated Kalman's pronouncement, the astonished officer and her colleagues were uncertain how to respond. Kalman broke the silence by removing the offending posters from the wall and calmly placing them in the trash.

Kalman then asked Ben to convey this message: "Should you encounter any trouble over this, please have your officer call us. We will take full responsibility and ensure your protection against reprisal." Meanwhile, Kalman smiled and handed his business card to each of the soldiers.

With that matter resolved, Kalman and Ben turned to the bureaucratic process at hand. It was, unsurprisingly, a seamless and swift resolution, and the two were soon back in the sun-drenched square outside.

"That was amazing!" Ben exclaimed. "How did you know the exact chapter and verse of that army statute?"

Kalman's eyes twinkled. "Oh, I just made it up," he confessed. "But women should not be degraded that way, and I had to do something about it."

Decades later, Ben reflects, "Kalman was a master out-of-the-box thinker. If something needed correcting, he'd go into battle mode – not with anger, but with creative tactics. He embodied the biblical maxim: 'With strategies you shall wage battle!'"

DEPUTY SHERIFF

Kalman once assisted a man in Atlanta, who showed his gratitude by arranging for Kalman the title of Special Deputy Sheriff in the State of Georgia. Kalman received an impressive badge and a letter from Richard Lankford, Georgia's High Sheriff:

> Having full trust and confidence in your dedication to the good welfare of all mankind; and whereas you have displayed a unique loyalty of service and further distinguished yourself as a courageous Ambassador of Peace and Good Will, you are hereby granted all rights and privileges associated with your commission.

While living in Jerusalem, Kalman kept the sheriff's badge in his car, waiting for the perfect opportunity to leverage his status. Soon after, Kalman was pulled over by the Israeli police for a small infraction. As the officer approached the car, Kalman whipped out his badge and said, "Good morning, officer! I am a sheriff in the United States. Perhaps you could take that into consideration."

The police officer stared at the badge, then called over his colleague. "Hey, Itzik. Look at what they do in the States. This badge is so cool!"

The police officer apologized to Kalman for any inconvenience, then wished him a nice day.

(The badge in now in the possession of Kalman's eldest grandson.)

COMFORT VERSUS PLEASURE

Confronting challenge always brought Kalman back to the classroom in 1973:

> "What is a parent's greatest pleasure?" Rav Noah asks.
> "Their children."
> "Correct. And a parent's greatest pain?"
> "Their children."
> "Correct. So how can pleasure also be the source of anguish?"

Rav Noah paused to let the question sink in, then asks, "What is the opposite of pain?"

"Pleasure," one student suggests. Others nod in agreement.

Rav Noah shakes his head. "Actually, the opposite of pain is 'no pain' – comfort. True, a hot bath and drifting off to sleep is comfortable and painless. But don't make the mistake of pursuing 'comfort' as the goal of life. That's not genuine pleasure. That's decadence!"

Rav Noah lowers his voice and leans forward. "Far from being opposites, pleasure and effort are two sides of the same coin. The Mishnah says, 'According to the effort is the reward.' Effort is the 'price tag' of pleasure. The more valuable the accomplishment, the greater effort is required to achieve. It's hard work to be an Olympic champion. It's even harder to be a champion human being."

—◆◆◆—

Kalman was constantly working to improve his parenting approach. One time, the Packouz's six-year-old son was late for dinner. After frantically calling the neighbors, Kalman finally located his son and got him on the phone. Frustrated and upset, Kalman asked gruffly, "Do you know what time it is?"

After a moment of silence, Kalman heard a small voice ask his friend's parents, "Excuse me. My father wants to know what time it is."

Kalman took the lesson to heart: An indignant tone is an ineffective way to communicate.

"Parenting is a challenge," Kalman once said. "There are no training courses, and by the time you finally know what you're doing, you're out of a job."

He then added a caveat: "Actually, parenting is a role that constantly evolves, and parents are never out of job."

TRASH BUSINESS

Kalman loved his children unconditionally and focused on the unique greatness of each. Never judgmental and always supportive, he encouraged them to "follow your passions and become your best self."

Kalman wrote, "The role of a parent is to make the child independent – to nurture their self-confidence and provide what they need to succeed in life. We hold their hands so they can walk, let go so they can run, and cheer when they fly!"

In Sanhedria Murchevet, the Packouz's apartment building had no elevator and no garbage chute. This meant that each family had to take their trash down the stairs, then schlep it to the large dumpster by the curb. Chana and David Packouz, ages seven and six, complained about the difficulty involved.

Kalman saw this as a teaching moment. "You're looking at this all wrong," he told them. "Besides being a challenge, this is also an opportunity to start your own business. Why not approach the neighbors and offer to take out their trash every other day. Make it a subscription service and charge one shekel (25 cents) a week. Ask them to commit to one week and see how it goes."

Chana and David enthusiastically agreed and pitched the idea to all the neighbors. Kalman's entrepreneurial instincts proved correct: Eight neighbors signed up.

The Packouz family had a small cart with wheels, so Chana and David would collect the trash, put it in the cart and schlep it down the stairs – *ka-chunk, ka-chunk, ka-chunk* – then dump it in the curbside receptacle.

After the first week, Kalman called for an evaluation session. "Dad, this is way too much work," the kids said. "We're young and this garbage is heavy. It's not worth it. We want to quit."

Kalman didn't want them to give up before acquiring some business skills. "Would you do it for twice the amount?"

Chana and David thought for a moment. "Twice the money? Sure, we'll do that!"

"So raise the price," Kalman suggested.

"We can't raise the price," they countered. "Just a week ago we set the price at one shekel."

Kalman explained, "You have a choice: Either quit and have zero clients, or try speaking with the neighbors and see what they say. They also have a choice: Yes or no. Find out if the price that's worth it to you, is also worth it to them. But stand firm on the price, even if people complain."

With this advice, Chana and David returned to their clients and announced the new pricing. Most said, "Fifty cents? No problem."

The garbage collection business did well, but eventually Chana dropped out – leaving David to double his money again. After a few months, he'd built up a few hundred shekels, kept in a Zip-loc bag in his parents' bedroom. David recalls, "Every day I'd hear the ice cream truck playing its jingle, and think to myself, *I'm rich! I can buy ice cream.* I soon became a fat little kid."

David reflects, "The garbage business taught me many lessons: To value my time, to offer a service that people value, to adjust as it goes ... and to watch my weight."

GOODWILL AMBASSADOR

Kalman was Rav Noah's first lieutenant in cultivating relationships with key partners, and Shabbos at the Packouz home was a popular destination for important visitors.

Dick Horowitz, a high-powered life insurance salesman, had read the Harvard Jewish Population Study predicting that American Jewry would nearly disappear due to assimilation. "I'm a numbers person, and the demographic research showed every stream except Orthodox heading toward zero," Dick explained. "For anyone hoping for proud Jewish children and grandchildren,

Torah is the obvious answer." This revelation prompted Dick to produce a chart entitled, "Will Your Grandchildren Be Jewish," which was presented to Jewish leaders and cited in the *New York Times*.

In the early 1980s, on one of his first visits to Jerusalem, Dick stayed at the Packouz home for Shabbos. Kalman and his family were welcoming, generous and made a wonderful impression. In the wake of that visit, Dick became president of Aish HaTorah International, and over the years personally donated tens of millions of dollars to Aish HaTorah.

———⟫•⟪———

In 1983, Harvey Hecker, an internationally known accountant, and his wife Sheila, visited their son Joel who was studying at Aish Jerusalem, to understand better what he was experiencing.

The Heckers rented an apartment in the Old City for two weeks. Rav Noah designated Kalman to speak with them at length about Aish HaTorah's goals and ideals.

Kalman and Shoshana hosted the Heckers for a beautiful Shabbos meal, and at one point Sheila exclaimed, "So many children! Why so many?"

"Allow me to quote a Chinese proverb," Kalman replied. "If you want one year of prosperity, grow grain. If you want ten years of prosperity, grow trees. If you want a hundred years of prosperity, grow people."

"But how do you give enough attention to each?" Sheila asked.

Kalman thought for a moment. "This reminds me of a joke about a child who swallows a coin. If it's your first child, you panic and take them to the hospital. If it's your fourth child, stay calm and take it off their allowance!"

Kalman continued, "But seriously, we give each child as much love and attention as possible. They know that whatever they need, we're here. And beyond what we provide as parents, the children help each other. We're a family."

Impressed with Kalman's idealism and commitment, the Heckers concluded, "This lifestyle would make any parent proud."

Upon returning to Toronto, Harvey organized a board for Aish HaTorah Toronto. Upon returning to Toronto, Harvey organized a board for Aish HaTorah Toronto. He involved his best friend, pharmaceutical tycoon Leslie Dan. Leslie became one of Rav Noah's closest partners and subsequently donated tens of millions of dollars.

Meanwhile, when Harvey was short-listed for chairman of a large global accounting firm, he withdrew his name from consideration in order to become chairman of Aish HaTorah International. He held the post for twenty-five years – due in part to Kalman making such a positive first impression.

⤜⬥⤛

When Yitz Greenman came to Aish Jerusalem to study in 1984, his parents were less than thrilled. Yitz was on track to becoming an upwardly mobile professional, and in their minds yeshiva was an unwelcome interruption. A few months later, Yitz's mother came to visit Jerusalem, hoping to persuade him to return to America.

To give his mother a positive impression, Yitz planned a first-rate Shabbos experience. The Packouz family – with meaningful discussions, scrumptious food and endless warmth – was his first choice.

That Shabbos proved a major success, transforming Mrs. Greenman into an avid supporter of yeshiva studies. "Rabbi Packouz is a caring and loving man," she told Yitz. "I love their family. And I want the same for you."

Soon after, Kalman typed an unsolicited letter to Mrs. Greenman, describing Yitz's progress and reiterating her wisdom in encouraging him to stay in yeshiva.

A few months later, when Yitz was visiting his mother, she showed him the letter, tearfully describing how much it meant to her.

Yitz went on to become a rabbi and master fundraiser, serving for decades as executive director of Aish HaTorah New York, then as strategic advisor to Olami – funneling tens of millions of dollars to Jewish educational programs.

Until her dying day, Mrs. Greenman kept Kalman's letter next to her bed. Says Yitz, "Kalman brought peace to our family and performed a huge *kiddush Hashem*."

HOME AWAY FROM HOME

Aish students in Jerusalem knew they could always find a "home away from home" with the Packouz family, who lived with the maxim: "To live with joy, care about the joy of others."

Rabbi Raphael Shore, who went on to lead various initiatives benefiting the Jewish people, describes his early days at Aish HaTorah:

> I had an open invitation to join the Packouz family for Shabbos, and I took them up on it with frequency. I can still taste the delicious chopped liver and mustard, the cold beer in frosted glasses, and the kids flying everywhere. Kalman's warmth and calm nature, as both a mentor and friend, was enormously helpful during those intense formative years.

⇒◆⇐

Chaim Feld grew up in New Jersey. After earning a business degree, he went backpacking through Europe. While running with the bulls in Pamplona, he realized there must be more to life. This began a journey that led him to yeshiva in Israel, and to one of his first Shabbos meals at the Packouz home. In his words:

> Shoshana displayed extraordinary patience and calm with what felt like three dozen children. They were so well-behaved and charming, but I didn't know how she could remember all their names!
>
> One of the kids dropped a dish, which shattered on the floor. I expected a whole ruckus after the crash, but there was barely a gasp. Nobody appeared annoyed or made a disparaging remark. Then, in a quiet and respectful manner, Kalman asked the child to get a dustpan.
>
> Kalman later told me, "Whenever I buy an item for the house, I immediately consider it broken. That way, when a child inevitably breaks it, instead of getting upset, I thank the Almighty for the gift of my child, and for use of the object until then. I also wonder why it took so long to break!"

Chaim recalls, "That incident made a deep impression and impacted my decision to become Torah observant."

Chaim went on to make his own remarkable impact on the Jewish people, as co-director of Aish Cleveland, co-founder of a national anti-gossip campaign, and patriarch of his own large family. Chaim quips, "That broken dish was well worth it!"

KNOW YOUR LIMITS

In hosting guests, Kalman's frame of reference was a class Rav Noah had taught on Genesis chapter 18:

> "Abraham was a wealthy man with a team of servants. Yet despite being elderly and weak from circumcision, Abraham welcomed guests into his home and served them personally.

"All else being equal, it is better to perform a good deed personally, rather than use a proxy. This way, in addition to providing for others' needs, it gets into our bones and changes us for the better," Rav Noah says, grinding his teeth for emphasis.

"What if I'm not on the level of Abraham?" a student objects.

"Judaism is not all-or-nothing, and you're not expected to be superhuman," Rav Noah says. "Part of greatness is knowing your limits and accepting them with grace and humor."

——◆——

Steve* was a yeshiva student who arrived at the Packouz home a few hours before Shabbos. Kalman graciously showed him to the guest room, then pointed to the clean sheets and towel lying folded on the bed.

"Have you heard the story about the great twentieth-century sage, the Chofetz Chaim?" Kalman asked rhetorically. "Even in old age, he personally served the guests in his home, attending to their comforts. One time, as he was making the guest's bed, the guest objected. 'Rabbi, don't trouble yourself!' Yet the Chofetz Chaim insisted, saying, 'If you saw me putting on tefillin in the morning, would you offer to put them on in my stead? Hosting you is my privilege, and I insist on making the bed.'"

Kalman looked at Steve and asked, "Isn't that an inspiring story?"

As Steve nodded politely, Kalman gestured toward the unmade bed, chuckled and said, "Well, I'm not the Chofetz Chaim!"

——◆——

As a purveyor of kindness, Kalman was reminded of the old joke: "Why does that person resent me? I never did them a favor!" Kalman explained, "Whenever you do someone a favor, there's unfinished payback. The other person feels indebted to you. So it's a kindness to give them an opportunity to 'give back' and not feel like an imposition."

In hosting guests, Kalman applied this principle with a unique twist of humor. When a guest would ask, "How can I help?" Kalman would reply, only half-joking, "Please make yourself at home. Wash the dishes and take out the garbage!"

The legendary Packouz hospitality was not limited to the walls of their home. In Aish HaTorah's study hall, Thursday evening was designated as *Mishmar,* a special learning session where students studied extra hours to finish the week on a high note. Attendance was motivated in part by the knowledge that at midnight, a delicious homemade cake would be served.

So it was, week after week: Shoshana Packouz baked a *Mishmar* cake that had the dual effect of encouraging Torah study, and offering students a small taste of home.

DISARMING TENSION

Kalman articulated his policy on interpersonal relationships:

> It takes two to argue. If someone is yelling and screaming at you, the issue is likely not about you. Perhaps some childhood and life experiences made them this way. They may simply be having a bad day and taking it out on you.
>
> You're dealing with emotions, not logic. Even with all the explaining and clarifying, you won't win. Instead, shower them with compassion and kindness. Even better, apologize! They'll simply be unable to argue after that.

Kalman took inspiration from a friend whose parking spot was positioned directly below a neighbor's air conditioner drainage hose. The car would regularly become covered in water mixed with dust – what Kalman called "a slurry mess that looked like modern art." Despite repeated requests that the hose be moved, the neighbor failed to comply.

After a number of helpful reminders and no resolution, Kalman's friend considered his options: Yell at the neighbor; call the police; or write a letter to the residents' committee.

Instead, Kalman's friend bought the neighbor flowers. He took a deep breath, knocked on their door and said with a big smile, "Here, these are for you."

The neighbor was completely baffled. "Why are you giving me flowers?"

"You're a good neighbor," he said softly. "I appreciate the effort you make to keep the air conditioner hose from dripping on my car."

The neighbor thanked him and shut the door. From that day forward, the air conditioner hose never again dripped onto the car.

Kalman's conclusion: "It's difficult to be angry at someone who brings you flowers."

———※———

Even when criticism came in the form of invectives, Kalman would defuse the tension with a short and sweet reply: "That's a good point. Thank you for letting me know."

In Jerusalem's Geula neighborhood, Kalman parked his car in front of Uri's Pizza and went in to pick up dinner for the family. A few minutes later, Kalman came out to find a man leaning against Kalman's car, with a scowling face and crossed arms. As Kalman approached, the man growled aggressively and shouted, "So you're the one!"

"The one *what*?" Kalman asked.

"The one who blocked my car!"

Sure enough, the man's car had no room to maneuver out of its parking spot. "I'm very sorry," Kalman said sincerely. "I didn't realize I'd blocked you. In the future, I'll be more careful. Please forgive me for causing you wasted time and aggravation."

At that, the man charged toward Kalman – and enveloped him in a bear hug. "I've never received an apology like that," he exclaimed. "You can block me any time!"

In recalling this true story, Kalman said, "This is a perfect example of why Israelis are called sabras – prickly on the outside, sweet on the inside."

ON THE LOOKOUT

On the street, Kalman would often pick up small coins. He explained, "Most people won't pick up a coin because it's embarrassing, demeaning or simply not worth the effort. Indeed, Jewish law regarding lost objects states that a person need not return an item that – were it their own – they wouldn't bother to pick up."

Kalman came to a unique conclusion: "Even if I wouldn't make the effort to pick up a coin for myself, why not make the effort for others?" From then on, whenever he saw a coin, Kalman would pick it up, put it in a separate pocket and, upon returning home, place it in a tzedakah box – his "bonus effort" to help others.

Kalman offered a second explanation for picking up coins: "U.S. coins are inscribed, 'In God We Trust.' It is disrespectful to leave God on the ground."

One day, Kalman saw an elderly man wandering around Sanhedria Murchevet who looked confused. Kalman recognized the man as the father-in-law of a great rabbi, who'd apparently gotten lost and couldn't find his way home.

In a precious act of *hashavas aveidah* (returning a lost item), Kalman patiently escorted the elderly man every step of the way – down the hill, between some buildings, and up four flights of stairs – till he was safely ensconced at home.

The rabbi was extremely grateful for Kalman's act of caring and asked, "How can I ever repay you?"

Rather than wave away the offer, Kalman had a wise retort: "When I have questions in Jewish law, I'd be glad to get a quick response."

The busy rabbi agreed, and from then on Kalman's questions always received priority treatment.

CONQUERING IMPATIENCE

1974. On their weekly ride to Bnei Brak, Kalman bemoans, "Rebbe, it bothers me that certain aspects of my character are holding me back."

"Kalman, that's normal," Rav Noah says. "Every person is born with a unique mix of traits to correct. Some struggle with arrogance; others with greed. Never say, 'I was created with certain negative traits and cannot change.' The soul has an innate yearning for perfection, and improving our character is the very reason we're sent to this world.

"On the other hand, animals live by pure instinct, with no imperative to change, and no ability to make ethical decisions.

"To win the inner battle, distinguish between the competing voices: cravings of the body and aspirations of the soul. Identify with your soul and train the body to reflect that reality."

Kalman had a tendency toward impatience, rooted in the false belief that we fully control our lives. Kalman learned that the Almighty sends challenges as a reminder that we don't run the show.

He also learned that when things work out contrary to our wish, it's not the end of the world. Kalman would say, "This moment is exactly where I need to be. My frustration is God's way of suggesting that I reconsider my approach."

CALM RESPONSE

In presenting an idea that might be viewed as controversial, Kalman would offer a disclaimer:

> Surely, some will be incensed by my suggestion and want to write, fax, email or call me. Please do so. If you have a good point that I haven't considered, I will gladly agree.
>
> Alternatively, if the only objection is that you happen to disagree, I will imagine money pouring into my bank account as a reward for standing up for my beliefs. This takes the sting out of any insult!

As a global ambassador for the Jewish people, Kalman became a lightning rod for angry pushback, suffering his share of humiliation. One recipient of the *Shabbat Shalom* newsletter faxed Kalman back twenty copies of the newsletter. Eager to defuse the tension and turn foe into friend, Kalman responded with a friendly note, asking, "Is there a problem? How can I help?"

The man's response was to fax back twenty copies of Kalman's note.

Whenever Kalman found himself on the receiving end of anger, he'd write a fiery letter in response. He'd then focus on the benefits of not retaliating and – like Abraham Lincoln – kept a drawer full of angry letters, written yet never sent.

Kalman wrote, "In one respect, humiliation is a good thing, because it humbles us. It's hard to be egotistical while being humiliated. Don't let a barrage of rage and insults chip away at your sense of self-worth. If you're truly humble, the humiliation won't affect you."

—◦—

On the rare occasion that Kalman lost patience, he was despondent at having stumbled. Early in married life, Kalman got angry with one of the children. Shoshana expressed displeasure, and since that day, Kalman never again raised his voice to the children.

Kalman did his best to control impatience, and typically appeared calm and even-tempered, even earning the moniker "Calm-man." He reasoned: "It's nobody else's problem. It's my problem and I have to deal with it. The only appropriate place for anger is the dictionary."

TRYING SITUATION

Despite a natural impatience, Kalman made great efforts to become more patient, and in his later years considered this his main goal in life.

According to Maimonides, a negative character trait can be repaired by going to the opposite extreme. To break the trait of impatience, Kalman employed a technique taught by Rabbi Pliskin:

> Assist someone, perhaps an elderly person, who moves slowly. Operate at their pace, without making them feel rushed. Calmly say, "Please take your time. Go at a pace you feel comfortable with." It's a form of respect that communicates, "Our time together has intrinsic value."

Kalman would put himself in situations that required patience – visiting hospitals, senior living facilities and prisons, where he'd listen for hours to long-winded recollections. Kalman sought out opportunities to build his "patience muscles" and master the next level of compassion.

⋙⬥⬥⋘

Kalman was close to someone with a difficult personality, who would berate Kalman with verbal abuse and cause him to suffer great indignity. Rather than do everything to avoid this person, Kalman saw it as an opportunity to work on patience. He went to the extreme and phoned this person nearly every day – for decades! This person would incessantly criticize Kalman, with never a kind word. Yet Kalman would just listen without arguing, astonished at the person's cognitive dissonance of the ill treatment. Day after day, Kalman made that call, as a way to achieve his goal of self-control.

Rabbi Yisrael Salanter taught that "repairing one character trait is more difficult than mastering the entire Talmud." Kalman, with his overpowering desire to change, "mastered the Talmud" several times over.

Shoshana says, "Kalman had an incredible ability to change and do what's right. For many years, he worked on conquering anger and impatience. I can testify that he finally conquered it – and it rubbed Kalman into a pearl."

ACCIDENTAL TRUTH

Kalman frequently cited the teaching that the Hebrew word for "falsehood" (sheker) is comprised entirely of letters with a small base at the bottom, whereas the letters of "truth" (emet) all have a wide base. The idea is that falsehood has no legs to stand on, whereas truth prevails.

One day, Kalman was at a stop sign near Dung Gate, the entrance to the Western Wall. A dump truck was trying to turn, but had no room to maneuver. To accommodate, a van filled with people backed up in Kalman's direction. Kalman blared his horn, but the van kept coming – smashing the front of Kalman's car.

The two drivers got out and exchanged information, which Kalman passed along to his insurance agent, Shalom Goldman.

A few days later, Kalman received a call from Shalom. "The driver of the van is claiming that you rear-ended him. And he has a van full of witnesses to prove it!"

Kalman was outraged at this brazen lie, yet took it as a test from God. "So how do you suggest we proceed?" Kalman asked.

Shalom thought for a moment, then said, "Let's invite the van driver and his insurance agent for a *sulkha* (Arabic for 'peace meeting') to discuss the incident."

A few days later, they all met at Shalom's office. After some small talk, cake and Turkish coffee, Shalom turned to the driver of the van and said, "As our honored guest, please go first. Tell us what happened."

"A dump truck wanted to turn," the driver began, "but he couldn't make it around me. So I backed up my van to let him in, and I hit the car behind me."

Kalman was astonished. The driver forgot to lie!

Shalom asked Kalman to confirm the events, and the brief meeting ended with the van driver agreeing to pay the damage. Kalman was thrilled to see justice prevail.

In telling this story, Kalman added a unique take-away: "This incident occurred because the van driver was doing a kindness for the dump truck. When doing kindness, be careful not to harm anyone in the process."

CERTIFICATE OF SANITY

As a master of interpersonal relationships, Kalman subscribed to the Jewish idea of *vitur* – relinquishing convenience for the sake of another. This involves yielding to others' wishes; going beyond the letter of the law; and not always standing on one's rights.

In the Old City of Jerusalem, the Jewish Quarter parking lot had a combined entrance and exit. Frequently, one car would be entering the lot at the same time that another wanted to exit.

One day, Kalman witnessed a verbal "tennis match" between two drivers, arguing about who should yield the right of way.

Neither succeeded in convincing the other. (They ignored one bystander's cynical suggestion "to duke it out.")

Finally, one of the disputants yelled at the other, "Do you have a certificate of sanity?!" *(Yesh lecha te'udat normaliyut?!)* The other fellow, at a loss for words, promptly backed up his car and yielded the way.

A few months later, Kalman was visiting a hospital, when a man asked for directions to a certain ward. "I'm sorry, I don't know," Kalman replied.

Immediately the man lashed out, "What's wrong with you?! Why don't you know?!"

The incident at the parking lot flashed into Kalman's mind, and he interrupted the man's tirade by asking, "Excuse me, do you have a certificate of sanity?"

The man looked at Kalman as if he was completely short-circuited – and walked away.

HORSE PLAY

Kalman was a paragon of transparency, always above-board and refusing to play games. His motto was, "What you see is what you get." He enjoyed telling this story:

> One day in a Russian village, a man observes the sale of a horse for the incredibly low price of 100 rubles. When the deal concludes, the bystander approaches the seller and says, "That horse was worth at least 1,000 rubles. Why did you sell it so cheap?"
>
> "That horse is lame," the seller sneers. "In a few minutes, the buyer will be carrying the horse on his shoulders!"
>
> The bystander runs to the buyer. "The horse you bought is lame!"

"I know," the buyer guffaws. "He's lame because of the nail in his hoof. I'll remove the nail and have a perfectly good horse for only 100 rubles!"

The bystander runs back to the seller. "The horse has a nail in his hoof. Once he takes it out, it will be perfectly fine!"

"Idiot!" The seller laughs. "I knew nobody would ever agree to buy a lame horse. So I put a nail in its hoof to trick the buyer!"

Huffing and puffing, the bystander returns to the buyer. "You've been swindled! He put in that nail to deceive you."

The buyer shrugs and throws up his hands. "It doesn't matter anyway. The rubles are counterfeit."

Kalman was like the bystander in this story, obsessed with integrity and always on the lookout to remedy a situation. On a visit to Ramat Beit Shemesh, a city with many roundabouts, he was concerned that one particular roundabout with deer figurines was improperly lit and therefore a hazard. To avoid the maze of municipal bureaucracy, Kalman went to the hardware store, purchased red reflectors and – with his wry sense of humor – attached a reflector to the nose of each deer in the roundabout.

CHILD'S PROMISE

Kalman's intolerance for falsehood was absorbed by his children from the earliest age. When Avraham Packouz was six years old, his friend knocked on the door with an invitation to play. "If you come to my house, I'll give you cookies and milk," the friend pledged.

Despite the attractive offer, Avraham's friend had used the "cookies and milk" gambit before and failed to deliver. "You're always making false promises," Avraham said indignantly. "I'm calling the police. They'll put you in jail for lying!"

As the words came out, it dawned on Avraham that he'd now made his own "promise," and Kalman's voice rang in his ears: "Say what you mean, and do what you say."

Avraham knew that he needed to follow through on his threat. He looked on the fridge and – lo and behold – his well-organized mother had posted a magnet with emergency numbers.

With trepidation, Avraham called the police. "Do you put people in jail for lying?" he asked, as the friend stood by shaking in fright.

"Yes, I understand. Thank you," Avraham said, hanging up the phone.

"Are they coming to get me?" the friend stammered. "Will they put me in jail?"

"No," Avraham said. "But the officer said that it's wrong to lie, and you shouldn't do it again."

SHISHKABAB JUSTICE

Kalman loved stories where perpetrators of injustice receive their just rewards. In his own life, this devotion to justice sometimes manifest in the extreme.

Kalman and Shoshana were celebrating their wedding anniversary at one of Jerusalem's finest restaurants. Shoshana ordered shishkabab, yet when the plate arrived it contained only one shishkabab.

"Where is the other shishkabab?" Kalman asked the waiter.

"This is how we serve the dish," the waiter replied.

Kalman asked to see a menu, then pointed to the English description: "Skewers of meat roasted to perfection on our grill." He then respectfully explained, "The word 'skewers' ends with the letter 's.' This indicates the plural form – a minimum of two."

The waiter was gracious, but reiterated, "This is how we serve the dish."

Kalman's inner lawyer came out and, with dramatic flair, pointed to the photo on the menu: a beautiful plate with *two* skewers of shishkabab!

The waiter remained firm. "This is how we serve the dish."

"Thank you for your assistance," Kalman said. "May I have a word with the maitre d'?"

The maitre d' glided over to the table and inquired, "How may I be of service?"

Kalman repeated his lesson in English grammar, describing the incongruity between the menu and what was served on the plate.

The maitre d' gave Kalman a look of pity, then dryly said, "This is how we serve the dish."

Kalman and Shoshana proceeded to enjoy their dinner. Yet in the back of Kalman's mind, the wheels of justice were turning.

The next day, Kalman wrote a letter to the restaurant manager, extolling the restaurant's virtues – fine decor, excellent service and delightful food. "Yet there is one matter which a restaurant of your high standards would want to know about," Kalman wrote, then proceeded to describe the misrepresented shishkabab and his by-now infamous English grammar lesson.

The letter concluded, "My understanding of prevailing standards in upscale restaurants is that, in such situations, the waiter is to immediately apologize and bring a second shishkabab. If the situation ever reached the manager, the couple would likely be invited back for a complimentary dinner."

A few weeks later, Kalman was pleased to receive a letter from the restaurant manager, with an apology and an invitation to return as guests of the restaurant.

Soon after, Kalman and Shoshana were back at the restaurant. Things went smoothly… until they brought Kalman's steak. "Excuse me, where is the baked potato?" he asked.

The waiter responded, "This is how we serve the dish."

Kalman held up the menu and pointed to a photo of the steak and baked potato.

The waiter went to consult with the maitre d'.

A minute later, Kalman had his potato.

(Postscript: Soon after, the restaurant removed photos from the menu.)

MEASURE FOR MEASURE

On occasions when Kalman found himself the target of an abusive outburst, he'd reframe the exchange by applying this scenario:

> Imagine walking down the street past a psychiatric hospital, when a patient wearing striped pajamas leans out the window and shouts, "You are the most disgusting creature to ever walk the planet!"
>
> Should I take this remark personally and have my ego crushed? No. I'll have compassion on the fellow, and tell myself, *It's sad there is so much insanity out there.*

⟹•⟸

One day, Kalman parked his car in Jerusalem's Ramat Eshkol shopping center. He returned to find the car's right side scraped from end to end. Spotting a note under the windshield wiper, Kalman was pleased that the driver had not just driven off. He opened the note to read, "I observed a woman in a black Mercedes, license plate #123-456, sideswipe your car and drive off. I am willing to testify to the police or in court." Signed was a name and phone number.

Kalman went to the police and, with the license plate number, obtained the woman's name and address. On the way, Kalman was reminded of the Mishnah: "Judge every person favorably."

Refraining from accusations, he went through a checklist of possibilities:

> • One small detail – exaggerated or omitted – can completely alter the scenario. Am I sure the details are correct?

> • Don't assume ill intent. Maybe a miscommunication or misconception explains their behavior – the result of innocent error, lack of experience, or being forgetful or distracted.

> • Do I know all the background? The person might be enduring great pain, frustration or stress – due to illness, financial loss or other deep concern.

Upon arriving at the woman's home, Kalman introduced himself and explained the purpose of his visit.

"It wasn't me who hit your car!" the woman shouted.

Kalman took a deep breath and reminded himself: *Don't escalate a quarrel, nor answer every insult.* "Are there any other female drivers in your household?" he said.

"No."

"Okay, have it your way," Kalman said. "I'm going to file a police report. Minimally, you'll lose your license. And there's the possibility of a large fine and jail sentence."

The woman went berserk. "That's unfair! Last month someone sideswiped my car and didn't leave a note. Why should I leave a note?"

Kalman was taken aback by the psychological linkage that made him the unfair object of revenge. Yet he avoided the urge to respond, focusing instead on the words of King Solomon: "A master of temper is stronger than one who captures a city."

As the woman continued to rage, Kalman dutifully nodded, maintained eye contact and made intermittent listening sounds.

Eventually she ran out of steam, but not before unleashing one final invective: "It's all your fault for parking so close to the white line!"

As Kalman drove home, he was left to ponder: *Why was I subjected to this person's extreme frustration, obstinacy and verbal abuse? Am I culpable in some way? What lesson does the Almighty want me to learn from this incident?*

Kalman concluded: "This taught me that people, including myself, often don't see our own faults and mistakes. As a rabbi, this is a good lesson in dealing with people."

Kalman filed a police report. In the ensuing weeks, the woman repeatedly phoned Kalman, screaming and threatening. She also had her friends call, pressuring Kalman to cancel the police report.

Finally, the woman agreed to pay. They met at the police station, where she handed Kalman an envelope with cash.

Kalman counted the money, then said, "There seems to be a mistake."

Her barrage came like a rocket blasting off. "I know your type! You've got me over a barrel and now want to extort more money! Who do you think you are? I'm not going to pay!"

Eventually, the propellant petered out and the litany stopped.

"Actually, you gave me too much," Kalman said softly, handing her a hundred-shekel note, which she took without a hint of remorse or embarrassment.

Kalman then inquired about the person who had sideswiped her car.

"I was able to track them down, but it's so frustrating," she said. "They're unwilling to take responsibility and pay for the damage. Some people can be so cheeky!"

In retrospect, Kalman wondered on what basis he merited that a witness left a note. He then recalled that a few weeks earlier while riding a public bus, the driver had sideswiped a car and continued on. Kalman had gotten off at the next stop and left a nearly identical note on the windshield.

Kalman smiled and thought, *The Almighty repays, measure for measure.*

KALMAN'S WAY: POSITIVE & PEACEFUL INTERACTIONS

- **Open.** Expose your convictions to the marketplace of ideas, to be analyzed and discussed. Validate other views that are rational and intelligent. Be willing to change in the face of compelling evidence. Let your motto be: "Convince me or join me!"

- **Listen.** Speak like you're right, and listen like you're wrong. Allow the other person to speak without interruption. To reassure they've been heard, repeat what was said.

- **Clarify.** Define your terms. How often have you gotten into a disagreement, only to eventually conclude, "Oh, if that's what you mean, I agree!"

- **Compromise.** Find common ground. Acknowledge areas of agreement, then build upon that. People of good will can reason together and reach a common conclusion.

- **Repair.** In the event you cause emotional pain, repair the breakdown and aim for full reconciliation. A little resentment multiplied many times over can create a wall of bitterness.

- **Respect.** Discuss ideas passionately, without attacking anyone's character.

- **Gentle.** Don't inflame the situation. Speak in a soft voice.

- **Truth.** Check your motives: Do you seek the truth, or just to defeat the other side? Rather than trying to "win the argument," try to understand the full picture – regardless of which side you're on. Being defeated by truth is itself a victory.

CHAPTER SEVEN

Shabbat Shalom – Fax of Life

FLORIDA-BOUND

In 1990, Kalman was at work in the Old City of Jerusalem when Rav Noah called him in for a meeting.

"A position has opened up to develop adult Jewish education in Miami Beach, as well as a regional office of Aish HaTorah's Jerusalem Fund," Rav Noah explained. "It requires someone with teaching, fundraising and administrative experience, who knows the ins and outs of the organization. I'm thinking of you, Kalman, because this position will allow you creative independence, and the flexibility to launch new initiatives."

Kalman was attracted to the idea and discussed it with Shoshana. She thought about it for a few days and concluded that, while difficult to leave their family and friends in Jerusalem, it was the right move for Kalman and the family.

The move proved prescient, as it kick-started Kalman's greatest period of creativity – the development of Jewish unicorns *Shabbat Shalom* weekly and the Western Wall webcam.

CENTURY-OLD TECHNOLOGY

Kalman was always one step ahead of the curve, on the lookout for innovative tools and techniques to be harnessed in service of God and the Jewish people.

In Miami, Kalman's next iconic project traced its roots to the mid-1800s, when the invention of the telegraph by Samuel Morse sparked an explosion of communication technology. Soon after, Alexander Bain made a breakthrough advancement by inventing the fax ("facsimile") machine, which enabled the transmission of documents along electric (and later, telephone) lines. Early fax machines cost tens of thousands of dollars apiece and, for over a century, fax technology remained confined mostly to news reporting and military operations.

Finally, in the late 1980s, the fax machine came into its own as a mass consumer product, a "must-have" device for businesses and homes. Market penetration grew tenfold overnight, launching the era of electronic document sharing, and crowning the fax machine as one of history's most influential communication devices.

Until then, bulk distribution of newsletters was confined to snail mail. Kalman took notice and pondered the potential of reaching a mass audience with history's first "electronic Torah mailing list." Yet limitations, such as the need for manual dialing and document handling, rendered the mass-mail potential of fax technology unfeasible. Kalman's dream moved to the back burner.

SEIZE THE MOMENT

Kalman's thoughts drifted back to Rav Noah in the classroom:

Everyone is looking for immortality, to impact the world. Some erect tall buildings and attach their name. Others set athletic records. Others create great works of art. Yet when all is said and done, it is the power of great ideas that lives on.

Everyone dreams about changing the world. But talk is cheap. Genuine change-makers are those who summon the courage to leave their comfort zone and follow their destiny.

The Torah tells us: Seven days after the Exodus from Egypt, the Israelites were trapped between the Egyptian army and the raging sea. As the Israelites cried out in fear, God said, "Instead of crying, go forward into the sea!"

Nobody wanted to go first, until the prince of Judah, Nachshon ben Aminadav, jumped in. He continued deeper and deeper, with the water reaching his knees, his chest, even his neck. Only when the water reached his nostrils did the sea split – paving the way for the entire Jewish people to pass through on dry land.

The lesson: The Almighty grants success to those who courageously undertake responsibility.

———◆———

In 1992, Kalman was browsing a computer magazine that described a technological advancement whereby documents could be sent – via modem – directly from a computer to a fax machine. The computer would do the dialing and eliminate the need to feed paper into the fax machine.

This was Kalman's eureka moment, an unprecedented opportunity to connect with an ever-widening audience. He immediately plunged in, investing long hours of research and brainstorming with computer experts, marketers and rabbinic colleagues.

Ultimately, Kalman conceived of a weekly newsletter of Torah thoughts: bite-size pieces of folksy, down-to-earth wisdom, witticisms, insights into life and stories with a message. He developed a six-part formula to keep things fresh and dynamic, week in and week out:

- **Educational.** Teach the basics of Jewish literacy and inspire further study.

- **Relevant.** Address contemporary issues from a Torah perspective – relationships, personal growth, spirituality, etc.

- **Universal.** Employ language, style, tone and content that is accessible and digestible, and appeals to all ages and backgrounds.

- **Timely.** Sync people with the rhythm of Jewish life by featuring short lessons based on the weekly Torah portion or upcoming holiday.

- **Fun.** Feature jokes and a pithy "quote of the week."

- **Practical.** Include Shabbos candle-lighting times for cities around the world.

Kalman entitled the nascent publication *Shabbat Shalom Weekly*. Then, to highlight the electronic medium and the element of "practical wisdom," he added the witty tagline: *Fax of Life*.

Kalman produced a prototype edition of the newsletter, then scoured his database for fax numbers of a few dozen supporters and friends. He purchased a computer modem – a novelty in pre-Internet days – then rigged it to his computer and performed test-runs to ensure the software worked without a glitch.

With his best efforts in place, Kalman said a short prayer – "May these efforts bring honor to the Almighty, to Torah and to the Jewish people" – and pressed "send."

SUBSCRIBER LIST

Reaction to that first, experimental edition of *Shabbat Shalom* was unanimously positive, giving Kalman validation to run with the idea. His first order of business: Scale the distribution list. In relentless fashion, Kalman began collecting fax numbers from whomever he encountered – engaging in conversations at the supermarket, or ambushing people as they perused the *smorgasbord* at a *simcha*. Fax numbers were duly noted in a small notebook and, one by one, the database of *Shabbat Shalom* subscribers grew.

What Kalman could not have predicted was the exponential growth fueled by avid readers volunteering as brand ambassadors. They shared *Shabbat Shalom* with family and friends, distributed copies in Jewish community centers and synagogues, and posted on office bulletin boards.

Kalman was walking in Miami when a man recognized him. "Look!" the man exclaimed, proudly opening his briefcase to reveal multiple copies of *Shabbat Shalom*. "I hand these out to whoever I meet."

LOGISTICAL CHALLENGE

As the subscription list grew, Kalman encountered a logistical challenge that had no precedent: how to send thousands of faxes. This was daunting for even the tech-savvy, yet Kalman embraced the challenge as a hurdle to overcome.

To create the infrastructure of an efficient distribution system, Kalman converted his home office into a veritable "fax factory," installing additional phone lines and outfitting multiple computers with multiple modems. When the prevailing software, an auto-dial system designed to send out faxes by the dozens, proved inadequate to satisfy *Shabbat Shalom's* hungry readership, Kalman innovated a method of "grouping" subscribers and sending out faxes in chunks at a time.

Shabbat Shalom was delivered in the forty-eight hours leading up to Shabbos, creating an enormous logistical challenge: insufficient time to send all the faxes. The delivery schedule was further constrained by Kalman's desire not to disturb anyone with the ringing, squeaking and whirring noise associated with receiving a fax. As a solution, he divided subscribers into two groups: homes and offices. During the daytime, with many people out and about, faxes were sent to homes. The remainder was sent to deserted offices throughout the night.

During those forty-eight hours, anyone walking by Kalman's home office in Miami Beach would hear the distinctive squeal of modems, spreading *Fax of Life* to all corners of the world.

The distribution system, however, was not without glitch. Approximately ten percent of transmissions ended in error – either the recipient's fax machine ran out of paper or the phone line was interrupted. Invariably, by midday Friday, Kalman's phone would ring incessantly, with distressed readers asking him to resend the fax.

Far from annoyed, Kalman cherished these calls. One Friday, a man phoned, frantic for help: "I distribute *Shabbat Shalom* to dozens of people in my office – and we can't enjoy the weekend without our favorite reading material!"

CONTENT IS KING

The popularity of *Shabbat Shalom* was driven by its first-rate content. Kalman's writing showcased a unique combination of warmth, sincerity, humor, wisdom and storytelling. Most of all, *Shabbat Shalom* explained Jewish concepts in a down-to-earth, relatable style – not above or below anyone's level of understanding.

"I'm not a tech wizard," he explained. "But I understand life. I understand Judaism. I understand people. *Shabbat Shalom* is my filter on life. It's what I find valuable, important and humorous. I write for myself, and hope that others find it helpful, too."

In his efforts to render Judaism relevant for today's generation, Kalman never compromised the integrity of Torah, nor pandered to make it more acceptable or appealing. Following Rav Noah's methodology, Kalman distilled various aspects of Torah to their conceptual essence, like a chemist breaking down materials into component parts. Short pieces such as "Five Reasons to

Keep Kosher" and "Why Not Cremation?" became instant classics. When Kalman wrote about the reasons and benefits of fasting on Yom Kippur, one reader wrote back to say that she was inspired to fast for the first time in forty years.

A perennial mainstay of *Shabbat Shalom* was insights from Rabbi Zelig Pliskin, Kalman's first Talmud teacher in 1974 and subsequent lifelong friend. Each week, Kalman would cull a nugget from *Growth Through Torah, Gateway to Happiness*, or another of Rabbi Pliskin's dozens of groundbreaking books on self-development and relationships.

"Kalman was a pioneer, totally dedicated to spreading Torah values," Rabbi Pliskin says. "Kalman was constantly asking himself, 'What can I do to help the Jewish people survive and thrive?' The fact that something was 'new' was not a negative factor to be feared, but rather an opportunity to courageously embrace."

One of *Shabbat Shalom's* most popular features was "Quote of the Week," drawn from a wellspring of Sages, philosophers and leaders – as well as Kalman originals such as:

- If you want to be happy, never miss an opportunity to be kind and grateful.

- If you want misery, expect everything to go your way, and protest when it doesn't.

- Never leave a loved one or a friend without saying, "I love you!"

The CEO of a famous toy company reported, "I love the weekly *Shabbat Shalom* and read it every week for the quote."

One year, *Shabbat Shalom* included tips for making the Passover Seder more child friendly: "During the Ten Plagues, use props. Throw plastic frogs for the plague of frogs, and ping-pong balls for the plague of hail." A few days later, Kalman went to a local toy store and asked an employee where to find plastic frogs.

The employee looked at Kalman strangely and said, "You're the seventh person to ask that today – and we're all sold out. We're also out of ping-pong balls." Kalman's conclusion: Do your holiday shopping early!

VIRAL REACH

Within a few months of its launch, the *Shabbat Shalom* subscriber list had snowballed into the world's first "viral fax," transmitted to far-flung locales from Hong Kong to Houston, Singapore to Caesarea. *Shabbat Shalom* grew into a global virtual congregation.

The *Miami Herald* profiled the local rabbi who pioneered the use of technology for Jewish adult education:

> Rabbi Kalman Packouz has eight children and eight computers. He loves his kids, of course. He's not so sure about the computers. But he's learned to live with his electronic gizmos and even, sometimes, to like them, because each week they let him educate more than 100,000 people worldwide about Judaism with his free Shabbat Shalom Fax.

Shabbat Shalom reached the highest echelons of government, C-suite executives, and rabbis of all denominations. Ambassador Stuart E. Eizenstat, chairman of the United States Holocaust Museum, who served in the administrations of U.S. Presidents Johnson, Carter, Clinton and Obama, reports that for decades, *Shabbat Shalom* was the basis for discussions at his family's Shabbos table.

Rabbi Eliot Pearlson of Temple Menorah in Miami Beach was an early *Shabbat Shalom* subscriber who encouraged members of his synagogue to subscribe. "I don't know of anything that reaches out on such a down-to-earth level," he told the *Miami Herald*.

Jacob Solomon, CEO of the Miami Jewish Federation, called *Shabbat Shalom* "a five-minute pause that, in an extremely accessible format, connects people proudly to their Jewish heritage."

⇒•◦•⇐

For every *Shabbat Shalom* fax sent, multiple people passed it along. One morning, Kalman's phone rang with a caller from Israel saying, "Mazel tov!" Having never before spoken to this person, Kalman was perplexed. Then the caller explained:

"For a few years, I've been forwarding my copy of *Shabbat Shalom* to a friend in England. That person in turn forwards it to a woman in Russia. The fax lit a spark and the woman subsequently became Torah observant. I'm calling with the good news that today she's getting married to a rabbi in Moscow!"

Such stories were repeated, with varying details, countless times over the twenty-seven years that Kalman produced *Shabbat Shalom*. One reader wrote:

> When our family became more interested in Torah, we looked for written content to share with our children. We live in a rural location and can't always make it to synagogue. We came across *Shabbat Shalom* and we all love it. We feel like Rabbi Packouz is our "other rabbi," when weather or other things keep us away from our own.

Over the years, Kalman received a steady stream of positive feedback:

- "This week's edition was exactly what I needed to get through the day."
- "My life has changed since I started reading your well-written and meaningful articles."

- "I always marvel at how you fit so much insight into short, easy-to-read communiqués."

- *"Shabbat Shalom* is easy to understand, written in clear language that isn't over my head."

- "I was one of the first fifty people to receive the *Shabbat Shalom* fax, and continue to enjoy it every week!"

Now primarily in email format, the typical "open rate" on *Shabbat Shalom* emails is twenty-five percent, far higher than industry standard. People still print hard copies and pass them around, increasing the readership far beyond the number of subscribers. For example, one large shul in London uses *Shabbat Shalom* as their weekly congregational newsletter.

TRAVEL ENCOUNTERS

Each edition of *Shabbat Shalom* featured a photo of Kalman's broad smile, together with a big "thumbs up." As such, he became a roving ambassador for the Jewish people, frequently recognized when traveling around the world.

Kalman was on a trip to Prague with rabbinic colleagues, when suddenly a menacing-looking man with a shaved head noticed the group and headed toward them rapidly. Kalman and his friends – openly Jewish at a time of rampant anti-Semitism in Europe – huddled together nervously. As the man drew closer, he suddenly stopped, pointed a finger directly at Kalman and with a friendly smile exclaimed, "Rabbi Packouz? I get your fax!"

One day, Kalman was traveling by public bus from Jerusalem to Tel Aviv. Sitting beside him was a young man whose distinctive accent identified him as native Australian. The two began to schmooze, but did not introduce themselves. The young man, sensing that his seatmate was a good listener, shared a bit of his story. "I'm Jewish by birth, but until recently I knew nothing about my Jewish heritage."

Kalman was intrigued and urged the young man to continue.

"A few years ago, I decided to read the Bible, to catch up on Jewish history and philosophy. Yet the text seemed confusing and irrelevant. I needed a guide. So I searched the Internet and discovered a wonderful newsletter called *Shabbat Shalom*."

Kalman marveled at the Almighty's sense of humor. Yet he didn't let on, and bit his lip to avoid laughing.

The young man continued, "I've been reading *Shabbat Shalom* avidly for years. The insights have literally changed my life."

Kalman suspected this meeting was a set-up, like some prank from "Candid Camera," so he began looking around for suspicious activity. Meanwhile, the young man leaned toward Kalman and spoke in serious, hushed tones. "*Shabbat Shalom* made such an impact on my life that I'm moving to Israel, to establish a non-profit that educates Jewish children in good values and character. My goal is to change the world."

With this, Kalman's eyes welled up with tears, overwhelmed with gratitude at having planted a seed to further spread the Jewish message and mission.

At this point, the young man stared intently at Kalman, then said with sudden realization, "You know, the photo of the rabbi in *Shabbat Shalom* looks a lot like you."

This was Kalman's cue. He broke into an ear-to-ear grin and flashed his trademark "thumbs up."

The young man's eyes widened, then his mouth dropped open. "Rabbi Packouz! I can't believe it's you!"

As the bus arrived in Tel Aviv, the other passengers could only wonder at the scene of the two men embracing with tears of joy.

BACK DOOR

Shabbat Shalom's clear and concise Torah message, flavored with humor and inspiration, resonated with readers across the spectrum. When one colleague observed that *Shabbat Shalom* is perfect for unaffiliated Jews, Kalman took it further. "What do you mean? Our mission to teach ethical monotheism is not limited to Jews. *Shabbat Shalom* is good for everyone!"

Kalman understood the imperative of bringing all humanity back to God, and non-Jewish readers account for nearly twenty percent of *Shabbat Shalom* subscribers. In a typical week, Kalman would receive letters from New Zealand and Iraq, from a priest in Ireland, and from a church group in the Midwest. One *Shabbat Shalom* reader wrote, "I'm not Jewish, but I truly believe that Rabbi Packouz fulfills God's promise to Abraham that, through the Jewish people, all the nations of the earth are blessed."

With its universal appeal and viral momentum, *Shabbat Shalom* often found a back door to a range of recipients:

- Kalman was contacted by a secretary who admitted that, though not Jewish, she loved reading *Shabbat Shalom* that was sent to her Jewish boss. "I've tried getting him to read it," she told Kalman earnestly, "but haven't been successful. What do you advise?"

- A non-Jewish caregiver who worked for a Jewish man became an avid *Shabbat Shalom* reader. Each week, the caregiver and the Jewish man discussed the content together – reconnecting him with his Jewish roots.

- A Jewish woman had *Shabbat Shalom* faxed to the Catholic school where she worked. The office manager objected and asked that it stop. The Jewish woman appealed to the head priest who, after reading a copy, told her, "You may continue receiving the fax, on the condition that I receive a copy every week!"

• Dr. Brian Lerman of Baltimore, who is not Jewish, began reading *Shabbat Shalom* in 1993 when it arrived at his office, earmarked for his Jewish partner. Everyone in the office knew that *Fax of Life* had to be placed in Dr. Lerman's inbox so he could read it first thing. "Rabbi Packouz's teachings were universally applicable," he says. "What a wonderful person to share this wisdom for the good of all."

• One *Shabbat Shalom* reader wrote, "I never met Rabbi Packouz. But as a Roman Catholic, I found his way of explaining the Bible to be life-changing. He was an exceptional human being who taught me many heartfelt spiritual lessons."

• One woman, an American of Spanish-Cuban descent, worked as a credit manager for a Jewish-owned company. Every week when *Shabbat Shalom* was due to arrive, she'd sit next to the office fax machine and secretly make a copy, then pass it along to the intended recipients. Though she worried about the ethics of this surreptitious interception, she couldn't resist. This practice continued for years, with *Shabbat Shalom* clippings often displayed on her fridge at home. She says, "The wisdom and inspiration of *Shabbat Shalom* made me wish I was Jewish."

• *Shabbat Shalom* was sent every week to a bank manager, whose non-Jewish secretary saw that her boss was uninterested. But she was – and read it week after week. Six years later, Kalman received a call from that secretary to say that, inspired by *Shabbat Shalom,* she had converted to Judaism.

SUBAQUATIC CONNECTION

A nuclear submarine, equipped with advanced weaponry and thousands of naval personnel, was patrolling underwater in the icy seas of the Northern Hemisphere. Sonar and radar sensors whirred and pulsed, tracking multiple objects above and below the surface – everything from hostile ships to humpback whales.

In the control room, a fax machine sprang to life and, with its telltale screech, rolled out the latest edition of *Shabbat Shalom*. The recipient? A U.S. Navy Admiral, the Jewish commander of the nuclear submarine, who would faithfully distribute copies to all the Jewish sailors on board.

Kalman was unaware of his subaquatic subscribers. Then, one morning, the admiral – stationed for a few days in the port of Fort Lauderdale – phoned Kalman's office, introduced himself, and asked about the possibility of "meeting the famous Rabbi Packouz."

Kalman was taken by surprise and respectfully asked for an explanation.

"Naval patrols take me underwater for months at a time," the admiral said. "Though I'm not religious, the weekly spiritual connection of *Shabbat Shalom* is a breath of fresh air."

Kalman knew that his faxes went all over the world, yet this was a new realm of maritime outreach.

The admiral invited Kalman and his family on a VIP tour of the submarine. The naval exercises – including a "full emergency blow" surfacing procedure – surpassed any amusement park, leaving Kalman and his children euphoric.

PERFECT MESSAGE

Knowing that people "judge Judaism by the Jews," Kalman was extra-careful in his behavior. He strove to always speak in a gentle, loving, upbeat tone. "Hello!" he'd answer the phone. "To what do I owe the pleasure of this call?"

One morning, while checking his voicemail, Kalman was startled to hear a belligerent voice shouting, "I never subscribed to *Shabbat Shalom*. I don't want this junk! Take me off your list immediately, or I'll have the Attorney General go after you for unsolicited faxes. Be warned!"

In his anger, the man neglected to provide either his name, fax number or phone number. Wishing to alleviate the man's emotional torment, Kalman cross-referenced the call log and phoned the man back. Kalman was immediately treated to a volcanic eruption of threats and name-calling. When things calmed down, Kalman said, "Please tell me your name and I'll gladly remove you from the distribution list."

The man gave his name, but Kalman could not locate it in the database.

"What is your fax number? Perhaps a data-entry error mistakenly directed the fax to you."

The man's fax number was not in the database.

Running out of options, and with tension exploding through the phone line, Kalman suggested, "Look at the small letters on the top-left corner of the page. That indicates who sent the fax."

"Oh, look at that," the man murmured. "One of my friends sent me a copy of your fax. I wonder why."

Kalman bit his tongue. The topic of that week's edition: "Conquering Anger."

FUNDRAISING ENGINE

Beyond its educational value, *Shabbat Shalom* enhanced Kalman's fundraising efforts. Fundraisers need to be in regular contact with donors and – while Kalman preferred one-on-one contact – as his renown and influence spread, *Shabbat Shalom* became his primary tool to stay in touch.

Kalman also leveraged *Shabbat Shalom* for numerous small donations. Though the newsletter was free, a note at the end of each edition reminded readers of the opportunity to donate in honor of a birthday, anniversary or memorial.

SHARE THE WEALTH

Rav Noah described the power of unity in achieving a goal:

Leviticus 26:8 says that five Jews will pursue 100 enemies. According to that 1-to-20 proportion, 100 Jews should pursue 2,000 enemies. Yet the verse goes on to say that 100 Jews will pursue 10,000 enemies – a proportion of one to 1,000. Why the proportional increase?

From here we see: There is no comparing the power of a small group versus a large group. Every individual, no matter how talented or dedicated, will always accomplish more through the exponential power of unity. We need to work as a team and help one another. One person's success is a success for us all.

The well-known verse, "Love your neighbor as yourself," concludes with the words, "I am God." Unity and friendship are so precious that God wants to be part of it.

Kalman was the consummate teammate fighting for the cause and over the years, trained many successful fundraisers. Rabbi Yitz Wyne of Young Israel of Las Vegas has raised millions of dollars over the years. As a newly minted rabbi, Yitz chose Miami as his first way station, in order to receive Kalman's patient and wise mentoring in the fine art of fundraising.

Kalman became a trusted sounding board for other fundraisers, always available to offer assistance and advice. The success of *Shabbat Shalom* presented a unique opportunity to help.

In the early 1990s, amid a serious economic downturn, Chanan Kaufman had taken on responsibility for the Jerusalem Fellowships, the touring-and-study program in Israel that was the precursor to Birthright. Yet success had its downside as well: the budget had swelled and Chanan was feeling stuck. One day, while commiserating on the phone with Kalman, Chanan expressed his frustration.

Kalman listened empathetically, then suggested, "Why not fly down to Florida? I'll set up some fundraising appointments, and we'll go together to solicit them for the Jerusalem Fellowships."

Chanan was taken aback. He'd never before heard of a fundraiser offering to make calls and take another fundraiser around.

When Chanan arrived in Miami, Kalman had already lined up a half-dozen meetings and was still making calls.

The next day, they headed out together. People were very receptive – some more, some less – but they all gave money. Chanan noticed an interesting pattern: The prospective donor would invariably mention an inspiring message or quote from *Shabbat Shalom*.

Suspecting some linkage, Chanan asked Kalman, "How did you get these meetings?"

"I send *Shabbat Shalom* to thousands of people," Kalman replied. "So I called some people up, explained that a friend is raising money for the Jerusalem Fellowships, and asked if we could come by and talk about helping out."

Chanan was shocked. "Are you saying that you cold-called these people, and they said, 'Sure, come on over,' like you're old buddies?"

"That's right!" Kalman said.

Kalman then offered a piece of advice that transformed Chanan's entire fundraising model: "How about a free 'franchise license' to send out *Shabbat Shalom* to your own network of supporters. I'll explain everything you need – computers, modems, additional phone lines."

Chanan was thrilled. "That sounds like a great idea. And I'll give you credit on the fax."

"No, sign your own name," Kalman said. "And better yet, put your picture on it."

Back home, Chanan immediately went to work, scouring *Crain's New York* for Jewish-sounding names of business executives. He called hundreds of offices to obtain fax numbers, then sent a copy of *Shabbat Shalom* along with a cover letter allowing people to opt-out. Approximately half of those contacted became subscribers, and the list grew to thousands.

"Over the years, *Shabbat Shalom* led to many major donations, and was the single most powerful tool for getting new people involved," Chanan says. "Today, thirty years later, I'm still sending out *Shabbat Shalom* – reaping the benefits of Kalman's talent, generosity and mentorship."

———⊰⊱———

Other fundraisers also adopted *Shabbat Shalom* as their weekly point of contact, sending out *Shabbat Shalom* under their own name, to their own lists. For decades, Mitch Mandel in Toronto, Aryeh Markman in Los Angeles, Steve Baars in Washington DC and others benefited from Kalman's largess.

Kalman's payoff was the satisfaction of knowing that his teammates had a good method for keeping in contact with students and supporters – without needing to recreate the wheel.

LONG DISTANCE DELIVERY

As the popularity of *Shabbat Shalom* multiplied, Kalman faced the growing problem of how to send thousands of faxes economically. The early 1990s were not like today, where cellphones connect people thousands of miles away with virtually the same ease and cost as calling next door. Back then, every out-of-town call incurred a long-distance fee, making global fax distribution prohibitively expensive.

Kalman's breakthrough came in 1996, when the Sprint Corporation launched a promotion called "Fridays Free." Anyone who subscribed to Sprint for a minimum of $50 in long-distance calls per month, would receive up to $1,000 monthly of free long-distance calls on Fridays, to anywhere in the world.

For Kalman, this solution was Heaven-sent, enabling him to aggressively scale his subscriber base at minimal cost. Kalman rigged his computer-and-modem system to take full advantage of the promotion. He transmitted long-distance faxes starting at 12:01 a.m. on Friday, and staggered them over multiple time zones to arrive before Shabbos.

With this breakthrough, Kalman was buoyed by his father's quip: "Luck is where preparation meets opportunity. The harder you work, the luckier you get."

DIGITAL GROWTH

Meanwhile, Kalman stayed on the lookout for the "next big thing," and in 1993 caught the first murmurings about the emerging Internet technology. Rabbi Yitzchak Berkovits, now the Rosh Yeshiva of Aish HaTorah and then Kalman's neighbor in Sanhedria Murchevet, first heard about the Internet from Kalman, who enthusiastically predicted the Internet would become "unquestionably the future of Jewish education."

Kalman wasted no time putting this theory into practice, again pioneering the use of technology in 1994 by sending *Shabbat Shalom* via the email server shamash.org. At the time, few people had Internet access, and Kalman dreamed of the day when email would become ubiquitous, obviating the need for *Shabbat Shalom* to rely on bulky machines that whined and squawked at all hours.

———⊰•⊱———

Shabbat Shalom's email list grew significantly in 1997 when – in the spirit of teamwork that Rav Noah constantly preached – Kalman joined forces with the Aish website and generously offered to merge his entire subscriber list. *Shabbat Shalom* became the website's single most popular page and helped propel Aish HaTorah to a position of online leadership in Jewish education.

Shabbat Shalom could now be sent – instantaneously, soundlessly and seamlessly – with the push of a button. The subscriber list continued to grow, and *Shabbat Shalom* became history's first Jewish e-newsletter to reach 100,000 subscribers and 300,000 weekly readers.

GLOBAL APPEAL

In 1996, Kalman was invited to speak to the Jewish community of São Paulo, Brazil, where the assimilation rate was alarmingly high. Near the airport, a billboard spanning the entire highway proclaimed, "Welcome, Rabino Packouz." Kalman stayed in São Paulo for a few days, engaging with young people, and counseling local rabbis and educators.

A few months later, Rabbi Gerson Farberas of Brazil spent Shabbos at the Packouz home in Miami. Kalman showed him a copy of *Shabbat Shalom*. Gerson was captivated by the accessible, engaging style, and offered to translate *Shabbat Shalom* into

Portuguese. The result was *Meor Hashabat Semanal*, which Gerson initially sent to a group of twenty people. The response was highly enthusiastic, and today *Meor Hashabat Semanal* reaches thousands of Portuguese-speaking readers throughout South America and beyond, proving the power of Kalman's insights to transcend boundaries.

———⟫·◦·⟪———

A man in Brazil owned a large company that manufactured notebooks and stationery. One Friday, anxious to read the latest edition of *Meor Hashabat Semanal*, he headed to the fax room. At that moment, a vicious gang of thieves entered the factory and stormed into the owner's office, with plans to force him to open the company safe and to kidnap him for ransom.

Finding the office deserted, the bandits spread throughout the building, ransacking the premises in their quest to find their prey. It never occurred to them that the wealthy, influential boss would be in the fax room, picking up his weekly dose of Jewish wisdom. Eventually, the thieves despaired and left empty-handed, sparing a devoted *Meor Hashabat Semanal* reader from potentially catastrophic financial and bodily harm.

———⟫·◦·⟪———

As the popularity of *Meor Hashabat Semanal* grew to tens of thousands of subscribers, Gerson published a collection of essays in Portuguese by "Rabino Packouz." For the launch, Kalman traveled to São Paulo and Rio de Janeiro for book-signing events. The book was a major success, and a second volume was published a few years later.

Soon after, Rabbi Avraham Serruya in Buenos Aires, Argentina, began translating *Shabbat Shalom* into Spanish.

Meanwhile, half a world away, Kalman was impacting another Jewish community. In 2005, he received an express mail package from Turkey containing a siddur – history's first Jewish prayer book with Turkish translation. Kalman smiled broadly, as if greeting a new grandchild. The siddur was produced by *Shabbat Shalom* subscriber Sami (Shmuel) Franco Blimen of Istanbul, who had previously met Kalman in Jerusalem and invited him to compose a foreword for the siddur, which today is the standard in Turkish synagogues.

PASSING THE TORCH

Of all Kalman's professional achievements, *Shabbat Shalom* remained his pride and joy. He was "thrilled and humbled" to have brought weekly Torah messages to thousands of homes and businesses – particularly the many readers for whom *Shabbat Shalom* was their only Jewish connection. One year at the Aish HaTorah International Meetings, Rav Noah declared, "*Shabbat Shalom* goes to hundreds of thousands of readers. Look at the power of what one person can accomplish. Kalman has the biggest yeshiva in the world!"

Kalman savored the pleasure of that success – not with the arrogance of "Look how great I am," but with gratitude to God for the opportunity to make a positive difference in the world.

At the same time, Kalman was sad that for many Jews, their only Jewish connection was a weekly newsletter. These dual emotions motivated Kalman to spend endless hours on developing content, upgrading the tech and marketing the list.

For twenty-seven years, under every conceivable circumstance, Kalman never missed sending out the weekly edition.

⇒◈⇐

In 2018, Kalman's looming sense of mortality prompted the creation of a "digital eternity project," with the *Shabbat Shalom* archives serving as a database for weekly emails in perpetuity. This work is now being continued by Rabbi Yitzchak Zweig, Kalman's long-time friend, who says, "I don't know of anyone who, every week for decades, affected millions of people like Kalman did."

Today, email and smart phones have collaborated to render the fax machine an antiquated cliché. Yet faxes offer one advantage over today's digital media: A fax is a tangible item that lands on a person's desk and invites them to engage. *Shabbat Shalom* still sends out 20,000 faxes – mainly to doctors and lawyers who require faxes to transmit and receive medical and legal records.

Thanks to *Shabbat Shalom*, the first mass-distribution of electronic content in Jewish history, fax technology remains forever etched in Internet lore.

KALMAN'S WAY: UNDERSTANDING GOD

Among the range of Jewish ideas that Kalman taught, he considered a relationship with God as life's primary value, and composed this short list of principles:

- God is One, the essence of everything. No reality is separate from God.

- God has infinite compassion and an endless, personal love for every individual.

- A person can become attached to God by directing their energy to loving God.

- God personally guides our life journey with infinite wisdom, tailor-made to our unique life mission and choices. Even our mistakes will not deter God from getting us where we need to go.

- When we "do the right thing" as defined by God, it mitigates the desire for a less-ethical choice.

- God's individual relationship with each person is synchronized to reflect that person's relationship with God.

- God has infinite power. If we make the right effort, God will move mountains.

CHAPTER EIGHT

Miami Beach

NEW CONNECTIONS

Some of Kalman's best years were spent in Miami Beach, where he developed Jewish educational projects, while raising substantial funds for Aish HaTorah – all in a friendly community with great weather.

One of Kalman's first meetings in Miami was with Rabbi Yitzchak Zweig, director of Yeshiva Elementary School. They shared a connection in that Yitzchak's esteemed father, Rav Yochanan Zweig, was a disciple of Rav Noah's older brother, Rav Yaakov Weinberg.

Yitzchak was in charge of the school's finances and discussed a tuition payment plan with Kalman. Rabbis typically felt entitled to a professional discount, because "we're in the same business." But Kalman told Yitzchak, "You're doing amazing work, and there's no reason that your institution needs to subsidize my institution. If I have to make more money, God will give me the money. But I'm going to pay full tuition."

Yitzchak puts this into perspective: "Kalman had a frugal life-style. He bought ten-dollar shirts. Yet he refused to take a discount for his children's schooling. He didn't look at tuition as spending money, but rather as fulfilling a responsibility. With nine kids, that's an annual tuition bill of nearly $100,000. Even wealthy parents don't pay that kind of money. Nine kids, full tuition. It's unbelievable."

Kalman and Yitzchak became close friends, and for the next twenty-seven years met every Wednesday for breakfast at Kalman's favorite meeting-place: Bagel Time Cafe, across from Talmudic University.

Yitzchak recalls one breakfast where Kalman was served his regular order: a toasted, scooped bagel filled with two eggs. Suddenly Kalman had the unpleasant sensation of biting into a piece of eggshell. He pulled the eggshell out of his mouth and declared: "Nice! They use real eggs, not the buckets of egg whites that most places use."

Yitzchak observes how this comment revealed Kalman's character: "Many people would see themselves as a 'victim' and start to complain. Yet Kalman's instinct was to appreciate the positive aspect of the situation."

Yitzchak says, "I learned a tremendous amount from Kalman over the years. He was a humble man who lived in the shadow of God, literally believing that God was on his shoulders. The better I got to know Kalman, the more I loved him."

CONNECTION MODE

Rav Noah taught the secret to loving all people:

The Talmud says that baseless hatred – *sinat chinam* – is the primary cause of the Jewish nation's exile today. *Sinat chinam* is hating people for being different or being imperfect.

The antidote, the first step toward peace and unity, is unconditional love.

Imagine being born on a desert island, never before having seen another human. When you meet one for the first time, you're thrilled! A fantastic "gadget" that walks, talks and thinks – with the ability to accomplish and create.

Yet we take people for granted. It's all a matter of focus. Parents love their children despite their faults. No matter how low a person has sunk, no matter how many imperfections, you can focus on the virtue common to all people: a Divine soul that seeks goodness and truth, is intelligent and full of potential. These are no small virtues!

⊰•◦•⊱

On his extensive travels, Kalman enjoyed connecting with different types of people. He'd greet people of every stripe with the warmth of a best friend – even those he was meeting for the first time. With fearless curiosity, Kalman would approach anyone who looked like they had a story to share. He was a great active listener and had a knack for making people feel they had an interesting life. He'd nod and gently probe: "Tell me about that. How did that feel?" People would open up and confide in Kalman. They'd become instant friends – and frequently, friends forever.

One day at a Miami gas station, Kalman was pleased to see a vintage 1950 Packard automobile. Kalman loved nostalgic reminders of his youth – particularly how this car conjured up a longstanding family joke about the "Packouz Packard."

Kalman sauntered over to the car and – in instant "friendship mode" – began enthusing to the owner. In the course of conversation, the man mentioned that he was Jewish. Kalman signed him up for *Shabbat Shalom* and the man became a donor. They became life-long friends and would meet every week.

Kalman said, "When I meet someone new, I try to show the same interest as if it's my long-lost cousin. I've learned not to be afraid to show enthusiasm. People respond quite positively to being the target of love!"

CLOSE ENCOUNTERS

Kalman's eyes were always open for what the Almighty was sending his way. His motto: "Truth is stranger than fiction. It has a more creative Author."

Daryl Brenner recalls an episode at a kosher restaurant in Macau, on the south coast of China across from Hong Kong. Kalman was talking about a project he was working on. "I need to speak with someone prominent in Washington DC," he said. "Do you know anyone I could contact?"

Just then a man walked in who looked familiar, yet they couldn't place him. After forty-five minutes of being baffled, Kalman finally went over to introduce himself, saying, "You look familiar. How do I know you?" It was former U.S. Vice President Walter Mondale.

Says Daryl, "Kalman needed a contact in Washington and – bam! – look who walks in. With Kalman, these things happened so many times it was uncanny."

Kalman was in Prague, eating at a kosher restaurant with a friend. The only other diners were a couple sitting near them. Kalman stared at the man, who looked eerily similar to a donor from Singapore who had recently passed away. Finally, Kalman asked him, "Excuse me, where are you from?"

"Milan," the man replied.

That didn't help. "Where were you born?"

"Afghanistan," the man replied.

Bingo! "By chance is your last name Khafi?"

"Yes! How did you know?"

Kalman explained his relationship with the brother and expressed condolences over the loss.

Kalman was conversing with a group of doctors. "Are you also a doctor?" one asked.

"Yes, I'm a doctor of the soul," Kalman wittily replied.

The man looked puzzled. "Oh, a podiatrist?"

Kalman was asked to perform a wedding on Grand Cayman Island. While checking into the hotel, he noticed the manager's last name: Schwartz. *Amazing!* Kalman thought. *Here in the middle of nowhere – a fellow Jew!*

Kalman's penchant for Jewish geography kicked in. "Where are you from?" he asked.

"Santa Monica," the manager replied, "a beach town near Los Angeles."

A light went on in Kalman's head and out came the words, "How is your brother Marc?"

The manager's eyes bulged. "Wow! How did you possibly know that?"

Kalman offered no response, preferring to milk the moment for dramatic effect. He waited patiently as the hotel manager looked down at his computer screen and began repeating Kalman's name. "Packouz... Packouz... Kalman Packouz! I haven't seen you in forty years!"

The hotel manager caught his breath and began unraveling the mystery. "Back in high school, you were regional president of BBYO, and my older brother Marc was vice president. But Schwartz is a common name. How did you make the connection?"

Kalman explained, "Whenever someone asked Marc, 'Where are you from?', he'd answer, 'From Santa Monica, a beach town near Los Angeles.' When you gave that same response, my memory bank connected it with Marc Schwartz from BBYO!"

Kalman called an 800-number to book a vacation in Orlando. While the agent checked prices and availability, Kalman casually asked, "Where are you located?"

"A little town in Oregon called Bend," the man replied.

"Ahh, Bend," Kalman responded pedantically. "Originally named 'Farewell Bend' by the Gold Rush pioneers who forded in the shallow part of the Deschutes River."

"Wow!" the man said. "How did you know that?"

"Because I grew up in Beaverton, Oregon."

"Funny! I also grew up in Beaverton."

"I graduated from Beaverton High School."

"I also graduated from Beaverton High!"

"I graduated in the class of 1968."

"I also graduated in 1968!"

For the next thirty minutes, the two enjoyed an impromptu forty-year high school reunion. This was possible only because Kalman was alert, interested and personable enough to ask, "Where are you located?"

Kalman later reflected, "With 300 million people in the United States, what are the odds of dialing an 800-number and getting a high school classmate? There's no such thing as coincidence. It's all a miracle."

HOME ATMOSPHERE

The name Packouz is so unusual that the family has a motto: "If there's a Packouz, you know it's us." Packouz means "horseshoe," as the family were farriers (horseshoe-makers) back in Europe.

The unusual name produced a slew of inside jokes. Kalman and Shoshana's nine-child family was a "Packed house." The family's twelve-seat vehicle was the "Pack-van." And for guests, refreshments were "on the house – the Pack-ouz!"

When introducing himself, Kalman would often exaggerate his lip movements to better enunciate and provide lip-reading assistance. That still didn't prevent mistakes like "Rabbi Pancake House."

———◆———

Kalman understood that, as head of the family, his mood at home sets the tone. "Some people go home short-tempered or impatient," Kalman said, "and selfishly expect their family to deal with whatever attitude they bring in the door." Before entering his home, Kalman would stop for a moment, look at the nameplate on the door, and align his mood.

Several times a year, Kalman traveled to fundraise for the Jewish people. On one occasion, following a grueling two-week trip to the Far East, Kalman called Shoshana. "I just landed here in Miami."

"That's great!" she said. "We're all excited to see you."

"And I'm eager to get home," he said. "But my fundraising trip wasn't as successful as I'd hoped. Plus, between flying thousands of miles, the change in time-zones, trying to make connections and not sleeping on the plane, I'm physically and emotionally exhausted. So I'm going to check into a hotel and get some rest. I'll see you in a few hours."

"But why not come home and rest?" Shoshana asked.

"I don't want to come home grumpy, tired and impatient," Kalman explained. "It's worth the money to get a hotel room, rest a bit, then come home full of love and joy."

Sure enough, a few hours later Kalman walked through the front door – refreshed, beaming a wide smile and thrilled to see his eagerly awaiting family.

Says Shoshana, "This happened on more than one occasion. Kalman was sensitive to how his mood affects others, and was unwilling to come home like a nutcase and take it out on everyone."

HAPPY MARRIAGE

In building a strong marriage, Kalman had excellent role models. His parents were married for seventy-two years, and were once awarded a prize for the longest marriage. "How did you stay married so many years?" they were asked. "We got married and tied the knot," Kalman's father quipped. "Not with a slip knot, but with a square knot."

Kalman viewed marriage as the training ground for sensitivity to others. He enjoyed telling the story of Rabbi Aryeh Levin, the beloved twentieth-century "Tzaddik of Jerusalem," who one day accompanied his wife to the doctor. "Please tell me the problem," the doctor said. Rabbi Levin spoke up: "*Our* foot hurts." Her pain was his pain.

Through forty-two years of marriage, Kalman strove for this level of sensitivity and unconditional love. Kalman had enormous respect and appreciation for Shoshana, whom he constantly praised and never criticized. Much of Kalman's professional success was due to Shoshana's support in every way – as sounding board, editor and bookkeeper. They were a true partnership, a meeting of souls.

Shoshana was extremely accommodating, giving Kalman the latitude to be a free agent and travel whenever needed. That included annual fundraising trips to Hong Kong and Singapore, which took him away for weeks at a time; visits to his parents in Oregon twice a year; trips to Israel multiple times a year; an annual get-together with friends on a cruise or at a lakeside cabin; attending various Aish conferences; and wellness retreats.

Kalman did all he could to show appreciation. Typically, a day or so after Kalman departed on a trip, Shoshana would receive a letter from Kalman in the mail – sent in advance, to arrive during his absence. "Though I am far away, I want to tell you how much

I love and care for you. You are always on my mind and in my thoughts."

With strength and wisdom, Shoshana ably handled nine children and the seemingly endless shopping, cooking, laundry, cleaning, carpools, homework and bedtime – while also managing to earn a black belt in martial arts.

THE GOOD FIGHT

Every marriage has its disagreements and friction. Yet Kalman never argued with Shoshana, claiming, "She refuses to argue with me." In truth, Kalman also refused to argue. He wrote:

> The first rule of marital happiness is: No fights. We marry someone because we love them and want to build a life together. Who is the last person on Earth you should be at odds with? Your spouse.
>
> Stay focused on the goal of a happy marriage. Discuss matters in a soft voice and don't get drawn into an argument. In the event of dispute, say nothing until the other person is through venting. Then in a soft voice say, "You've made some good points. Let me think about it and we can discuss it again later."
>
> Walk away if need be. But no matter how upset you are, never launch a verbal attack. Insulting your spouse is insane. Don't be insane.

In all interactions, Kalman refused to be pulled into a negative, adversarial position. One friend recalls, "I'd sometimes try to get Kalman angry, to throw him off his game and bring him down to my level. Yet I never succeeded. He would masterfully defuse a tense situation by telling a joke or maneuvering the conversation.

He'd lower the emotional pressure and get people talking with their head as well as their heart."

On one occasion, a man tried to draw Kalman into an argument by insisting, "I'm right!"

"Of course, you're right. You're always right," Kalman replied, knowing that by agreeing, there is no argument.

"No! I am not always right!" the man angrily rebutted.

Kalman's response: "You're right again!"

CREATIVE ENCOURAGEMENT

In order to stir his children's imagination, Kalman would play the "Ding Game." He'd begin telling a story, then stop in the middle and say, "Ding!" This signaled the next person to continue the story, in whatever direction their imagination led. The game would continue, with each child taking turns expanding the creative and unpredictable story that Kalman had set on course.

———◦◦———

As a parent, Kalman's priority was to encourage his children's success. One child recalls, "When I was young, we enjoyed playing checkers. My father would always maneuver his pieces to set me up for a dramatic triple- or quadruple-jump to win the game. He took pleasure in my pleasure!"

———◦◦———

When David Packouz was eight years old, he read a book about Nikola Tesla, the inventor of our electrical system. "This is amazing!" David exclaimed. "I want to be an inventor, just like Nikola Tesla."

Thrilled at his child's initiative, Kalman purchased a small notebook and wrote on the cover: "Invention Book." He gave it to David, saying, "Put all your inventions in here."

David let his imagination run wild, filling the notebook with outlandish ideas like flying shoes with propellers. Kalman loved it and encouraged his son.

Years later, David patented a piece of musical equipment, which achieved commercial success. "My dad deserves full credit," David says. "It all started with the Invention Book."

———✦———

Kalman encouraged his daughter's art from a young age, offering to purchase her completed drawings for ten cents apiece. He also encouraged her to undertake more challenging drawings by offering to pay a higher price.

As a young adult, she studied business management. Yet seeing she was unhappy, Kalman encouraged her to pursue her passion for art instead.

———✦———

On Shabbos, Kalman would ask his son David for a shoulder massage. Kalman enjoyed it immensely and said, "The Talmud instructs a father to teach his child a trade. You're good at massage and I think you could do it professionally."

"Dad, we still have time," David replied. "I'm only eleven years old!"

A decade later, David obtained his massage therapy license.

"You see?" Kalman said. "Don't ever accuse me of not teaching you a trade!"

———✦———

When Yedidya (Jay) Packouz was nine years old, he developed a passion for magic. "I thought it was the coolest thing in the world," Yedidya says. "I'd learn new tricks and couldn't wait to show people."

Every Friday, Kalman would visit terminally ill Jewish patients at Mount Sinai Hospital, and came up with the idea to have Yedidya come along to perform magic tricks. Kalman saw this as a win-win opportunity to encourage his son's magic hobby and to spend quality time together.

Most of all, Kalman saw this as a way to bring joy to the terminally ill. For him, it was not enough to go through the motions of showing up, wishing people a speedy recovery and moving on. Kalman wanted to lift them into a state of joy.

That Friday, with Yedidya toting a suitcase filled with magic props, the patients were treated to an amazing live magic show. At the end of the visit, Kalman – who knew how to incentivize a nine-year-old – bought Yedidya any candy bar of his choosing. The visits continued week after week.

⇒·⇐

One time at the hospital, Kalman and Yedidya were making the rounds to visit patients. One patient mistakenly assumed Kalman was an orderly and handed him a full bedpan. Most people would recoil, feeling it beneath their dignity, while saying, "It's not my job. I'll call someone to take care of it."

Yet on instinct, Kalman dutifully took the bedpan, cleaned it out, and brought it back with a smile.

Yedidya was flabbergasted. "Dad, why didn't you just say you don't work here?!"

Kalman's modest reply: "If I can help someone who is sick, I'm happy to do it."

FAKE SPANK

When is it instructive to spank a child? When Kalman was growing up, the inevitable answer was, "When your father gets home!" Kalman's father would take him to the bedroom, close the door and spank him. One time, Kalman had the clever idea of putting a book in the back of his pants, whereupon his father spanked him "without noticing" the book.

—————————

Young David Packouz committed a punishable offense, so Kalman took him to a bedroom and closed the door.

"Do you realize what you did was wrong, and why it was wrong?" Kalman asked in a voice loud enough to make an impression on David's siblings, standing expectantly on the other side of the door.

"Yes," David replied remorsefully.

"You won't do it again?"

"No," he solemnly promised.

Kalman lowered his voice to a whisper. "Here's what we'll do. When I slap my knee, you yell."

David loved the idea. Kalman hit his knee and David cried out, "Ahhhh!"

Kalman slapped his knee again; David dutifully yelled.

"Okay, one more time," Kalman said, smacking his knee. David cried out even louder. Kalman put his hand on David's shoulder and whispered, "This is our little secret. When we leave the room, look solemn and regretful."

For the next twenty-five years, Kalman enjoyed sharing this clever story of father-son bonding. One day, he received an email from a *Shabbat Shalom* reader: "To spank or not to spank is a valid question. Yet teaching your son deception is hardly a lesson in proper behavior. I respectfully urge that you rethink this approach."

Blinded by his own self-righteousness, Kalman had never considered that point. "I agree a hundred percent," he wrote back. "Thank you for setting me straight."

In all areas of life, Kalman welcomed criticism as a path to self-improvement. "Please criticize me," he would often say to close friends. "What can I do to be a better person?"

ROAD STORIES

Ten-year-old Hizkiyahu Packouz was thrilled to win a brand-new bicycle in a Purim raffle. On his first ride, two bigger boys perpetrated a "bike-jacking" by shoving Hizkiyahu off the bike and riding away. Hizkiyahu came home crying.

Kalman and Hizkiyahu drove around the neighborhood looking for the bike and the perpetrators, but came up empty. Kalman then took Hizkiyahu to the store and bought him a new bike.

For years, Kalman felt anguished over having missed a teaching moment about dealing with disappointment and growing from the situation, and the reality of cruel, selfish people who hurt others to get their way.

Twenty years later, Kalman shared that regret with his now-adult son.

Hizkiyahu differed. "You felt my pain and taught me how to be a loving, caring parent. I'll remember that lesson forever."

<hr>

As a teenager, Chana Packouz visited a friend's house and lost track of the time, staying late into the night. In those pre-cellphone days, Kalman and Shoshana had to call various homes late at night before finally locating Chana. They were relieved to find her safe and wanted her home immediately.

Chana said goodbye to her friend and left in the dead of night. While walking home, she noticed a car slow down and follow her. Chana sped up her pace and moved as far away from the car as possible. Suddenly, the car window rolled down and Kalman – who'd left the house to pick her up – called out.

Chana got into the car, expecting a speech about time management and responsibility. Instead, Kalman praised her for practicing "good stranger avoidance and safety awareness." Kalman held back his disappointment at having to leave the house in the middle of the night, instead choosing to keep the interaction loving and positive.

TRANSCENDENT CONNECTION

Rav Noah was teaching about the power of prayer:

God is all-knowing and all-powerful. So why do we have to pray for our needs?

The purpose of prayer is not to "change God's mind." Prayer is not where you submit a request, press a button, and God automatically fulfills it.

Rather, prayer is a tool to clarify your desires, to focus on what you truly want out of life. Before asking God for something, check yourself: *Why do I want this? Is it coming from a place of humility and compassion? Does the Almighty want me to have this?*

Everything in this world is a tool to help us connect with God, the transcendent dimension. This is the greatest pleasure possible, because it encompasses literally everything.

When you align your will with God's will, every aspect of life is alive with energy and meaning. It is a totally different plane of existence. Nothing else can compare.

——⊱◈⊰——

Part of Kalman's greatness was being a "regular person" who took the Almighty seriously. He believed it a mistake to pray only for "big things" like medical emergencies. In the flow of everyday life, Kalman was in tune and connected with God's imminent, loving presence. Whether at the supermarket check-out or interacting with a neighbor, Kalman would stop for a moment and speak with God, seeking to clarify how to be more kind and patient. In this way, he elevated even mundane activities to a higher, spiritual realm.

Before heading to an important meeting, Kalman would offer a short prayer to arrive on time and not run into traffic. When approaching his destination, he'd pray for a good parking space, saying: "Almighty, I'm working on behalf of the Jewish people. I don't want to walk two blocks and show up sweaty and harried. Please help me succeed."

<hr />

The Talmud says that reciting blessings faciltates a close relationship with God. Kalman was a role model for speaking with God mindfully. Before eating, he'd slowly say a blessing with focus and concentration – as if saying a blessing for the first time. "It was inspiring to hear Kalman get an aliyah to the Torah," one friend says. "He was focused on every word, literally talking to God."

Kalman would gently remind others to slow down and not mumble their blessings. "Not only for your sake," he'd say, "but so that I can answer 'Amen' to a better blessing."

<hr />

A leader of the Christian community invited Kalman to share his perspective on an important communal matter. They met at a kosher café and after eating, Kalman recited the Grace After Meals.

The man watched with keen interest and excitement, repeatedly interjecting with shouts of, "Yes! Yes!"

After finishing, Kalman remarked, "I know what I was saying. But what were you doing?"

"I was agreeing with you!" the man explained.

<hr />

"With all the craziness in the world these days," Kalman said, "it's enough to drive some people to pray." To help facilitate more prayers, he composed a short, standard prayer for all occasions:

> Almighty, Master of the Universe, Who gives me all good things – life, health, family, friends, and potential to grow as a human being and come close to You – please [insert request here].
> Thank You for this and for all that You give me.

JOKE COLLECTION

Kalman subscribed to the dictum: "You don't stop laughing because you grow old. You grow old because you stop laughing."

Kalman was always ready with a good story or joke, as a way to make people feel good. Rav Noah would often phone Kalman and say, "I just had a difficult meeting. I could use a good joke right now, to help shake this off and get me back in the right frame of mind."

Kalman collected jokes like a weapons arsenal and took every opportunity to try out a new joke – or an old joke on someone new. He had a particular penchant for groan-worthy jokes. For example:

> Did you hear about the dyslexic agnostic insomniac, who stayed up all night contemplating the existence of "dog"?

Since the Packouz family often had guests at the Shabbos table, Kalman's favorite jokes would elicit a round of groans from the Packouz children, who'd heard them hundreds of times. Yet Kalman relished every time with fresh enthusiasm, especially his series of "groan jokes" for the Jewish holidays:

> On Rosh Hashanah, a man needs to deliver an important message to a friend at the synagogue. Yet with no ticket, the usher refuses to let him in.

"Please," the man pleads. "I need one minute to relay a message."

"I'm sorry," the usher says. "No ticket, no entrance."

"Please," the man begs. "I promise not to pray!"

A house painter had been stealing from his clients by diluting the paint while charging full price. On Yom Kippur, the painter goes to the synagogue and pours out his heart. Suddenly a booming voice calls from Heaven: "Repaint, repaint... and thin no more!"

A Jewish man is waiting in line to be knighted by the Queen of England. Protocol calls for the person to kneel, then recite a phrase in Latin. When it comes his turn, the Jewish man kneels, as the Queen taps him on the shoulder with a sword.

Panicked, the man forgets the Latin line. Thinking quickly, he recites the first foreign language phrase that comes to mind, from the Passover Seder: *"Mah nishtanah, ha'lailah ha'zeh, mikol ha'leilot."*

The puzzled Queen turns to her adviser and asks, "Why is this knight different from all other knights?"

POSITIVE MOTIVATION

Kalman was keenly focused on connecting Jews with Jewish wisdom, and resisted efforts to make anti-Semitism the focus of Jewish identity. "There is little attraction in being part of a people historically persecuted," he said. "It's better to offer a positive answer to the question: 'Why be Jewish?'"

Kalman was once visiting a man in the hospital. "I don't know much about being Jewish, and I haven't spoken with a rabbi in fifty years," the man told Kalman. "But I'm the proudest Jew you'll ever meet!"

"What gives you this feeling?" Kalman asked.

"Rabbi, if anyone says anything negative about Jews or Israel, I'll beat 'em up!"

Kalman pressed to understand. "What is it about being Jewish that gives you this feeling?"

"Didn't you hear me, Rabbi? If anyone speaks against another Jew or Israel, I'll beat 'em up!"

Kalman realized: The horrors of anti-Semitism had engraved a strong Jewish feeling on this man's soul – yet he was unable to articulate a positive, affirming reason for being Jewish.

BE MY GUEST

Rav Noah taught the importance of hosting guests:

Abraham was a master of kindness and hospitality. His entire life was devoted to teaching the ideals of ethical monotheism and walking in God's path of kindness. Abraham's home was actually a hospitality inn, a tent that was open on all four sides. And to welcome the most guests, it was strategically pitched at an intercity crossroads.

Abraham understood that physical resources, when used for indulgence, are bound to the physical realm. So he'd prepare a nice meal as a way to feed the needy. By sharing with those in need, we don't lose out. Rather, our resources are elevated into higher pleasures of kindness and connection.

⇒·◇·⇐

Over the years, Kalman and Shoshana hosted hundreds of guests. Kalman often invited strangers for Shabbos, even at the last minute. When people would ask, "Are you sure it's okay?" Kalman would reply, "It's perfectly fine. This is what we agreed on when getting married."

Unfortunately, not all guests were well-mannered and appreciative. To avoid resentment, Kalman told himself:

Some people are slow, stubborn, sloppy, moody, argumenta-
tive, incompetent and generally imperfect. But so am I! Instead of
complaining about others' shortcomings, I remind myself: Just as I
am imperfect, yet still love myself, so too I can love others despite
their faults. So I choose focus on their virtues and show them love.

The Packouz hospitality was extended in even the most challenging circumstances. For many years, they'd frequently host
a blind, paraplegic man for Shabbos and holidays. Since the man
could not ascend the stairs to a guestroom, Kalman would convert
his tech-sensitive home office into a comfortable bedroom.

Additionally, Kalman went out of his way to include this
guest – who had strong political opinions – in the Shabbos table
discussions. Kalman would invite him to "have the floor" and
explain his view of the topic at hand.

<hr/>

In Miami, it is common for *tzedakah* collectors to go door-to-door.
As a professional fundraiser, Kalman was sensitive to the pride that
collectors have in their institution or cause. Whenever a collector
rang the doorbell, Kalman would rush to greet the itinerant fundraiser with a warm smile.

"Please come inside," he'd say. "What can I get you? Something
to eat or drink? Would you like to use the washroom?"

Kalman would then call out to his children, "We have an
important guest!" The children were dutifully trained to attend to
the guest's needs: "Would you like milk in your coffee? Ice cubes in
your cold drink?"

Kalman would then take out his checkbook and – to make
the collector feel good after a long day – tried to give more than
expected. Yet beyond money, Kalman gave his time, listening to
tales of woe and offering encouragement. He'd then honorably

escort the collector out, showering them with blessings for success. This scenario would be repeated multiple times, every evening.

⟫◈⟪

A typical Shabbos afternoon at the Packouz home found Kalman enjoying a festive lunch with family and friends. Just as typically, he'd be in the middle of a favorite song when – out of the corner of his eye – he'd spot the mail carrier coming up the front path.

Kalman's face would light up as he sprang into action and made a beeline for the door, where a stack of water bottles awaited weary delivery people. Kalman would throw open the door to greet the mail carrier, pressing a bottle into his grateful hand.

"Perhaps you'd like to come inside to rest for a few minutes," Kalman would implore. "Please, enjoy the air conditioning and a bowl of delicious cholent!"

EXPERT GIVING

A class from Rav Noah about building relationships made a lifetime impact on Kalman.

> A great rabbi once said that he understood the essence of "love your neighbor" upon hearing a slightly drunk farmer ask his friend, "Do you love me?"
> "Of course!" the friend replied. "I love you very much."
> "Do you know what I need?" the farmer asked.
> "How could I possibly know?" the friend replied.
> "If you don't know what I need, how can you claim to love me?"

⟫◈⟪

Kalman was quintessentially outward-focused, with a sixth sense for the needs of others. One of Kalman's friends had undergone back surgery and was just starting to walk. Kalman phoned and said, "I know that after back surgery it's important to go for walks. So I'm coming over to walk with you."

Kalman's friend reflects, "None of my other friends came to help. But Kalman was there for me."

⇒⋅◆⋅⇐

If Kalman knew of someone looking for a job or needing to earn money, he'd figure out a way to help. He knew that providing financial assistance goes beyond simple "good intentions" or even writing a check. Maimonides lists eight levels of *tzedakah*, Of which the highest level is helping someone achieve financial independence – with a gift, loan, partnership or job. As the saying goes, "Instead of giving him fish to eat, teach him to be a fisherman." This way the person can feed himself, plus ten others besides. That's truly fixing something.

One friend reports, "When I became unemployed, Kalman was constantly on the lookout for income opportunities for me. He arranged job interviews with contacts who needed my skill set. On at least one occasion, Kalman donated to an organization and earmarked the funds to hire me."

⇒⋅◆⋅⇐

One school administrator relates:

> Many people operate with an agenda of: *How can I maneuver to get what I want from this other person?* But Kalman was different. Anyone in need could call him for help. Yet he didn't wait to be asked. He'd anticipate others' needs, and upon recognizing a need, take action.
>
> Kalman was constantly asking me, "What does the school need? Give me a list and I'll try to get it for you." If he heard that we needed

a printer, he'd run out and buy a printer, then drop it off at the school office.

———≫◦≪———

Chaim Silberstein recalls:

Kalman was advising our organization – pro bono, of course – and joined a fundraising meeting where I presented a video clip on my laptop. After the meeting, I quipped that a mini-projector would be more professional. "Order a mini-projector," Kalman told me. "I'll pay for it."

Another time, Kalman asked for our bank details, "so that someone could make a donation." A few days later, a significant donation appeared in our account – from Kalman himself. I assumed that he'd rerouted a donation on behalf of a third party, so I called to inquire. After a bit of back-and-forth, Kalman confessed to being the mystery donor. "We recently sold our house," he said, "and decided that your organization should share the profit."

All this kindness was done without fuss or expectation of thanks. On the contrary, Kalman thanked me for the opportunity to support our cause.

———≫◦≪———

On another occasion, Kalman asked Rabbi Pliskin for guidance on how to "be a giver, not a taker."

Rabbi Pliskin explained: "When meeting another person, takers tend to think, *What can this person do for me?* Those with a critical tendency think, *What can I find negative about this person?*

"Kalman, when you meet someone, let your first thought be, *What can I do for this person?* This way, every encounter becomes a kindness opportunity."

Kalman took this advice to heart, repeating this question so often that it eventually popped into his mind automatically. Upon meeting someone, Kalman would hear himself say, *What can I do for this person?* Invariably, the first words out of his mouth were, "How can I help you?"

⟫◦⟪

People often say, "If you need anything, give me a call." Chances are they'll never actually do anything. But when Kalman offered to help, he sincerely meant it – and would keep asking until he found a way to help.

> A friend was visiting Miami. "What do you need?" Kalman asked.
>
> The friend thought for a moment. "I don't need anything, thank you."
>
> "Come on," Kalman said. "I want to get you something. Think! What do you need?"
>
> Not being able to come up with anything, the friend finally said, "A stapler."
>
> "Wonderful!" Kalman said, clapping his hands – and immediately whisked the friend off to buy a stapler.

⟫◦⟪

When Kalman wanted to give a gift and anticipated resistance, he'd "trick" the person into revealing what they really want. This way, Kalman was able to avoid any uncomfortable discussion or argument of, "I don't need anything."

When Rabbi Yaakov Burstyn got married, Kalman told him, "I always have my ears open for people getting rid of things. What do you need?"

"I have a lot of books, but they're sitting in boxes because I have no bookshelves," Rabbi Burstyn said. "If someone is giving away a bookshelf, I'd be grateful."

In truth, Kalman was not interested in what secondhand goods the Burstyns needed. Rather, he was engaged in sly detective work in order to buy them a firsthand wedding gift.

A few days later, Rabbi Burstyn was pleasantly surprised to see a truck pull up to his home with a nice set of bookshelves, courtesy of Kalman and Shoshana. He was doubly surprised that the delivery included a second matching bookshelf, courtesy of a benefactor whom Kalman had tipped off.

MAGIC UMBRELLA

Rav Noah taught the principles of "expert giving," per Maimonides:

A high level of charity is to give anonymously – where neither the recipient nor the donor knows the other's identity. This has double benefits:

- The recipient is not embarrassed to take.

- The gift is more altruistic, since it's not about accolades, but "feeling good about doing good."

———⟫•⟪———

It was a warm, sunny day when Tehila and Donny Mocton set out on a relaxing stroll down 41st Street in Miami Beach, their baby comfortably tucked into a stroller. Suddenly, without warning, the skies erupted into a torrential Florida rainstorm. The couple was caught unprepared.

"What should we do?" Tehila said, anxiously bending over the stroller and doing her best to block it from the downpour.

"Let's run for it!" Donny said, hastily snapping on the stroller's rain cover, hoping it wouldn't leak. Heads down, the hapless couple strode faster and faster in the pelting rain, as passing cars splashed them with puddles.

Suddenly, a car slowed down and pulled up to the curb. Before the Moctons knew what was happening, the window opened and the driver thrust an umbrella into Donny's hand – then drove off with no time for them to say "thank you."

Donny was stunned. This was no ordinary umbrella, but a sturdy model with a broad canopy that offered blessed protection from the deluge. With this act of kindness, the young family made their way home, safe and relatively dry.

The next day, Donny, who had glimpsed the face of their savior and knew Kalman from the neighborhood, visited the Packouz home to return the umbrella.

"Rabbi, thank you very much," Donny said, handing back the umbrella. "You really saved the day!"

Kalman's eyes grew wide in surprise. "You mean that was *you* in the rain?"

"Yes, didn't you know?" Donny replied, shaking his head in amazement.

"No, I had no idea," Kalman said. "It was raining so hard I couldn't tell."

Now it was Donny's turn to be confused. "But if you didn't know who you gave the umbrella to, how did you expect to get it back?"

Kalman's ear-to-ear grin said it all.

TRUSTED ADVISOR

As a rabbi, Kalman was a magnet for people seeking sage advice. He became accustomed to people often ignoring the advice, especially when it contradicted their desires and predilections. (Kalman's grandfather prepared him for this, saying, "Free advice is worth what you pay for it.")

Many people, however, clung to Kalman's advice as a lifeline. One woman recalls:

One evening, I had a dilemma and someone suggested that I speak with Rabbi Packouz. I went to their house and knocked on the door. Despite whatever important matter he was tending to at the time, Rabbi Packouz welcomed me in and gave me his time, attention and care. It was as if speaking with me was the only thing he had to do.

Kalman lived by the dictum: "If it's important to you, it's important to me." He would imagine two words written on everyone's forehead: "Important Person." Status, wealth and popularity did not matter. He treated everyone with equal respect and sought to make everyone's day better, especially those often ignored or overlooked:

- At a take-out window or toll booth, Kalman would make conversation and invariably put a smile on their face.

- Kalman always found ways to compliment people and build them up. When visiting a modest home, he'd describe it as a "palace."

- In Israel, Kalman would speak to taxi drivers in Hebrew and ask how to say various Hebrew phrases. This built a small connection and made the driver feel good.

- Some of Kalman's grandchildren enjoyed ice hockey. Though not a hockey fan, he brushed up on hockey trivia and peppered his language with hockey terms.

- Kalman was allergic to cats. When one of his family members got a cat, Kalman bought cat toys as a gift.

When encountering difficult people, Kalman would think, *If this was my own child, how would I act?* This focused him on treating everyone with the care and respect befitting of God's children.

BANQUET PREP

As executive director of a Jewish day school, Rabbi Yitzchak Zweig was accustomed to pressure. But today was over the top. That evening was the school's annual scholarship banquet – the year's biggest fundraiser and the culmination of months of planning and effort.

Not only was Yitzchak the brains behind this massive effort, but also much of its brawn. Without much budget for administrative staff, most of the event's myriad details fell on him. But Rabbi Zweig was good at his job, and as one detail after another fell into place, he breathed a sigh of relief.

That breath soon became a gasp with the realization that he hadn't yet prepared his speech. It couldn't be off the cuff; Yitzchak had to express proper appreciation to the many people who support the school.

Yitzchak flopped into his desk chair, hoping that his spinning head would manage to focus on the urgent task at hand. Suddenly the phone rang. In those days, without caller ID, he picked up the receiver, hoping the call would not consume precious time.

"Hi, Yitzy!" came Kalman's cheerful voice. "I know this is a pressured time for you, and I called to see how I might help."

"Thank you," Yitzchak replied with exasperation. "I can't think of anything right now. I'm busy scribbling notes for my speech."

"Perhaps it would be easier, and you'd be more relaxed, if the notes were neatly typed out," Kalman said.

"I wish," Yitzchak sputtered. "But there's no time. I'm still working on last-minute details for the banquet. I barely have enough time to jot these notes, no less type them up."

A few minutes later, Yitzchak's doorbell rang.

It was Kalman, wearing a magnificent smile. "I'm here to type your notes!"

Yitzchak was dumbfounded. Kalman knew that Yitzchak would never dream of asking him to do a menial task, so Kalman created a *fait accompli* and simply showed up.

"Kalman, you have more important things to do than typing my notes," Yitzchak protested.

Kalman insisted. In the end, not only did he type the notes, but his keen editing skills vastly improved the speech.

Yet that wasn't all. After the typing, Kalman said, "You and your wife need to get ready for the banquet. I'll stay and babysit your children."

Yitzchak was stunned. "Kalman, you've got nine kids of your own. You don't have to watch someone else's kids!" But Kalman insisted.

Yitzchak reflects, "I didn't ask Kalman for anything. He dropped whatever he was doing and showed up out of the blue. It's incredible, not only how much Kalman cared, but how he put those feelings into action."

GIVING, GIVING, GIVING

Kalman derived inspiration from Rav Noah's teaching about friendship:

> The Mishnah says: "Acquire a friend." Rabbeinu Yonah explains that friendship is so valuable that, when necessary, we should even spend money to "acquire friendship."
>
> This doesn't mean to "buy friends" who are not real friends. We're talking about gifts as a tangible expression of friendship, especially when the gift is unconditional and unrelated to any special occasion or obligation.

In spending money on friends, Kalman took this idea to the extreme. He was constantly buying gifts, on the lookout for interesting things that others might need or enjoy. If he saw something online that someone might like, he'd send a link saying, "Can I get you this?"

When Kalman saw a unique object that fascinated him, he'd buy it – not for himself, but for the greater joy of giving it to a friend… another drop in the ocean of goodness.

One friend recalls that Kalman came and said, "Here, I want to give you my favorite pocketknife." The next day, Kalman gave the same friend an expensive pen that someone had sent him.

The more Kalman enjoyed something, the more he desired to give it away and share the pleasure. He explained, "More than the pleasure of owning something is the joy of giving it away. If I enjoy something, I have that pleasure for an hour or two. But if I give it to someone else to enjoy, I have that pleasure forever."

If someone expressed interest in something that Kalman owned, he'd offer it as a gift. One surprised recipient asked, "Why give it away? Don't you like it?"

"Actually, I love it," Kalman replied, without missing a beat. "But I love you even more!"

———✦———

With the mindset of striving to bring people joy, Kalman spared little expense:

- In shul, Kalman met a man who mentioned that he enjoys metaphors. A few days later, a package containing two books of metaphors appeared on the man's doorstep.

- Rabbi Gil Eisenbach was in charge of the yeshiva library and was always fixing torn pages. He preferred a certain high-quality tape that was unavailable in Israel. Unsolicited, Kalman sent fifteen rolls of that tape.

• As a practical matter, Kalman always carried a pocketknife. If he saw a thread hanging from a friend's shirt, he'd pull out the knife and trim it.

PEACE FUND

One day, Kalman's friend was complaining about having been ripped off by a car mechanic. "You always seem so calm," the friend said. "How do you handle the shysters trying to rook you for another dollar?"

Kalman leaned in to reveal his secret. "Life always has disappointments – someone cheats you, or you buy a lemon of an item. Every year, I budget several hundred dollars for what I call the Shalom (Peace) Fund. In the event that someone – a plumber, auto mechanic, storekeeper – takes unfair advantage, I deduct money from the account. Rather than get upset at being cheated, I simply dip into my Shalom Fund. A few dollars is a small price to pay for peace of mind."

Kalman concluded, "Every year I review the account: If it has a decent balance, that's an encouraging sign that people have been honest with me!"

MULTIPLE LAYERS

Rabbi Yaakov Burstyn gives a short Torah lesson following morning prayers at Talmudic University, which Kalman attended daily. In 2014, Kalman was going to Israel for ten days and asked Rabbi Burstyn to record the class and send it. Other people heard about the recordings and asked to receive them, too. Today, hundreds of people receive the daily class, and Rabbi Burstyn has an archive of thousands of recorded classes – thanks to Kalman.

Always thinking of ways to do more, Kalman suggested that Rabbi Burstyn offer sponsorships of the daily class, as a way to subsidize a high school graduation trip.

"I'm skeptical if the idea will work," Rabbi Burstyn said.

"To prove it will work," Kalman replied, "I'll sponsor the first week."

"That's very kind and generous," Rabbi Burstyn said. "Is there someone special you'd like to honor or memorialize with the sponsorship?"

"Yes," Kalman replied, "I'd like to sponsor it in honor of Rabbi Yaakov Burstyn."

Looking back, Rabbi Burstyn says, "Some people give money. Others give guidance and advice. Others provide encouragement. All are important. But seldom does one person do everything. That was Kalman – a seemingly everyday person, filled with multiple layers of caring and righteousness."

SPREADING POSITIVITY

Residents of Miami Beach were accustomed to seeing twelve-year-old Ari* riding his bike at all hours of the day and night. Riding was Ari's passion, and his enthusiasm for motion and speed were undeterred by inclement weather or encroaching darkness.

One evening, Ari's mother answered the doorbell to find Kalman standing there holding a package. "Allow me to explain," Kalman said in his warm and disarming manner. "I know your son loves riding his bike after dark, so I bought him this reflective vest."

As the boy's mother gratefully accepted the package, she stopped to consider: *Who besides Rabbi Packouz would care more about my son's welfare than even I do!*

⇒—◆—⇐

When traveling, Kalman carried a bag of chocolates to distribute to airport and airline employees – what he called "the invisible faces who perform the myriad tasks of supporting my pleasure of air travel." At the ticket counter or gate, he'd ask the agent's name and how their day was going. Then he'd proffer a chocolate, along with wishes "for a sweet day."

Kalman was always looking for innovative ways to bring sweetness to others' lives. He produced a business card that said, "You are special. In the next twenty-four hours, please pass this on to another person who is special."

BUILDING RELATIONSHIPS

In Jerusalem, Kalman witnessed a constant stream of people coming to Rav Noah's office to "meet a wise man."

> "Why do you spend so much time speaking with visitors?" Kalman asks Rav Noah.
>
> "If it was your own child," Rav Noah replies, "you'd find the time and patience. I look at every Jew as a beloved member of my family."
>
> Rav Noah then shows Kalman a little black book, in which he recorded the name of every person he'd met. Each entry includes a few keywords to help Rav Noah remember that person.
>
> Kalman flips through the book, stunned to see that it contains over ten thousand names.

⟫◆⟪

Kalman invested heavily in relationships, making extraordinary efforts to stay in touch with thousands of relatives, friends, colleagues, donors and students. Not satisfied with a simple email message, Kalman kept a lengthy list of people to call regularly – weekly or monthly. One friend relates, "When I'd see Kalman's video call coming in, I'd think, *Isn't he busy?* He had heavy responsibilities and was working toward big achievements. With all the people Kalman was in touch with – and he continuously added to that roster – how did he find the time and energy to maintain so many relationships?"

The answer: Just as some people have a demanding job and family, yet manage to find many hours a week to devote to a hobby they're passionate about, so too Kalman loved people and invested enormous time, energy and resources in building those relationships.

Says one friend, "Though Kalman had hundreds of friends, he always made me feel like the most important one."

ATTENTIVE LISTENING

Most people are either the type who accomplish or who invest in relationships. Kalman was a rare individual who excelled at both. He treated everyone, of all ages and walks of life, with unconditional love. Kalman was a master of pastoral counseling, making the rounds at hospitals, prisons and retirement homes. He'd comfort those who were often ignored, and provide an empathetic ear to those most prone to complain.

Kalman lived by the credo: Be a good listener. He explained, "Allowing another person to be heard is a great act of kindness. Turn off your cellphone. Send verbal and nonverbal signals that say, 'I understand and I care.' Ask open-ended questions, even if the result is a ten-minute unburdening of the soul."

On multiple occasions, Kalman guided people through emotional traumas, serving as a trusted confidant to help the person rebuild. One man reports that during a particularly difficult period, Kalman called him every day to share a joke.

Kalman encouraged people to "adopt a senior" to shower with love and attention. One person wrote:

Your suggestion brought tears to my eyes. I work for a medical transportation company, and many of our clients are seniors. I printed out your words and placed copies in the company break room. If this helps even one of our drivers think about how they interact with seniors, it will have made the world a better place.

———

Kalman, accompanied by friend and colleague Boruch Rabinowitz, had a fundraising appointment with a prominent heart surgeon in Miami. They were speaking about Jewish educational projects, when suddenly the doctor received an urgent call: "We need you for emergency carotid artery surgery!"

The doctor leapt to his feet. "Sorry, rabbis, I've got to go. Do you want to observe the surgery?" Kalman demurred, but Boruch was given scrubs and told to wash up.

The surgery took an hour, after which Boruch emerged. "I'm sorry it took so long," he said. "How did you pass the time?"

"I was speaking with the patient's wife," Kalman said. "I listened, comforted her, and reassured her that everything will be okay."

HOW ARE YOU?

As a student of human behavior, Kalman was fascinated by people's response to the standard greeting, "How are you?" He interpreted the response "I can't complain" to mean, "Thank you for the courtesy of asking, but I doubt you have the time or interest in the details of what I'm going through."

When Kalman asked, "How are you?" he sincerely wanted to hear about the person's challenges and help solve them. In response to, "I can't complain," Kalman would say, "Sure, you can. As a rabbi, I have all the time you need, and a full box of tissues."

In contrast, when Kalman was asked, "How are you?" his preferred replies were: "Fabulous, thank God," "Wonderful, thank God," and his friend Alon Tolwin's answer: "Life is perfect... but will get better!"

Kalman explained the essence of his reply:

> God has an individualized plan for my (and everyone's) growth in spirituality and character development. Everything that happens is ultimately from God and, by definition, is for my good. Things are sometimes painful and challenging, but the Almighty determines the best situation for me – every time. I acknowledge this reality with boundless gratitude and appreciation.
>
> We cannot always control what happens to us. We can only control our attitude. Life is ten percent "what" happens, and ninety percent "how" we view it.
>
> A response of "Fabulous, thank God!" is an opportunity to focus, be thankful, and be an uplifting example to others.

One day, Kalman met a friend who asked, "How are you?"

"Magnificent, thank God!" Kalman replied cheerfully.

At this, the friend exploded, "You're brainwashed!"

Without missing a beat, Kalman countered, "Better a clean mind than a dirty mind."

Kalman then turned serious and addressed the friend's annoyance. "How do you prefer that I answer the question, 'How are you?'"

"Just say, 'Can't complain,' like everyone else," the friend replied in a huff.

PRISON TIME

An acquaintance of Kalman's, despite protestations of innocence, was sent to prison for a lengthy term. Since prisoners are only permitted a limited number of visits, Kalman became the man's "designated rabbi," allowing for visits that did not diminish the prisoner's family time.

Kalman did not merely make a lone appearance or offer perfunctory words of encouragement. For years, Kalman was dedicated to bringing solace to this one person. Every Friday, Kalman drove to the prison, over an hour in each direction. He'd typically wait an hour or two to be checked into the visitors' area. The prison sometimes had lockdowns and, depending on the situation, Kalman might need to wait two hours to get out. The actual visit was limited to twenty minutes.

The prison food did not supply the man with enough calories, but prisoners weren't allowed to touch money. So every week, Kalman brought a roll of quarters to buy the man a pile of treats from the vending machines.

Upon returning home, Kalman would walk through the door and, with wry humor, call out, "I'm back from jail!"

———

In order to use his time effectively, Kalman would visit the prison on Fridays and spend the entire car ride calling a lengthy list of people to say, "Shabbat Shalom." Kalman began with widows and others who lived alone, then proceeded to family, friends, donors and colleagues.

"For years, every Friday I received a sweet call from Rabbi Packouz," one widow recalls. "In his soothing and melodious voice, he'd wish me 'Shabbat Shalom.' That meant so much to me!"

———

A former prisoner in state penitentiary says:

Rabbi Packouz generously committed his time to speak with me every week. I was not allowed to receive phone calls, so Rabbi Packouz instructed me to call him collect, every week. He bore that expense, just so I would have someone to talk to.

No matter how busy he was, he always accepted my call. I'd often catch him at an inconvenient time – in a meeting or on a family outing – but he always gave me undivided attention, full of patience, concern and abundant love.

One time, I was unable to make the weekly call. The following week, Rabbi Packouz said how much he'd missed speaking with me the week before. He wasn't just placating me; he genuinely looked forward to our calls.

He'd conclude our talks by saying, "Much love." I feel that he truly meant it.

TEFILLIN ADJUSTMENT

Rav Noah taught:

Beyond our own self-improvement, we must encourage positive actions in others, according to our ability to make a difference. If you can influence your family, yet don't, you're accountable for the mistakes of the family. So too, if you can influence your city – and even the entire world.

On the other hand, the Talmud says to fix yourself before trying to fix others. The great ethicist Rabbi Yisrael Salanter said, "I wanted to change the world, but found it too difficult. So I tried to change my city. I couldn't do that, so I tried to change my family. I finally realized that I could change only myself."

⤙⬥⬦⤚

Kalman hoped to fix the world, but knew that it's not about asserting moral superiority or venting anger at others' behavior. Rather, effective correction must be with love and for the other person's benefit. When admonishing, Kalman did so in a soft and pleasant voice, conveying patience, warmth and care. He lived by the credo: "Only when someone knows how much you care, do they care how much you know."

Kalman also knew that constructive criticism goes beyond pointing out mistakes; it includes offering a solution. For example: The mitzvah of wearing tefillin involves many details, and Kalman was meticulous in observing this. When seeing someone wearing tefillin improperly, he would help position it correctly. Kalman even carried tweezers to help adjust the knot on the tefillin's straps.

Rabbi Stephen Baars relates:

> When Kalman visited Washington DC, we went together to shul. Although Kalman didn't know anyone there, he went around ensuring that everyone's tefillin was on properly.
>
> Commenting on the positioning of someone's tefillin can often come across as pushy and imposing. But no one objected or even felt criticized. People sensed Kalman's love and sincerity. They even thanked him.

PRAYER TIME

Kalman took his relationship with God seriously. Every morning, he'd come to shul early and say all the prayers from a siddur, enunciating each word. After prayers finished, Kalman would recite the Mishnah that lists actions that "a person enjoys both in this world and the next" – honoring parents, doing kindness, hospitality, peacemaking, etc. He'd say each item aloud, adding a few words to highlight each item's importance.

Kalman often said, "Life is fragile – handle with prayer." In the synagogue, he was vigilant with the Jewish law about not talking during prayers. Besides the distraction it causes, Kalman saw side conversations as an affront to the Almighty's honor.

Though Kalman was careful not to think negatively of others, he occasionally dreamed at night about getting angry at people for talking during prayers. Kalman took these dreams as a sign to find a different shul with less talking – which he did on more than one occasion.

———⬥———

For twenty-five years, Kalman maintained an email list called "Refuah," a collection of names of sick people in need of prayers. Kalman leveraged his influence by sharing that list with thousands of subscribers. Today, such lists are common, but Kalman pioneered the idea of a large-scale, organized effort to pray for individuals in need.

One subscriber wrote, "I had a family member who was critically ill. Rabbi Packouz put her name on the Refuah list and hundreds of people prayed for her. I live in Spain and know very few Jews. This was an amazing kindness."

Kalman put great effort into compiling and updating the list every week. He'd check back intermittently for an update on how the sick person was doing. One subscriber relates, "Kalman thanked me for sending a sick person's name – as if I was doing him a favor!"

RIPPLES OF INFLUENCE

Kalman was deeply impacted by the 9/11 terror attacks, which he saw as a sign of global instability and confirmation of Rav Noah's exhortation: "The fight for life is the fight for sanity."

Shortly after 9/11, Kalman was inspired to write a guest column for the *South Florida Sun-Sentinel*, describing the Jewish mission of *Tikkun Olam*. Kalman called on all Americans to take responsibility to make the world a better place. "Giving of your time and money to help others is a basic human responsibility," he wrote. "It is a statement that says, 'I will do whatever I can to help repair the world.'"

Kalman was upset to see the term *Tikkun Olam* sometimes applied to ideals that run contrary to Jewish tradition. "As we say in the *Aleynu* prayer at every service," he'd point out, "*Tikkun Olam* is predicated on the Almighty's sovereignty. How can we expect to achieve world peace if the most important ingredient is missing?"

<hr />

Suzanne Lasky Gerard, a self-described "three-day-a-year Jew who married a nice Jewish boy," moved to Miami Beach to work for NBC News. Years later, when the Jewish Federation planned a national Jewish cable network, Suzanne was hired to spearhead it. "That was an awakening," she says. "I never realized how little I knew of my Jewish background. And I had to catch up quickly."

A friend arranged for Suzanne to meet Kalman. "Realizing we were on opposite ends of the religious spectrum, I was defensive at first," Suzanne says. "But I learned differently. Rabbi Packouz was brought up in a Reform environment similar to mine, so he understood. He never proselytized, never made me feel uncomfortable, and was very kind and caring. Our conversations were inspiring, intellectual and plain fun."

Suzanne later wrote and produced *March of the Living*, a documentary for PBS that followed youngsters as they traveled to the Holocaust death camps and then to Israel. Her discussions with Kalman about the Holocaust seeped into the documentary, which won a coveted Emmy Award. Says Suzanne, "I attribute that success to the inspiration and knowledge I gleaned from Rabbi Packouz."

——➤➤➤——

In the 1980s, Ricky Turetsky was asked by the Miami Jewish Federation to lead a young leadership mission to Israel. Ricky put together an eclectic program that included a Shabbos dinner at Aish HaTorah, where he met Kalman, at the time executive director of Aish Jerusalem. The two kept in touch and reconnected when Kalman later moved to Miami.

Given their shared passion for Jewish literacy, they partnered in a promotion whereby Ricky purchased multiple copies of Rabbi Aryeh Kaplan's *The Living Torah,* and Kalman publicized this offer: "Commit to ten minutes a day of Torah study. After thirty days, we'll send you a free Chumash."

Says Ricky, "People strengthened their Judaism significantly through this promotion. It transformed generations!"

MEANINGFUL COLLECTIONS

As a child, Kalman amassed a prized collection of hundreds of first-edition comic books. His collection was inspired by an article he'd read about the high price of real estate, which quoted people lamenting, "If only I'd invested in property when I was young and it was inexpensive!" Kalman's 25-cent weekly allowance did not afford the possibility of purchasing real estate, so he opted for comic books.

At age twelve, Kalman returned from summer camp to discover that his comic book collection had been inadvertently thrown out. Upon recovering from the shock, Kalman purchased a lockable steel file box to safeguard future purchases.

Decades later, when Kalman related this incident to his children, they asked, "Whatever happened to the steel box? Which comic books were in it?"

"The box is in my closet," Kalman replied. "But I haven't opened it in years. I have no idea what's in it."

The children were unable to contain their excitement, so Kalman obligingly retrieved the steel box. He wiped away the dust, turned the key and – voila! – inside were eighty perfectly preserved first-edition comic books, including #1 *X-men*, #1 *Spiderman* and more.

Kalman took advantage of the teachable moment. "There is something intrinsically meaningful in collecting," he observed. "Yet I've discovered that no matter how much a person collects, there is a feeling of existential angst, like something is missing. That's because we have a need for spiritual completion – which no amount of material items can ever satisfy."

Seeing his children's puzzled look, Kalman tried a less philosophical route: "It's good to collect things. But channel that desire in a productive direction. Be sure that what you're collecting is more meaningful than comic books."

PRICELESS CHILDREN

Kalman was profoundly affected by Rav Noah's perspective on parenting:

> Imagine you're married with three children. Would you agree to give up one of those children for $100 million dollars? (Perhaps the child who's always kvetching... and you'll still have two left!) Think of all the pleasure you can buy with $100 million – yachts, vacations, homes and every gourmet meal imaginable.

Of course, no sane person would ever sell their child. A child is worth more than $100 million. So spend more time with your children. Learn how to enjoy them – and get your money's worth!

<hr>

Upon meeting someone new, Kalman would occasionally announce, "I'm a billionaire." In response to their astonishment at how a rabbi became mega-wealthy, Kalman would explain, "Nobody would sell their child for $100 million. With my wife and nine children, that makes me a billionaire!"

Ricky Turetsky was familiar with Kalman's approach and tried it on a friend who had two daughters. "Are you planning to have more children?" Ricky asked.

"No, my wife and I decided it's enough."

With Kalman's voice ringing in his head, Ricky gave it a try. "What if I offer you $100 million for one of your daughters. Would you give her to me?"

"That's ridiculous," the friend said. "Of course not."

Ricky pushed forward. "But imagine what you could do with $100 million. You could change the world!"

The friend was getting impatient. "Ricky, what's your point?"

"If you agree that each of your children is worth more than $100 million, then why not increase your portfolio?"

Those words reverberated. Within a year, the friend had a beautiful son, who became the apple of his eye.

Ricky reflects, "It's all because of the wisdom that Rav Noah taught Kalman, who then passed it on to me, and that I shared with my friend. Another $100 million in the bank!"

PARENTING MOMENTS

Though Kalman was very busy with teaching, writing and fundraising, his family remained top priority. Kalman worked long hours in his home office, yet if any family member came by, Kalman would fully engage, swiveling his chair 180 degrees and putting his feet on a stool to relax, totally present in the moment to assist with whatever was needed.

Kalman understood there is no greater pleasure – and no better investment – than spending time with one's children. He wrote:

> Love your child. Spend time with your child. If you spend more time at work or in front of the TV than with your children, they'll get a loud and clear message about your priorities.
>
> Quality time is quantity time. The more time you spend with your child, the more they know that you love them and are a priority. The best presents for your children is your presence.

Kalman never let a day go by without telling his children, "I love you," along with a warm smile and ready hug. He'd then ask, "Wait! Did I say 'I love you' today?"

Kalman wrote:

> What a wonderful epitaph that your children remember you for "driving them crazy" with hugs and kisses. Nobody ever complained that their parents hugged them too much, or told them too many times, "I love you." (Except maybe teenagers...)

Kalman learned from Rav Noah that the most important lesson to teach children is that the Almighty loves them. Every day, Kalman would ask his children, "Who loves you?" – to which they'd respond, "Mommy and Daddy." Kalman would then ask, "Who loves you most of all?" – to which they'd respond, "God."

LOYAL FRIEND

Kalman was a devoted friend whose loyalty was unbreakable. He believed that no matter the circumstances, even if paths diverge, a friend is for life. Over the years, despite geographic distance and radically different lifestyles, Kalman kept in touch with his Jewish high school friends, a loyal "Gang of Seven" who stuck together and looked out for one another. Every year, they'd hold a reunion to celebrate life, catch up with one another, laugh, cry and reminisce. Today, fifty years later, the tradition continues.

One of Kalman's childhood friends – a Jew who observes Christianity – describes their friendship:

> We had a supportive, respectful acceptance of one another, despite Kalman's sometimes strident advocacy that butted up against my life path. We had numerous quirky dialogs about ethics and social behavior. We offered plain-speaking feedback to one another. The tone was always warm and constructive, with friendship prevailing over dogma.

Indeed, they remained lifelong friends, and Kalman never gave up hope of the friend returning to his Jewish heritage. Many people would say, "Why waste time on a lost cause?" Yet Kalman, the perennial optimist, never gave up.

——— ◆ ———

If a friend or colleague was having an out-of-town *simcha* or funeral, Kalman would make every effort to attend. Rabbi Mitch Mandel recalls:

> When my children got married, I sent invitations to all my friends and colleagues. I had no expectation that they'd bear the trouble and expense of attending. Yet Kalman was different. He flew in especially for two of my children's weddings.

Kalman's commitment to friendship knew no bounds. One longtime friend recalls:

Kalman was fiercely loyal. Once you became his friend, it was a lifetime commitment through thick and thin. Kalman went to the end of the world for his friends, even risking personal harm. He had the strength to follow his beliefs, no matter how painful or challenging. He was loyal to the point of, "I'll give my life for you."

In one particular situation, Kalman went out on a limb and stood up for me one hundred percent – and got hurt because of it. Yet he had the integrity to do the right thing… and let the chips fall where they may.

Another friend describes:

I spoke to Kalman almost every day. His standard line was, "How can I help you today?" My relationship with Kalman was never about him. It was always about my challenges, my needs, my goals, my physical, emotional and spiritual wellbeing.

I solicited Kalman's advice on everything, from fundraising scenarios to technical issues with my computer. He would listen to what I was struggling with and offer tactics and advice to help solve the problem. I'd present a fundraising scenario, and he'd drill me with questions: "What's the person's background? Their profession? Their hobbies?"

Kalman was a wealth of insights and wisdom , a walking encyclopedia who loved dispensing information. He always had a great joke or a perfect story to loosen things up. And he gave me the confidence to succeed. Always without judgment, only love.

Kalman signed his emails: "Much love, beloved friend. You are a blessing in my life!" And he meant it.

TO SAVE A LIFE

Kalman had a deep desire to help people – no matter who they were, poor or powerful – and would go to incredible lengths to provide it.

The Ostrovsky family emigrated from Russia to Israel in 1990, when their daughter Lisa was one year old. The father, Dr. Ilia Ostrovsky, is an ecologist dealing with water-quality issues in the Sea of Galilee.

At age ten, Lisa was diagnosed with cystic fibrosis and needed a double-lung transplant. The procedure could only be performed in the United States, with medical costs totalling one million dollars. Israel's Cystic Fibrosis Foundation and an insurance company provided some financial subsidy. Private donations totaled approximately $170,000, and one wealthy individual who read about Lisa's condition underwrote a large portion of the medical care – anonymously. Yet $350,000 of unpaid bills remained, without which the surgery could not be performed. And Lisa was running out of time.

In desperation, Lisa's father sent letters and emails to anyone who might help. One letter reached Kalman. Though he had never met the Ostrovskys, he recognized the chance to save a life.

Kalman sprang into action, harnessing his large *Shabbat Shalom* subscriber list with an email campaign that emphasized one of the Torah's earliest and most important lessons: "I am my brother's keeper." He explained, "If we want to live in a humane world, we need to share the burden of those who suffer. This means not just empathizing with people's problems, but getting involved in the solution."

Kalman's efforts sparked a wave of care and compassion, and the remaining money, in denominations large and small, was raised.

Meanwhile, a forty-eight-year-old, non-Jewish janitor named Ron Johnson was in a London supermarket and happened to pick up a Jewish newspaper publicizing Lisa's plight. The serendipity hit Johnson like a ton of bricks. He'd recently visited Auschwitz and resolved: "While Jews were being decimated by the millions, few people did anything to help. If I ever have the opportunity to save a Jewish life, I'll do so."

The newspaper featured an appeal for money to help with Lisa's medical costs, and after reading the article, Johnson realized: "I can't help financially, but maybe I can donate my lung." Johnson underwent the requisite medical tests and was identified as a match.

Johnson, a married father of two teenagers, explained, "I've had a wonderful life. This is a chance to give something back. I'm not looking for praise, and certainly not looking for money. It's not often that an ordinary chap like me gets the opportunity to save a life."

Meanwhile, Kalman reached out to the Ostrovskys and became their family rabbi – networking for their needs and providing emotional and spiritual support. Prior to the double-lung transplant, Kalman flew to St. Louis to serve as the family's advisor, therapist and media spokesperson.

Lisa's surgery initially appeared successful and she was able to breathe without a respirator. Her condition, however, quickly deteriorated. She remained unconscious for a few weeks, then passed away.

After the funeral in Israel, Kalman hosted a lunch in Jerusalem to help console Lisa's parents, who had fought so hard to save her life. As a final act of gratitude, Kalman raised funds to have a grove of trees planted in Israel in honor of the lung donor, Ron Johnson.

Kalman said, "Although Lisa did not survive this ordeal, nobody lost out by extending the effort to help. Lisa touched many lives and caused many people to grow."

One of Kalman's email readers wrote: "All your updates about Lisa, filled with overwhelming love, make me proud to be a Jew. This effort has made an enormous difference in all our lives."

PRAGMATIC OPTIMIST

Kalman liked to joke about the difference between a pessimist and an optimist. "A pessimist says, 'Things can't get any worse.' An optimist says, 'Yes, they can!'"

As a social experiment, Kalman asked people to read the following phrase: "opportunityisnowhere." He'd then ask: Did you read "opportunity is nowhere" or "opportunity is now here"?

With his optimism, Kalman was sometimes accused of being "pie-eyed, Pollyanna-ish, naïve, childlike in trust and honesty, and living in la-la land." Yet Kalman's long list of achievements proved his ability to combine idealism with pragmatics.

Kalman trained himself to look at the positive side of every situation. He wrote:

> Who is better off: the "optimistic idealist" who persists against all odds, or the "pessimistic realist" who views life cynically and fears the worst?
>
> My philosophy is to never blame or complain. Why invest time and energy in worry or regret, all for nothing and to our detriment? "Worry" is interest paid in advance on a debt that often never comes due.
>
> Rather, give thanks to the Almighty, and ask, "How can I help?" This perspective obligates us to improve the world from a position of humility and agency, and to live with constant appreciation for God's gifts.

Kalman shared an amusing, apocryphal story about maintaining a positive perspective:

There once was a king, whose assistant subscribed to the attitude of: "No matter what happens, this too is for the good."

One day, the king and his assistant were out hunting. The assistant erred in loading the king's rifle, causing a misfire and blowing off the king's thumb.

"This, too, is for the good," the assistant exclaimed.

"No, it's not," the king replied – and promptly threw the assistant in jail.

A year later, the king was out hiking in the jungle and was captured by cannibals. As they we're preparing to cook him for dinner, they noticed the missing thumb. Since cannibalistic ritual disallows eating such a person, they let the king go.

Immediately, the king went to the jail and freed his assistant. "You were right. This was for the good!" the king said. "I'm sorry you spent the last year in jail."

"No problem," replied the assistant. "Jail was good for me."

Puzzled, the king said. "But you were away from your family and suffered harsh conditions."

"True," the assistant replied. "But if I wasn't in jail, I'd have been captured by cannibals along with you. And I've got both my thumbs!"

⋙◆⋘

Kalman was sensitive to certain noises, such as chalk on a blackboard, the rapping of fingers on a table, and the honking of car horns. He wrote about overcoming annoyance through the power of reframe:

On Israeli roads, there is a lot of horn-honking. The joke is that scientists found a new way to measure a millisecond: the time from when the light turns green, until the person behind you starts honking.

Kalman found this noise disconcerting, yet over time learned to view it in a different light. He'd imagine the horn-honker saying, "Good morning, beloved friend! I hope you slept well. In the event you're a bit drowsy, I lovingly remind you that the light is about to change. Don't miss it and be late to where you're going. Have a wonderful day!"

With this paradigm shift, the horn-honking became a pleasant (or at least bearable) experience.

LOVE OF ISRAEL

Kalman had a strong connection to Israel, and visited multiple times a year. He was astonished to witness, after two thousand years of exile, the fulfillment of God's biblical promise to ingather the exiles and return the Jewish people to their ancestral homeland. Kalman cherished the mitzvah of settling the Holy Land and his heart was always there, fulfilling King David's edict to "raise Jerusalem above my highest joy." At his home in Miami, Kalman proudly displayed a set of antique keys from Ottoman-era Jerusalem, symbolizing his dream to return there permanently.

During a trip to Israel in 2014, Kalman joined a geopolitical tour that explored the Jewish origins of Jerusalem. Kalman believed in the importance of educating people about Jerusalem and, after the tour, pledged to help the organization.

Kalman filled the role of strategic advisor, sharing practical advice and ideas for advancing the mission. He coached the organization's director in the fundamentals of fundraising, and provided encouragement during challenging times. Kalman personally introduced the organization to donors, and connected marketing and creative people who became invaluable assets to the organization's growth.

One time, Kalman was on the phone with the organization's director, trying to dictate some information. It was taking time because the director's computer keyboard was malfunctioning. "You can't run an organization like this," Kalman said. "I'm buying you a new laptop. Send me a link."

A few days later, a new computer was delivered to the organization's office.

UNWITTING SMUGGLER

Rav Noah was teaching the foundations of Jewish ethics:

The Talmud says that the angel appointed over conception takes the seed to God and asks, "Will this person be strong or weak? Wise or foolish? Rich or poor?" Notice that the angel doesn't ask if the person will be "righteous or evil," because ethical choice depends entirely on our free will. That is the only "true" choice we have. Everything else is circumstances.

Choosing to do the right thing – even when nobody knows about it – is a key to emotional and spiritual health. The prophet asks rhetorically, "Can a person hide where God can't see? Does God not fill all spiritual and physical reality?" If you're in the presence of a tiger, a bee poses no relative threat. So too, nothing compares to being in the awesome presence of God.

Do you act differently in private when no one is looking? The Mishnah says that to keep on the straight path, "know what is above you – a seeing eye, a listening ear, and all your deeds are written in a book."

◆

Kalman strove for the highest level of integrity and transparency. One time, on an outing with his son at the amusement park, a sign at the ticket counter said, "Half-price for twelve and under." The ticket agent asked the child's age. "Thirteen," Kalman replied.

"That's okay," said the agent. "I'll give you the cheaper youth fare."

In such a situation, many people would say, "Thank you very much. I appreciate that." But not Kalman, who asked the agent, "Are you authorized to do that?"

"Not really," the agent replied.

"Okay," Kalman said. "So we'll pay full price."

———❖———

One time, Kalman was flying to Israel and, in response to a friend's request, purchased a huge five-liter bottle of whiskey at the airport's duty-free shop. Kalman assumed this was within Customs Authority guidelines entitling the duty-free import of one bottle of liquor.

Upon landing in Israel, Kalman put his luggage on a cart and placed the whiskey bottle atop the suitcases. He then passed through the customs "green line" for those with nothing to declare.

"Hold it right there!" the customs agent said, pointing to the whiskey bottle. "This is too big to be considered 'one bottle.' We'll need to confiscate it."

Kalman was sad to disappoint his friend, but shocked at the agent's next words: "We're issuing a $500 fine for smuggling."

Smuggling?! Kalman was aghast. He stared at the whiskey bottle perched on the inspection table, and imagined the customs officials taking it into the back room for an unofficial party. Kalman gritted his teeth as he squelched a fantasy of the bottle "accidentally" falling off the table.

In the end, Kalman's whiskey-less friend wrote a letter to the Customs Authority, explaining the misunderstanding, and the charges of "smuggling" were cancelled.

LIKE ROTHSCHILD

Rav Noah was teaching the principles of effective giving:

"Imagine you designate $100 for *tzedakah*. All else being equal, which is better: to give one individual the entire $100, or to give one dollar to a hundred people?"

A hand goes up. "Giving the entire $100 to one person makes a bigger impact."

"That's true," Rav Noah says. "Yet there's another factor to consider: the impact it has on *you*. With one large donation, the impact dissipates – whereas the repetitive act of giving, even one dollar, makes you more compassionate, sensitive and accustomed to giving."

From a young age, Kalman learned the value of giving charity. His father, Raymond Packouz, was legendary for starting each day by writing at least a dozen charitable checks. Though not large amounts, Raymond made literally thousands of charitable donations every year.

Kalman role-modeled this idea. In the course of a single year, he wrote six hundred checks to charity.

In fundraising as well, Kalman affirmed the power of small checks by encouraging people to make any size donation – and he received thousands of small donations annually.

———◆———

On one trip to Israel, Kalman attended a wedding where he sat next to an old friend. Often at weddings in Israel, poor people walk around collecting *tzedakah*. Kalman's friend was put off by the continuous barrage of outstretched hands. Whenever a collector approached, he'd pull inward, put up a shield and do his best to appear invisible.

Kalman saw an opportunity to share his perspective. "These *tzedakah* collectors are fantastic!" Kalman said. "Look at all the opportunities to give. Back in Miami, I don't feel good unless I give $18, minimum. Here in Israel, I can make someone happy with one shekel – and I feel like Rothschild!"

UNPUBLISHED CHOFETZ CHAIM STORY

Rabbi Motty Berger, a popular teacher in Jerusalem, visited Miami to teach classes and accompany Kalman to fundraising meetings.

Together they visited a middle-aged donor whose family had escaped from Europe prior to World War II, gone to Cuba and finally settled in Miami, where they built a successful printing business. The donor worked alongside his elderly Polish father-in-law, whom Motty – himself of Polish origin – recognized as a Socialist, Bundist or Communist who had long since abandoned allegiance to Torah. Motty made little effort to interact with the man, certain he'd make no headway with someone who ostensibly had little sympathy for reuniting Jews with their heritage.

Yet Kalman, "Mr. Congeniality," eagerly followed the octogenarian around the shop, asking questions.

"Where are you from originally?" Kalman asked.

"From a small town in Poland," the man replied.

A huge smile filled Kalman's face. "Really? Poland! Did you ever meet the saintly Chofetz Chaim?"

At this, Rabbi Berger cringed and rolled his eyes. The Jewish population of Poland before World War II was three million, making Kalman's question analogous to, "Oh, you're from New York? You must know my cousin!"

Yet Kalman had struck a chord. At the mention of the Chofetz Chaim, intense emotion swept across the old man's face. He quickly grabbed a newspaper and folded it into a makeshift kippah – apparently regarding the Chofetz Chaim so holy that merely speaking about him demanded a head covering.

The man looked Kalman in the eyes and proudly declared, "It has been many years since I've spoken about my meeting with the *heilige* [holy] Chofetz Chaim."

The man took a deep breath and continued, "I grew up in a small town in the mountains of Poland, where I attended *cheder* [Torah day school]. In those days without air conditioning, people would visit our region to enjoy the cool mountain breeze.

"One day, my rebbe excitedly told our class that the world-famous tzaddik, the Chofetz Chaim, was spending the summer nearby. Excited to meet the elderly sage, our entire class piled into a wagon and rode to another town. We arrived at the shul and our rebbe went into a side room, while we waited expectantly in the sanctuary.

"We overheard a murmured conversation and what sounded like some protest. Suddenly the door burst open and out came our rebbe – accompanied by an elderly Jew, not much taller than us ten-year-olds, wearing a *tallis* over his head.

"With tears in his eyes, the Chofetz Chaim approached us and said, '*Kinderlach* [children], why are you asking for me for a *bracha* [blessing]? You study Torah and are *tei'ere Yiddishe kinderlach* [precious Jewish children]. You should be giving *me* a *bracha*!'"

Standing in the print shop, wearing a newspaper yarmulke, the elderly man shed a tear, awash in memories of that profound encounter. "The Chofetz Chaim gave each of us a short *bracha*. When he came to me, he gently tapped my face and blessed me to be a good Jew. Then he walked quickly back into the side room, closed the door and continued his Torah studies."

The old man got a faraway, dreamy look, as if reliving that magical moment. "I can still feel that touch on my face," he said.

After the meeting ended, Motty said to Kalman, "That was amazing! This man obviously dropped out of Torah observance long ago, yet that story reconnected him back with a special time."

Kalman replied with matter-of-fact confidence and infinite optimism. "We're in the business of bringing Jews back, one small step at a time. And that's exactly what we did."

TRIP TO POLAND

In 2006, Rav Noah took a group of sixty disciples to Poland to visit the concentration camps. He believed that by confronting the terrible loss of the Holocaust, today's crisis of assimilation would become more tangible and urgent. Standing at the site of the Auschwitz crematoria, Rav Noah said:

> Imagine this was 1943. Would you stop everything you're doing right now and try to save Jewish lives? What if you'd left your entire family and town behind in Europe? Would you be able to sleep at night?
>
> Today, people look at their grandparents and wonder, *What were you doing during the Holocaust?* It was no secret that millions of Jews were being put into ovens. Were your grandparents out raising money to help ransom Jews? Were they organizing secret rescue efforts? Were they demanding media attention and marching on Washington?
>
> Today, the Jewish people are fighting wars on many fronts. The existence of the State of Israel is questioned in world forums. Terror and anti-Semitism afflict Jews around the world. And due to assimilation, every year 50,000 Jews in their twenties opt out of the Jewish people, lost to us forever.
>
> So what will you do about it? Because one day, your grandchildren will look at you and wonder...

In Poland, Rav Noah spoke at the famous Yeshivas Chachmei Lublin, a citadel of Torah study inaugurated in 1930 (and tragically destroyed by the Nazis nine years later).

Rav Meir Shapiro was criticized at the time for building a unique and innovative institution. At the inauguration ceremony of the yeshiva, he responded to the critics and said, "I'm not sure if the criticisms are valid. But of one thing I am certain: Even if I don't succeed, I will be rewarded for my efforts to try to improve the situation – while you will be held accountable for having stood idly by."

Imagine a situation where your child, God forbid, is terminally ill. Since you love that child and are desperate to save him, you will try even things that are highly experimental.

If we love the Jewish people like a parent loves a child, we'll have the courage try new ideas – even if there's only a chance it will succeed. Some people might call our ideas crazy and unrealistic, but it's crazier just to stand by. If we're serious, we have to try.

TRIBUTE TO A FRIEND

In 2012, Kalman wrote an essay in memory of a dear friend, community activist and fundraiser Jerry Burstyn. The words reveal what Kalman held most dear and valuable – words that could easily have been written about Kalman himself.

When I first met Jerry, he immediately asked, "Who do you want to meet, and how can I help you?"

When we moved to Miami, Jerry approached me and said, "I have some dressers and beds. Do you need any?" The next thing I know, Jerry is driving up with a truck and a helper to move dressers into my home.

Jerry was like a brother to me – always there to listen, advise and assist. I suspect that everyone who knew him felt the same way. He never rushed and always had time, as if he had nothing else to do but talk with me. To be in his presence was to be filled with caring, love and warmth.

Jerry pockets were stuffed with notes and reminders to help people. He had warehouses filled with things that someone might need. He once gave a man thirty wrecked bikes to fix – one to keep, and twenty-nine to give to needy children.

If he could help another person, no task was too small or too difficult. Jerry once spent three days visiting used car lots, helping a widow on a tight budget buy a car.

One elderly woman, alone in the world, mentioned that she wanted to be buried with her family in Connecticut. She had no living relatives and no money. When she died, Jerry made all the arrangements, accompanied the body back to Connecticut, and performed the burial service.

Jerry's kindness produced miracles. One time, as a parking officer approached the expired parking meter of a Rolls Royce, Jerry put a coin in. The owner of the car – who had many times rebuffed Jerry's requests to meet for a donation – came running out, huffing and puffing, having seen the parking officer and wanting to spare himself a ticket.

Perplexed by Jerry's generosity, the man asked, "Why did you do that?"

"It was my small way to help spare you a ticket," Jerry replied.

"Come to my office," the man said. "I'd like to get to know you better."

Jerry walked out of that meeting with a $25,000 donation.

Jerry selflessly helped others. When he heard of someone's passing, he'd immediately go to the family to help with funeral arrangements, run the *shivah* (mourner's) home, and be there every day. For months afterwards, he'd call or visit the mourning family, letting them know that someone cares.

Before every holiday, Jerry would call a list of widows and orphans. He said, "It's important to call before the holidays, when the loved one is often missed the most."

Most of us have limits of how much we'll help. We think, *Enough! I need to look out for myself.* Jerry had no limits.

KALMAN'S WAY: FRIENDS

- Money is like manure. If you let it pile up, it stinks. If you spread it around, it helps things grow.

- Make your motto: "Care and share." The best vitamin for acquiring a friend is 2B1.

- The Sages say: *O chavruta o mituta* – Either friendship or death!

- A friend is someone who knows everything about you – yet likes you anyway.

- "Friend" is not a label. It's a lifetime promise.

CHAPTER NINE

Fundraising:
The $15 Million Man

MISSION POSSIBLE

Beyond Kalman's educational projects, his primary focus was fundraising. As the Mishnah says, *"Im ein kemach, ein Torah –* Without bread, there is no Torah." Building a global revolution is invariably tied to raising vast sums. Rav Noah taught:

> Imagine your child needs an expensive operation. Will you be able to fundraise? Of course! Because when you're fully dedicated to the mission, you'll do whatever is necessary to accomplish it. It's all a matter of how much you care.

With this perspective, Kalman never hesitated to approach anyone, at any time or place, for financial support. For forty years – as executive director of Aish HaTorah's first U.S. branch in St Louis; as executive director of Aish HaTorah Jerusalem; and in Miami as director of Aish HaTorah's Jerusalem Fund – Kalman worked the phones, pounded the pavement and honed his craft. He parlayed an exceptional array of talents: dedication, fearlessness, professionalism and personality, to help fund and promote Jewish educational programs in Jerusalem and around the world – Discovery seminars, trips to Israel, campus outreach, digital content, and construction of Aish HaTorah's headquarters across from the Western Wall.

The collective result of Kalman's efforts: $15 million raised.

ESTABLISHING RAPPORT

Kalman was not an aggressive fundraiser, nor was he driven by the treadmill of success. He looked at fundraising meetings as more than securing a donation. "My goal is to awaken people and open their horizons," he explained. "I want donors to get involved, to appreciate their potential to make a difference in the world, and to cast their lot with the eternal Jewish nation."

Kalman was a people-lover with a knack for talking about different subjects. Fundraising gave him the opportunity to meet new people and engage in conversations about life. His approach: "Care about the prospective donor – and the money will raise itself. Fundraising is not transactional. Fundraising is all about developing personal relationships. You've got to like people. Otherwise, stay away from fundraising. You'll do more harm than good."

A donor recalls, "Kalman called me to meet me, which I assumed was to solicit a donation. Yet that wasn't even on the agenda. He had another matter to discuss. When I offered him money, he didn't want it. How many people in the world are like that today?"

Before any meeting – fundraising or otherwise – Kalman would prepare by using Rav Noah's "love game." He'd focus on the person's positive qualities, saying to himself: *I am about to meet Mr. Smith. He has a kind heart and is devoted to the Jewish people.* Kalman would then enter the meeting with a positive vibe.

Kalman treasured the art of listening. He explained, "Many people go into a fundraising meeting and talk, talk, talk. Finally, the prospective donor says in desperation, 'Please, take a check!' – and gives the absolute minimum. In my early years of fundraising, I fell into that trap of talking excessively about my mission. I probably bored people to death. The best tool a fundraiser has is silence. Most people prefer to talk than to listen. Be fascinated with people. Listen and learn about their interests and their problems."

Whenever visiting a prospective donor's home or office, Kalman would scan the walls for clues about the person's interests. In one instance, the walls were filled with photos of Arabian horses. Kalman inquired about it, and the man gave an animated description of his farm with dozens of horses. Kalman shared that he'd recently read an article describing how, three thousand years ago, King Solomon had bred Arabian horses in his Jerusalem stables, and how that breed was being revived in Israel today.

After a few minutes of lively discussion about Arabian horses, the man stopped, cocked his head, took a long look at Kalman and said, "Rabbi, please tell me about yourself."

Kalman received a sizable donation – because he noticed the walls.

MERIT OF *TZEDAKAH*

Rav Noah taught Kalman to view fundraising not as an act of taking, but as giving donors the opportunity to partner in a noble cause and earn eternal merit. "The biggest beneficiary of giving is the one performing it," Rav Noah said. "Imagine a parent's investment of energy and resources: feedings, diapers, sleepless nights. The greater the investment, the greater the feelings of love. It is truly better to give than to receive."

Whenever meeting prospective donors, before discussing a specific project, Kalman would first establish the importance of philanthropy: "When it comes to wealth distribution, many people ruin their children with too much money," Kalman would say. "A wiser option is to give your money to a meaningful cause that you believe in. By empowering those on the front lines, you activate their success."

Kalman would then explain: "I'm presenting an opportunity to become involved in humanity's most noble cause: connecting Jews to their heritage. It's a triple-win: Judaism enriches personal lives, adds vitality to the Jewish people and makes for a better world. I'll help you share this opportunity."

The consummate professional, Kalman countered the stereo-typical image of a *schnorrer* (moocher) by presenting himself as a "philanthropic investment counselor." When meeting a prospective donor, he'd present a tightly written proposal (three pages maximum) to establish credentials, define the problem, and offer a solution. For transparency, a financial statement was included. And, as a personal touch, the prospective donor's name was printed on the cover.

Kalman liked to tell donors about Rothschild, the wealthy French Jew once asked by a visitor to reveal his net worth. Rothschild reached into his desk drawer, pulled out a ledger and handed it to the visitor.

"I don't understand," the visitor said. "This is a list of your charitable donations."

Rothschild nodded and explained, "My financial assets are not guaranteed. I could die tomorrow, or the government could decide to take away my money. But these charitable donations are mine forever."

Kalman succeeded in educating many wealthy Jews about the importance of supporting Jewish causes. One of Kalman's donors told him, "Thank you for introducing me to the pleasure of giving *tzedakah*. In fact, many organizations have you to thank!"

COUNTERING OBJECTIONS

Fundraising involves countless hours of cold-calling prospective donors. On these initial conversations, Kalman would try to get people in touch with how much they care about the Jewish future. "The Jewish people are experiencing a crisis of assimilation," Kalman would say. "Does that bother you?"

"Yes."

"Would you like something done about it?"

"Yes."

"If there was a formula to succeed, would you want to be part of it?"

"Yes."

"In that case, let's meet for fifteen minutes. That's all I need to demonstrate that not only does a solution exist, but is *already* successfully being done."

Kalman would present the Jewish cause in investment terms: "Do you have a stock portfolio? Imagine it's 1986 and I tell you about a small company called Microsoft, selling for ten cents a share. Wouldn't it have been worth fifteen minutes of your time to hear a pitch about that company? Would you later kick yourself at the missed opportunity?"

Kalman continued, "I'm coming on behalf of the Jewish people. We've been around for over three thousand years. Torah is a boom stock, the best philanthropic investment you can make. It has the highest return on investment, and pays dividends for generations."

Kalman developed ready replies for the litany of objections:

> Objection: "I'm busy."
> Kalman's Way: "Fantastic! I don't deal with people who aren't busy, who have nothing better to do than twiddle their thumbs."
> Objection: "I don't have any money right now. It's all tied up."
> Kalman's Way: "Wonderful! You can consider our programs objectively, with no fear of having to give something."

Objection: "I already give to many worthwhile causes."

Kalman's Way: "Of course! The reason to meet is because you're a proven philanthropist."

THE ASK

Kalman's first serious fundraising attempt was in 1976, while still a yeshiva student. He was visiting Portland and approached a prospective donor, extolling Rav Noah's educational programs in Jerusalem.

"How much do you want?" the man asked.

Kalman was flustered. He hadn't realized that to get a significant contribution, you need to specify an amount, then let the other person respond. He also had yet to learn a basic truth of human psychology: the tendency to give the absolute minimum.

"I don't know how much," Kalman stammered. "I mean, people give $18 and $36."

The man broke out laughing.

"I appreciate a good joke," Kalman said, bewildered. "But what's so funny?"

"I thought you were going to ask for $5,000," the man said. "You want $18? No problem!"

"Are you telling me that if I had asked for $5,000, you would have given it?"

"Yes."

"Well, actually," Kalman said with a wink and a smile, "I made a slight mistake. I intended to say $5,000, but it came out as $18."

"Nice try, but no go," the man said, handing Kalman a check for $18. "Let this be a lesson for you. The more you ask for, the more you get."

A few years later, Kalman met the same man in Portland. "We have a building facing the Western Wall," Kalman said. "It's the Beverly Hills of Jewish real estate! Millions of people visit the Wall each year. They all turn around and see our building. Your name can be on it for five million dollars."

Again, the man started laughing. "You certainly learned your lesson well," he said.

In the end, the donor didn't go for five million, but gave a substantial gift of $50,000. Says Kalman, "Had I asked for the $5,000 figure we'd discussed a few years earlier, he'd have given me that, too. But I wouldn't have gotten $50,000."

Kalman's conclusion: "Shoot for the stars and you'll get to the moon. Don't be afraid to ask for a high number. You never insult somebody by asking for too much."

THE DEAL

Back in college, when Kalman had plans to attend law school, a criminal lawyer shared what he called "the most important rule for success": "Always get the money up front. Because if your client is acquitted, he'll say, 'What did you do for me? I was innocent anyway!' And if convicted, he'll say, 'Why should I pay you? I'm going to prison!'"

Kalman applied this principle of "get the money up front" to fundraising. When meeting with a donor and agreeing on an amount, Kalman would say, "Is it possible to write a check while I'm here? When I leave, you'll be busy with a hundred other things, and neither of us will want to spend valuable time on reminders. Writing a check now is the quickest and easiest for everyone. And it will help the organization by putting the money to work as soon as possible."

Kalman had another reason for getting the money up front. "People might later incur financial problems, and regret not having given the money sooner. If the donor's stock drops, you've done a tremendous service by having them fulfill their pledge as soon as possible."

For Kalman, "get the money up front" was by no means an iron-clad rule. One donor dedicated an edition of *Shabbat Shalom* in memory of her parents. The following year, Kalman asked her to do so again. "I'd like to," she said, "but I'm financially strapped this year."

"Don't worry," Kalman said. "We'll do the dedication anyway. How would you like it to be written?"

DIVINE TRUST

Kalman was playing phone tag with a donor from Miami Beach, oncologist Dr. Mark Pomper. Mark said he'd call back by 10 p.m., but when he called at 10:30, Kalman didn't answer.

The next day, Kalman called Mark to explain: "I didn't wait up to see if you'd call, because fundraising is completely in God's hands. The Almighty can arrange anything, at any time. I didn't want to question that by staying up late."

Mark reflects, "Even if it meant losing a donation, Kalman would not compromise his faith in God. By not waiting for the call, Kalman proved that he trusted more in God than in me."

⇒◦◦◦⇐

One day, Kalman had a fundraising appointment at the office of a local attorney. Kalman began by asking about the man's family, then described his latest educational project. The conversation inevitably led to talk of a donation, and Kalman suggested an amount.

"That's far more than I've ever given," the attorney said. "I don't even have that much!"

"I understand," Kalman said. "But if you had the money, would it be the right thing to do?"

"Yes," the attorney nodded suspiciously.

Kalman paused for effect, then said, "So do the right thing and become God's partner in perfecting the world. The Almighty repays every good deed – in this world and for eternity."

The attorney hesitated to consider such a donation, which by all appearances was risky and even irresponsible. Yet inspired by Kalman's sincerity and assuredness, the attorney shocked even himself by writing a check – on the spot – for the large amount that Kalman requested.

The meeting concluded with warm goodbyes, after which the attorney's secretary brought him the mail. One of the envelopes caught his eye; it was from a client for whom he'd performed legal work a few years prior. The client had never paid, and the attorney had forgotten the whole thing. Now, moments after Kalman's assurance that the Almighty repays every good deed, the attorney opened the envelope from that long-forgotten client. It contained a check for the exact amount he'd just given Kalman.

FAR EAST

Kalman was an experienced traveler who knew the ins and outs of passport control, seat selection, ground transportation, hotels and – most importantly – the local kosher restaurants. To supplement his travel diet, Kalman was fortunate that a college buddy, Daryl Brenner, owned a kosher delicatessen and often sent a suitcase full of food to accompany Kalman around the world.

Kalman made an annual fundraising trip to the Far East, visiting wealthy Jews in the commercial centers of Hong Kong, Singapore and Malaysia. He met with a broad cross-section of business and political leaders, including the Chief Justice of Singapore's Supreme Court.

In Hong Kong, Kalman and Daryl had dinner with a high-level graphic designer. "Is there anything famous you designed?" Daryl asked. "Pull out your wallet and look at the Hong Kong currency I designed," the man replied, pointing to his name on every bill.

⇒◆⇐

Kalman treasured small donations, believing that once a person became a giver, it put them on the right side of the ledger.

In Hong Kong, Kalman regularly visited a wealthy man who refused to donate anything. "Just give *something* for the Jewish people," Kalman prodded. "Even five dollars." With persistence, Kalman eventually obtained a commitment for a small donation. Yet before he could collect, the man passed away.

After the mourning period concluded, Kalman spoke with the widow and delicately informed her about the unpaid pledge. To Kalman's surprise, she refused to pay. Since it wasn't a large amount, he considered letting it go, but concluded that because the man so rarely gave charity, this small gift could be a source of everlasting merit. So Kalman went to great effort, making multiple requests, until the widow finally honored the pledge – then refused to speak with Kalman again.

⇒◆⇐

On a trip to Hong Kong, Kalman was riding in a taxi. "Are you Jewish?" the Chinese driver asked.

"Yes, I am," Kalman replied. "How do you know what Jews look like?"

"From television," said the driver. "The Jewish people are very wise."

Kalman returned the compliment: "The Chinese people are also very wise."

"True," said the driver, "but the Chinese use wisdom only for themselves. Jews use wisdom for the whole world."

In the back seat of that taxi, Kalman uttered a prayer of gratitude for his good fortune of being Jewish, and reaffirmed his conviction that Torah is humanity's most valuable commodity.

———⊰•⊱———

Initially, Kalman enjoyed the novelty and adventure of trips to the Far East. Yet as years went by and the travel became more taxing, he started dreading the trips. To make things more palatable, he invited friends to join him and share a room. Kalman spent his days fundraising, while the friend went sightseeing. Daryl Brenner recalls:

> For years, Kalman wanted to meet in Hong Kong. I finally agreed. Kalman flew in from Israel, and I flew in from the U.S. My flight was scheduled to land eight hours before Kalman's. In the end, I missed my connection and landed in Hong Kong four hours late. Meanwhile, Kalman's flight arrived four hours early. The eight-hour gap was reduced to zero. Imagine my surprise to see Kalman at baggage claim!

HONG KONG SUBWAY

While traveling the world, Kalman found that wearing a kippah in public invited interesting conversations. He was once riding the Hong Kong subway when a young man approached. "Excuse me, are you a stranger here? Do you need any help?"

"No, thank you," Kalman replied. "I've been here several times and know my way around." Yet not one to let an opportunity pass, Kalman engaged the young man in conversation. It turns out that Dan* was a Jew from Texas who'd started his own company in Hong Kong. As the train pulled into the station, they exchanged business cards, and eventually Dan became one of Kalman's donors – all in the merit of the kippah.

As a bonus, Dan also passed Kalman's business card along to a friend who – in a fundraising rarity – called Kalman and asked to meet. He was a former U.S. Army colonel, whom Kalman described as "a tough-as-nails guy with a heightened Jewish consciousness."

At the meeting, the colonel shared some background about their mutual friend Dan: "We had business dealings together, and one day Dan told me, 'I have some news. I'm marrying my Christian girlfriend and converting to Christianity.' 'Convert to Christianity?' I shouted. 'Like heck you are!' Then I stood up and punched him in the teeth, just like it says in the Haggadah."

Kalman was taken aback by the colonel's extreme approach, which bore no resemblance to the loving and levelheaded methods described years earlier in Kalman's marriage book.

The colonel continued, "After losing my cool like that, I was afraid of legal trouble and immediately phoned my lawyer. He told me to wait and see what happens. Two days later, Dan called me and asked to meet. 'I want to thank you,' Dan said. 'My entire life, nobody ever cared enough to knock some sense into me. I've barely slept the past two days, thinking about all the blood, sweat and tears that my ancestors invested in keeping Judaism alive. I don't want to cut that chain. So I broke up with my fiancé.'

"Now you understand," the colonel concluded, "how special Dan is."

Kalman developed a relationship with the colonel, who also became a donor (and pledged to work on anger management).

TORAH STUDY HABIT

A pillar of Kalman's fundraising approach was to establish the credibility of Torah wisdom, knowing that it is the fount of Jewish vitality. Additionally, Kalman would encourage his donors to become personally involved in Torah study. "People think you only want their money," Kalman advised a young fundraiser.

"That's not true. Primarily, you want to give people an appreciation for the joy of being Jewish."

At fundraising meetings, Kalman would say, "I'd like to ask a
personal question. Are you planning to eat today?" Invariably, the
answer was a skeptical "Yes."

Kalman would continue, "Life is not about how many steaks
you eat, or how many restaurants you visit. Life has meaning
and purpose. Torah is our 'instructions for living,' the Almighty's
wisdom for getting the most out of life. If you're careful to feed
your body every day, doesn't it also make sense to feed your soul?"

Kalman's favorite donor gift was *A Fire in His Soul*, the biography of Irving Bunim, a twentieth-century Torah scholar and
businessperson who fought valiantly to save Jews from the Holocaust. Kalman saw this book as a way to inspire people about the
power of what one person can – and should – do to help the Jewish
people.

Kalman would also present donors with a copy of Bunim's
Ethics From Sinai, bite-sized pieces of Jewish wisdom. Kalman
would suggest, "First thing every morning, when you come into
the office, open this book and read one page. Then, whenever you
speak with someone that day – family, friends, business associ-
ates – share a piece of meaningful wisdom. It will transform your
entire day."

For many of Kalman's donors, this entrée into the world of
Torah study blossomed into a lifelong connection with Jewish
thought and practice.

WORDS FROM THE HEART

Kalman lived with Rav Noah's advice on achieving self-esteem:

> Don't make your happiness contingent on external factors like
> popularity and status. That puts your happiness in the hands of
> others, who can choose to supply approval or withhold it.

Genuine self-esteem comes from within, independent of any external factor. This guarantees a happy life.

Though fundraisers are the frequent target of insults and rejection, Kalman's inner esteem helped him achieve what others might shy away from. To maintain dignity in the face of harsh treatment, Kalman composed this affirmation:

> I represent the Jewish people, the Torah and the Almighty. Nobody has the right to push me around or besmirch me. What I have to say, and what I represent, is too important.

Kalman was visiting the office of a prospective donor and requested quality time with no interruptions. "Would it be possible to please ask your secretary to hold calls for the next fifteen minutes?" Kalman asked.

"What kind of arrogant moron are you?" the man shouted. "I'm the boss around here. If I want the secretary to hold the calls, that's my decision!"

"Of course, you're the boss," Kalman said calmly, thinking he may have been misunderstood. "That's why I politely asked you – the boss – to ask the secretary."

"You won't be here in fifteen minutes," the man shot back. "You'll be out in two! Now what do you want!"

Kalman made a quick strategic decision. Instead of a fundraising pitch, he shifted to pastoral mode, gently guiding the man to share the source of his obstinance. With patience and compassion, Kalman exemplified the Jewish teaching, "Words that come from the heart, enter the heart."

They spoke together for ninety minutes, at which point the man wrote a generous check.

Kalman was meeting a prospective donor in Singapore when the man began furiously screaming. "I wanted to marry a non-Jewish woman and my mother insisted that she convert. You rabbis are ruining the world!"

Kalman wasn't angry, but went with the flow and yelled back.

The man was stunned. "Why are you yelling?"

Kalman shrugged innocently. "I assumed that yelling is your preferred tone of communication."

"I'm sorry," the man said. "Let's speak softly."

They did. And the man became a donor.

While reviewing Aish HaTorah's fundraising records, Kalman noticed that two years prior, Rav Noah had met a man for lunch and received a $1,000 donation. Yet somehow, things fell through the cracks and no one had followed up since.

Kalman phoned the donor's office and the secretary put through the call. "Who the heck is Rabbi Packouz?" was his novel way of answering the phone.

Kalman stayed calm and professional. "I work with Rabbi Noah Weinberg at Aish HaTorah," he explained.

The man began hyperventilating. "I once met Rabbi Weinberg for lunch – and it cost me $1,000!"

"That is correct," Kalman said. "What are your lunch plans today?"

The man had no interest in becoming a continuing supporter. "You're doing great work," he said, still hyperventilating. "Goodbye!"

DELINQUENT PLEDGE

On occasions when a donor neglected to honor a pledge, Kalman reluctantly assumed the role of collection agent. He regarded this unpleasant task as doing the donor a favor, since Judaism treats very seriously the commitment to a charitable pledge.

To get his point across, Kalman occasionally shared this macabre joke:

> A wealthy, but very cheap, man gets married. Soon after, he goes to a rabbi and says, "I didn't anticipate how expensive married life is. I want out! Rabbi, could you pray that she die?"
>
> "I can't do that," the rabbi replies. "That's not the Jewish way."
>
> "So what do you suggest?" the man asks desperately.
>
> "I have an idea," the rabbi says. "The Talmud says that if someone habitually makes charitable pledges and refuses to pay, their spouse could die."
>
> "Thank you, Rabbi!" the man says. He rushes out the door and down the street to an orphanage, where he promptly pledges thousands of dollars, then follows this with a dozen other large charitable pledges.
>
> For an entire next month, despite repeated attempts by the charities to get paid, the man steadfastly refuses. Yet it has no negative affect on the bride. Distraught, the man returns to the rabbi. "I did exactly as you suggested, but it's not working. She's strong as an ox!"
>
> The rabbi thinks for a moment and says, "I think I know the problem. This is a curse, but you want it as a blessing. So I have a different way to fix the situation. Buy your wife an assortment of nice gifts. It may sound strange, but trust me on this."
>
> The man is skeptical, but at this point willing to give anything a try. He runs out and buys his wife a diamond pendant. The next day, he brings her flowers, perfume and chocolate. Feeling appreciated and loved, she begins to respond in kind.
>
> Before long, they're madly in love.

Soon after, the wife gets sick, and with each passing day, sicker still. The man is distraught. The doctors report, "There is nothing we can do."

The man runs back to the rabbi, eyes filled with tears. "Rabbi! My beloved wife is sick and dying! Please help!"

Calmly, the rabbi says, "Pay your pledges."

FUNDRAISING LESSONS

Kalman was scrupulously honest in administering the millions of dollars that crossed his desk.

One time, Kalman was sorting through the morning mail when he saw an envelope from a regular donor. The enclosed check for $1,800 did not fit that donor's typical pattern of giving. Kalman checked the computer records and, sure enough, this was an unusually large gift. He immediately picked up the phone and said, "I'm calling to thank you for the very generous gift. And I want to be sure there was no mistake in the amount."

———❖———

One time, Kalman's request for a donation of $1,800 was met by peals of laughter. After the man calmed down, Kalman said, "In many years of fundraising, my requests for support have evoked a range of reactions: derision, stunned disbelief, anger, irritation – and even an occasional word of appreciation. Yet this laughter is a first."

"Allow me to explain," the man said. "A few weeks ago, I made a deal with God: 'If my business deal goes through, I'll give $1,800 to the first person who asks.' And you're the first!"

Kalman's face lit up, savoring this manifestation of Divine love. "If that's the case," Kalman said, "then I look forward to more laughing and giving!"

———❖———

At a community event, Kalman's friend proudly introduced him to a successful businessperson: "This is Rabbi Packouz, who knows people from all over the world. Tell him where you're from, and he'll name someone from there."

Kalman was taken aback by this on-the-spot game of "Jewish geography," but went along for the ride.

The man thought for a moment, then named a small town in Alaska, located in the middle of nowhere.

Kalman's grin flashed ear to ear as he named someone from that town. The man was so impressed that he became a donor.

NON-TERRITORIAL

Rav Noah's operating principle was: "We're all on the same team, working together to help the Jewish people." To this end, Rav Noah provided seed funding for dozens of other projects and institutions – a rarity in a fundraising world that tends to be parochial and territorial.

"Torah is a universal enterprise," Rav Noah would say. "You don't work for Aish HaTorah. You work for the Almighty."

The most guarded asset of every fundraiser is their donor list. Yet Kalman generously made his network of contacts available to other fundraisers – with no expectation of return. "I'm on board with whatever is good for God and the Jewish people," Kalman explained. "When I share my contacts, it benefits everyone, myself included. You can't lose by helping people. It doesn't take away from me, because the money comes from Above. I'm just the conduit. Whatever the Almighty gives me, He can give to others as well. He can afford it!"

One long-time fundraiser recalls, "I never met someone with Kalman's degree of trust that his own success was tied to helping others and contributing to the greater good. On one occasion, he arranged an appointment for me with one of his donors, and accompanied me to the meeting. Unfortunately, it resulted in no donation. So Kalman donated the money himself."

Rabbi Yochanan Zweig, one of the premier Torah figures of our generation, testified, "Kalman Packouz did not work for Aish HaTorah. He worked for God."

WESTERN WALL REAL ESTATE

Kalman's fundraising skills were put to the test when Aish HaTorah had a unique opportunity to secure a building directly facing the Western Wall. To seal the deal, Rav Noah had to come up with all the construction money up-front. Kalman and the other fundraisers worked overtime to help make this happen.

Their efforts produced an unexpected miracle: When the Israeli shekel underwent a major devaluation, the Israeli government suddenly owed Aish HaTorah an enormous sum of money. To call it even, then-Housing Minister David Levy gave Aish HaTorah the building that today houses the Aish World Center.

Astounded, Kalman asked Rav Noah, "Did you ever imagine such a prestigious location?"

Rav Noah's immediate reply: "When you work for the Almighty, things get done."

Over the years, Kalman secured substantial gifts to help facilitate the building's construction and programming.

RUSSIAN PROGRAM

Rabbi Shalom Schwartz was Kalman's friend from the early days of Aish HaTorah. In the 1990s, Shalom was directing Jewish educational programs in the former Soviet Union and made fundraising trips to Miami. Shalom would stay at the Packouzes' guesthouse, which many out-of-town friends and colleagues considered their "home base" in Florida. Kalman would pick up

Shalom at the airport and care for all his needs, asking, "What dry cleaning do you need done? What gifts do you need for your family?"

During one trip to Miami, Shalom received a disturbing letter from an important donor, critiquing his program and challenging the data and assessment of results. Kalman literally stopped everything for two days to help Shalom research and compose a response. Kalman then personally typed it and faxed it to the donor.

Shalom comments, "Who would do that, besides Kalman? He was the most considerate person I ever met. Nothing was too big or too small for him."

In 1995, to raise money for Shalom's Russian program, talk-show host Larry King hosted an event called "Help Our People Know," a live broadcast from Paramount Studios in Hollywood. In those pre-Internet days, the program utilized satellite technology to connect Jerusalem, Moscow, Los Angeles and other locations around the world.

To benefit the program, Kalman arranged an event at a restaurant in Miami. He invited a range of important and wealthy guests, but in the end, only a handful showed up. The restaurant's air conditioning system was faulty, making the event hot and noisy – and deflating the presentation by Vitaly Pruss, a young Jewish leader in Belarus.

Yet despite such difficulties and unlikely odds, the event proved a huge success. When Vitaly mentioned the lack of a kosher Torah scroll in all of Belarus, entrepreneur Sol Zuckerman – whom Kalman barely knew but had called to invite – offered to donate a scroll.

Vitaly then explained there was no permanent facility to house the Torah scroll. On the spot, Zuckerman agreed to purchase a building, which became the Minsk College for Jewish

Leadership – a critical factor in the movement to rebuild Judaism in Belarus.

Till today, the ripple effect of Kalman's Miami event impacts thousands of Belarus Jews.

DIVINE PAYMENT

In 1974, Rav Noah was teaching a class:

"In Exodus chapter 2, baby Moses is floating in a basket. Pharaoh's daughter Batya comes to bathe in the Nile, and sees the basket far away in the reeds. Even though Moses is beyond reach Batya stretches out her hand to grab it – and her outstretched hand miraculously extended. Think about it: Why did Batya even try reaching an impossibly long distance to save Moses?"

Rav Noah lets the question sink in, then explains:

"Since she was determined to reach Moses' basket, Batya made no calculations. The lesson for us: When success seems impossible, our only task is to try. Ordinary effort can have extraordinary impact. The result is in God's hands."

Kalman subscribed to this principle – and merited to see his efforts have extraordinary impact.

Kalman was meeting a supporter for lunch. After catching up on each other's lives, they discussed the state of the Jewish people. Kalman then requested a renewal of the donor's $2,000 annual support.

"My current income precludes giving that amount," the donor said. "But I can give $500."

Kalman didn't give up easily. He graciously thanked the donor for continued support, then said, "The great twentieth-century sage, the Chofetz Chaim, offers advice for how to succeed in any financial or commercial enterprise. Before entering a venture, estimate your projected profit. Then write a check for ten percent of that amount and set it aside, to eventually be given as *tzedakah*. Then say, 'Master of the Universe, it is my privilege to invite You to be my partner in this endeavor. If I fail to realize a profit, I will have nothing to share with You, my partner. However, if I gain the anticipated profit, then the ten percent I've set aside is Yours.'"

Kalman paused, then asked the supporter, "How much income would you need in the coming year to enable a donation of the full $2,000?"

"Hmmm," the donor said, doing a quick mental calculation. "I'd need to double my annual earnings."

"Great!" Kalman said. "Then we have a deal. Please let me know if you make that amount in the coming year."

Over the course of the year, Kalman tried valiantly to maintain contact with the donor – via phone calls, emails, and sending packages of interesting information and books. The response was deafening silence.

At the end of the year, Kalman wrote to inquire about the status of their deal. Zero response.

A few months later, the donor's secretary called Kalman to schedule a lunch meeting. *Why would he want to meet after ignoring me an entire year?* Kalman asked himself. *He probably wants pastoral guidance for a personal problem.*

A few days later, the two met for an enjoyable lunch, filled with pleasant small talk. Toward the end of meal, the man asked, "Do you remember our financial deal?"

"Yes," Kalman said poker-faced, but anxious to see where this was headed.

"Well, Rabbi, you won't believe it. After we made the deal, my phone rang off the hook with more business than I could even handle. In the past year, my earnings didn't double – they tripled. I made more money than I ever imagined!"

"That's wonderful!" Kalman enthused. "But why did you avoid contacting me until now?"

"Because I was skeptical whether this bonanza was the result of our agreement, or mere coincidence. So I decided to wait and see what happens next. It turns out that the first quarter of this year has been a financial disaster. My worst ever! That's when I knew it was a mistake not to have made good on my pledge."

The donor handed Kalman a check, then added hopefully, "Rabbi, could we make the same deal for next year?"

Kalman chuckled. "Just tell me how much and I'll try to arrange it!"

KALMAN'S WAY: FUNDRAISING

As one of the Jewish world's most respected fundraisers, Kalman developed this recipe for success:

- Build rapport. Be genuinely interested in people.

- Convey the eternal merit of giving *tzedakah*.

- Articulate the problem, and that we are fighting humanity's most important cause.

- Connect donors to Torah study.

- If you don't ask, you don't get.

- The more you ask for, the more you get.

- Get the money up front.

- It's all in God's hands. As messengers, we only make an appropriate effort.

- The donor, the fundraiser and God are philanthropic partners.

CHAPTER TEN

Western Wall Webcam

LIGHT OF TORAH

1973. Rav Noah is at the Western Wall, speaking to yeshiva students:

"We're standing at the foot of Mount Moriah, the international symbol of hope and redemption," Rav Noah says. "Millions come to this site, the spiritual center of the universe. What makes it so special?"

Kalman suggests, "It's a symbol of the Six Day War that Israel just won."

"Actually, it starts back on the first day of Creation," Rav Noah explains, "when spiritual light became physical matter. Mount Moriah was the starting point. Jerusalem is literally 'where God is seen,' the bridge between Heaven and Earth. Here on Mount Moriah, Abraham brought Isaac onto the altar. Here on Mount Moriah, Jacob dreamed of the ladder ascending to Heaven. King David purchased Mount Moriah 3,000 years ago, and this is where the Holy Temple stood for 900 years. Throughout our nearly-2,000-year exile, we directed all prayers to this spot, with the cry of 'Next Year in Jerusalem!'"

Kalman asks about history. "Today there's a mosque on Mount Moriah, and before that were Crusader churches. Ancient maps show Jerusalem as the center of the world – the intersection between Asia, Europe and Africa. How did Jerusalem become such a focus of the non-Jewish world?"

Rav Noah explains, "When King Solomon built the Jerusalem Temple, he asked God to heed the prayers of non-Jews who were drawn by the Temple's magnetic spiritual power. Non-Jews brought offerings to the Temple and it was, in the words of the prophet Isaiah, 'a house of prayer for all nations.'"

"That sounds like a nice ideal," a student interjects. "But did that bear out historically?"

"When the Temple stood, the world was filled with appreciation for God and Torah," Rav Noah explains. "The Bible describes how the Queen of Sheba came with a large entourage to meet King Solomon in Jerusalem. She presented ethical and political scenarios, and Solomon's answers prompted her to say, 'Your wisdom and goodness surpass even your reputation.'"

"That was then," a student says. "What about today?"

"The prophet Isaiah says that 'Torah shall come forth from Zion, and the word of God from Jerusalem,'" Rav Noah says. "The ethical foundations of the Western world are all from Torah: Care for the widow, the orphan, the poor, the powerless and the oppressed. Universal education and the right to a fair trial. Genesis 1:27 is the source for the U.S. Declaration of Independence that all people are created equal and endowed by their Creator. Leviticus 19:18 is the universal Golden Rule, 'Love your neighbor as yourself.' Leviticus 25:10 is the source for 'Proclaim liberty throughout the land,' inscribed on the Liberty Bell. Isaiah 2:4 is the source for 'Beat their swords into plowshares,' etched on the United Nations' 'Isaiah Wall.'

"This is an enormous impact – and the Jewish people have accomplished it by miraculously breaking every sociological and historical rule. We are few in number – yet we've made a massive impact. We've been scattered to the four corners and persecuted – yet we're the eternal nation, fulfilling our mission as a 'light unto the nations.'"

"That's great about the Temple," a student says. "But what's so special about the Western Wall?"

"The Sages prophesied that even after the Temple's destruction, the Divine Presence would never leave the Western Wall," Rav Noah explains. "Jerusalem was destroyed and rebuilt nine times, and through it all, the Western Wall remained intact. It symbolizes how, against all odds, we've not only survived but thrived – impacting the world more per capita than any other people in history. We are one five-hundredth of the global population – and have won one-quarter of the Nobel Prizes. That's punching above your weight!"

Rav Noah raises his hands skyward. "Abraham's undertaking was the first progressive, liberal movement the world had ever seen. And look how it succeeded. The Jewish people are the greatest story ever told. And it starts right here."

CONCEPTION

One evening in 1998, Kalman was walking with a friend on the boardwalk in Miami Beach, enjoying the fresh ocean air. In those relaxed moments, Kalman shared a personal thought: "I take joy in my accomplishments, and am grateful for the good fortune of doing meaningful work for the Jewish people. Maybe it's a midlife crisis, but I feel a lot of untapped potential."

Kalman's friend put the ball back in his court: "What could you do to make an exponential impact?"

Kalman thought for a moment. "Rav Noah always says to go with your passion, which for me is technology. The Internet is going mainstream and is ripe for groundbreaking projects."

As they continued walking, Kalman's thoughts drifted to Jerusalem, thousands of miles away. He waxed nostalgic for his formative years at yeshiva, when he lived one minute from the Western Wall, the heart of the Jewish world.

"Jerusalem is geographically distant," Kalman told his friend, "but close to my heart. I suspect that many others feel the same. If only there was a way to use the Internet to connect people with Jerusalem."

Soon after, Kalman read an article about a growing phenomenon: 24-hour website cameras. Yet infrastructure for live transmission was expensive, and the only webcams at the time were at global icons like Times Square, the Eiffel Tower and Niagara Falls.

Suddenly, Kalman's eyes popped wide with an epiphany: "I'll make a live, 24-hour webcam on the Western Wall! It could be a virtual 'Window on the Wall.' People could tune in at all hours of the day and night to see worshippers praying for the health and safety of their families; to see brides and grooms from all corners of Israel on their wedding day, seeking the Almighty's blessing; and to see thousands of tourists visiting the spiritual center of the world. Best of all, the Wallcam can be a springboard to connect with the Almighty and learn more about Jewish heritage."

Kalman was not sure how to pull this off, but he was determined to try.

IMPLEMENTATION

It's one thing to imagine a creative new idea; bringing it to fruition requires a very different skill set. Kalman possessed both. He did a deep dive into the world of Internet cameras and transmission, with the goal of creating a breakthrough that he called "the intersection of high technology and high spirituality."

Kalman's biggest challenge was adequate connectivity to upload photographs 24/7. Back then, Internet connection was limited to slow dial-up modems, making it difficult to upload even low-quality photos. At the time, the fastest modem was a thousand times slower than the fiber optic networks of today. Compounding the problem was the fact that Internet lines in the Old City of Jerusalem were notoriously unstable.

Kalman purchased the largest bandwidth package available – sufficient for uploading one photo every thirty seconds.

Top-of-the-line camera equipment was donated by a non-Jewish fan of *Shabbat Shalom* (who upgraded the cameras over the years). Determining the camera location was obvious: It was mounted outside the Aish HaTorah building, directly facing the Western Wall. And for variety, Kalman arranged for a yeshiva student to adjust the camera angle once a day.

The final link in the chain proved the most challenging: a website server that would beam each single image to potentially tens of thousands of simultaneous users worldwide – without crashing in heavy traffic. In those fledging days of the Internet, Israel lacked such infrastructure.

So Kalman conceived of an out-of-the-box workaround: transmit the live Wallcam images to a more robust American-based server, and from there to a global audience. After an extensive search for a partner to solve this challenge, Kalman settled on Icanect – a small, innovative company at the forefront of Internet communications. Incredibly, Icanect was based in North Miami Beach, a fifteen-minute drive from Kalman's home. Deal done.

LAUNCH

With all the technology in place, there remained the all-important element of marketing. Jay Kaplowitz, a public relations professional in New York, had met Kalman and was attracted to his creativity and idealism. Working pro bono, Jay developed a PR plan to launch "Window on the Wall" with a bang, by leveraging Kalman's massive base of *Shabbat Shalom* subscribers.

A few days before Passover 1997, Kalman held a press conference at Icanect headquarters and announced:

> For the first time in nearly 2,000 years since the existence of the Holy Temple, the entire Jewish people will be able to experience *Birkat Kohanim*, the Priestly Blessing from the Western Wall during Passover. "Window on the Wall" will broadcast the event live via the Internet.

In 1997, this was a high-tech novelty and – fueled by Jay's PR playbook and Kalman's prayers – the story garnered extensive news coverage in South Florida. And within days, "Window on the Wall" was picked up by national media, including *CBS Evening News*.

"Kalman and I watched the site's visitor counter ring up thousands and thousands of hits," Jay recalls. "At the time, it was unimaginable that people were sitting in their home or office, thousands of miles away, watching these activities in real time. 'Window on the Wall' was making history."

Momentum quickly built and "Window on the Wall" was featured on CNN, MSNBC and the *New York Times*. Then the grand prize: "Window on the Wall" was selected by *USA Today* as "Internet Site of the Day."

"Window on the Wall" became the first "viral" sensation in Jewish Internet history. This precious digital real estate, integrated into the Aish HaTorah website, hosted millions of visits and funneled them to Rav Noah's online teachings – while catapulting Aish HaTorah to the forefront of online Jewish education.

SUCCESS

Lovers of Zion around the globe, of all religions, would keep the Wallcam open all day on their browser, to check in and maintain spiritual connection. As Rabbi Judah HaLevy, the fifteenth-century author of *Kuzari*, said, "I am in the west, but my heart is in the east" – in Jerusalem.

In the days before smart phones, "Window on the Wall" served another imaginative purpose: enabling a primitive version of "live streaming" from the Western Wall. This spawned a phenomenon whereby, at a pre-designated time, humongous banners would be unfurled at the Western Wall Plaza, as a "virtual greeting card" to a celebrant somewhere on the other side of the world… sitting in front of their PC… with the browser set to "Window on the Wall."

[With the advent of broadband, Kalman upgraded "Window on the Wall" to include 24-hour streaming video, which today enables millions of people to see Judaism's holy site in real-time.]

NOTES IN THE WALL

One evening in Miami, while pondering how to expand the impact of the Wallcam, Kalman thought back to something Rav Noah had taught about the power of Jerusalem:

> When the Temple was destroyed, all the Gates of Heaven were closed, except for the Gate of Tears. The Western Wall became known as the "Wailing Wall" because of centuries of endless tears, shed by Jews pouring their hearts out to God.
>
> The Midrash says that all prayers from around the world ascend to the Wall, and from there to Heaven. From here came a tradition to place written prayers in the cracks of the Wall.

Kalman had a eureka moment: *Why not create a virtual "Note in the Wall," where online visitors can type a note, have it printed out in the Old City of Jerusalem, then placed into the cracks of the Western Wall!*

Kalman created this digital "Note in the Wall," further strengthening people's connection to the holy site. Additionally, Kalman leveraged this to solicit voluntary donations and defray the cost of equipment and web hosting. The site noted: "This is a free service. However, there is great merit in making a contribution to assist in making this available to others, and to help fund our Jewish educational programs."

The feature proved wildly popular, and to date, "Note in the Wall" has facilitated tens of thousands of prayers and notes placed in the Wall.

SITE MANAGEMENT

One of Rav Noah's founding principles was to give people autonomy to run projects, with the confidence of a secure lifetime position. Though Kalman was by nature not "territorial," since he'd conceived of and built the Wallcam, he wanted to retain creative control.

Kalman worked closely with the Aish Internet team to maintain and upgrade the Wallcam page. On one visit to Israel, a friendly disagreement arose about the page design, and Kalman went together with Aish.com co-founder David LeVine to speak with Rav Noah.

David spoke first. "In my professional opinion, Kalman's design would make for a less desirable user experience."

"It's Kalman's site," Rav Noah replied. "Please accommodate his requests."

After the meeting, Kalman reflected on the Torah teaching: "Be a judge, not a lawyer." A lawyer argues for one side only, with the goal of winning the discussion. A judge objectively weighs both sides, with the goal of reaching an objective conclusion. Kalman understood the importance of striving to understand what is rationally true, not what you wish to be true.

In the end, few if any changes were made to the Wallcam site. "Kalman was not into exerting power," David says. "He balanced the fine line between 'being right' and 'giving in.' Once it was his decision to make, he deferred to our expert opinion."

Upon Kalman's passing, the Wallcam was bequeathed to Aish HaTorah. On the Wallcam webpage, a permanent "virtual plaque" greets visitors, crediting Kalman as founder, and noting his "innovative genius and lifelong commitment to connecting every person to their Creator."

In the annals of Jewish Internet history, "Window on the Wall" broke new ground and demonstrated the power of digital media for the Jewish people. With traffic in the millions – numbers unimaginable during the Internet's infancy – "Window on the Wall" became the Jewish world's first iconic online venture, an exclamation point in Kalman's spectacular life.

KALMAN'S WAY: CHECKLIST FOR GREATNESS

Kalman was a big thinker who enjoyed entertaining the notion of a perfect world. He wrote:

> We all have our rules to live by: Brush and floss. Shop wholesale. Apply sunscreen liberally. Yet while these rules make our lives comfortable and pleasant, we need greater goals to nurture our souls.
>
> Here is my personal "Checklist for Greatness." Try making your own list of rules to live by. After all, it's your life!

(1) Clean Speech. Gossip is a verbal atomic bomb that destroys marriages, businesses and friendships. Just because something is true doesn't mean you should say it. High-level people speak about ideas; average people speak about things; inferior people speak about people. Take the high road. A kind word at the right time can change someone's life and inspire greatness.

(2) Integrity. Your word is your bond. In the short term, you may gain in money or success, but dishonesty costs you in loss of respect, trust and relationships. As a rule, avoid anything that you'd be embarrassed were it found out.

(3) Respect. Every human is created in the image of God. Respecting people respects God. Rabbi Hillel said it best, "Don't do unto others as you wouldn't want done to you."

(4) Kindness. Every day, go out of your way to help others. Hold the door for someone; help carry groceries into the house; offer a listening ear when you'd rather run away; smile at others; find something nice to say.

(5) Wisdom. Torah is a compendium of wisdom, the instructions for living. The Sages say, "An uneducated person cannot be righteous." Study wisdom in order to know what (and what not) to do or say. Wisdom connects you with values, keeps you focused and helps you grow.

(6) Meaning. On their deathbed, everyone reflects back on life. Do you want your life measured by hamburgers consumed and air miles logged? Or would you rather it be measured by how you helped others and made this a better world? Find a meaningful cause and be bigger than yourself.

(7) Humility. Humility is not defined as "letting others walk all over you." Rather, humility is recognizing that your capabilities are Divine gifts. Just as it's ridiculous to say, "Hey, look at me – I can move my hand!" so too it's inappropriate to brag about being tall, handsome or mathematically inclined. Make your talents and skills a source of gratitude, not arrogance.

(8) Prayer. God doesn't need our prayers. Prayer is for our sake – a tool to help us focus on the Source of all blessing. By doing so, we become fit to receive more. Prayer also clarifies an important truth: We're not God!

(9) Consequences. Our actions have consequences. There is ultimate reward for good actions and penalty for transgressions – if not in this world, then in the next.

(10) Awareness. Rather than treating problems as obstacles to avoid, see them as opportunities to improve. Don't let decisions "just happen." Take control and monitor your choices. In the moment, if your ethical moorings drift, ask yourself: *Is this the higher choice?* If not, change it.

(11) Gratitude. The word "Judaism" *(Yahadut)* derives from the name Yehudah, meaning "to give thanks." Give up the illusion that you alone are responsible for your achievements. Appreciate that even simple things – breathing, eyesight, gravity, etc. – are a gift from God, the Source of all.

(12) Commitment. Stay focused. Relentlessly pursue your goals with discipline, strategy and follow-through. Put aside anything that unnecessarily detracts from you. Be prepared to forgo short-term pleasure in favor of long-term gain.

CHAPTER ELEVEN

Departure

MORTALITY REALITY

1974. Rav Noah was teaching on the topic of "death":

"Mortality" presents a great opportunity. When you have a literal "deadline" – an unknown expiration date – it's a constant reminder to think about life. If we'd live forever, we could always put off making the effort till tomorrow... and the next day... and forever. Death gets us to take life seriously and use our time wisely.

Some people expect to live forever, thinking, *There's a certain "club" of people who die – and I'm not a member.* That's an absurd denial of reality. Everyone dies. It is said that Baron Rothschild paid a servant to remind him every hour that he was one hour closer to death.

The Sages say, "Always keep your last day in mind." And since you don't know when that will be, treat every day as your last.

Kalman took this idea seriously. In Miami Beach, he reserved a memorial plaque in the shul and looked at it every day, thinking, *This might be my last day. God, please help me not waste a moment.*

Kalman imagined a bank account of $86,400 that had to be spent that day – or lost forever. "Every day we're granted 86,400 seconds," he'd say. "Use it or lose it!"

Kalman would encourage people, "Don't wait till late in the game to prioritize your cherished values. Do it now and live by them. Imagine a clock on top of your television, counting down the days, hours and minutes of your life – from now till the moment you die. At which point will you get up from the chair, turn off the TV, and do all the important things you've been putting off?"

As a practical tool for setting priorities, Kalman would suggest, "Try writing your own obituary. How would you like people to remember you? What do you want written on your tombstone?"

END OF AN ERA

In 2008, Rav Noah was diagnosed with lung cancer. This was a challenging time for Kalman. He'd enjoyed a thirty-five-year relationship with Rav Noah, whom he regarded as his trusted mentor, guide and partner – and admired as "the role model of a genuine God-loving Jew who lives in reality."

During Rav Noah's illness, Kalman made extra efforts to express his appreciation. Kalman put together a book entitled, *Thank You, Rav Noah,* containing photos and memories gathered from hundreds of students, past and present.

Writing in the book, Kalman expressed his deep gratitude to Rav Noah:

> Without your teachings, idealism and enthusiasm, who knows how my life would have turned out. Because of you, I am blessed to work for the Almighty and the Jewish people. Because of you, I have the most wonderful wife in the world and nine gorgeous children.
>
> You are a one-man cheering squad of love and encouragement, always helping me to break through self-imposed barriers.

All my accomplishments were with your guidance, acceptance and unconditional love.

"Thank you" is what you say when someone holds open the door for you. What do you say to the one who helped you find purpose and meaning in life? My gratitude is eternal.

Rav Noah cherished the book and kept it beside him.

———✥———

In their final meeting, Kalman requested a blessing for success. "Feel how much the Almighty loves you," Rav Noah said. "This will give you the power to accomplish anything in the world."

With Rav Noah's passing on 11 Shevat 5769 (February 5, 2009), Kalman felt like the bottom had fallen out of his world, leaving him orphaned and bereft.

In Jewish tradition, one comforts a mourner by saying, "May God – *HaMakom* – comfort you among the mourners of Zion and Jerusalem." *HaMakom* means "The Place." A person's death leaves a vacuum of the "place" they filled in this world. By emulating the qualities of the deceased, we can help fill the unique "place" that the deceased occupied and connect us with their essence. In this way, the mourner finds comfort.

In mourning Rav Noah's passing, Kalman pledged to emulate Rav Noah's qualities:

- Rav Noah had a twinkle in his eye; love in his heart; humility; and total commitment to the Almighty and the Jewish people.

- Rav Noah had unconditional love for every human being. He detected the Divine spark and greatness in each of us.

- Rav Noah's smile lit up the room with warmth and love – radiating the feeling that all is well in the world.

- Rav Noah helped others fulfill their potential by identifying their unique contribution to the Jewish people.

- Rav Noah's clarity, wisdom and authority enabled me to ask for advice – and to know, intellectually and intuitively, that his answer was correct.

- Rav Noah lived with sanity. He broke through petty squabbles and knew how to conquer obstacles, within and without.

- Rav Noah gave corrective advice *(tochacha)*. With laser sharpness, he could identify what was holding me back, and get me to focus on the big-picture problems facing the Jewish people.

After Rav Noah's passing, thousands of tributes poured in. Kalman, the ever-loyal disciple, compiled and arranged all the letters, articles, photos and eulogies into a 400-page volume entitled, *Remembering Rabbi Noah Weinberg*. With gratitude, Kalman presented the book as a gift to the Weinberg family.

Kalman recalled:

In the thirty-six years I knew Rav Noah, I heard only positive, uplifting words. He never focused on what I "could have" or "should have" done. Instead, he praised, encouraged and took pleasure in my victories and successes.

Rav Noah would greet me with a huge smile and call me *"tach'sheet"* (jewel) and *"neshamala"* (precious soul). I always knew that anytime, anyplace, with any problem, I could turn to him. He was there for me, 100 percent.

Everyone felt they were Rav Noah's most beloved student. Though I knew the truth: It was me.

INITIAL DIAGNOSIS

In 2015, Kalman encountered his own health trauma: a diagnosis of Stage 4 prostate cancer, asymptomatic. Kalman was suddenly plunged into a world of biopsies, MRIs and PSMA scans.

When the cancer was discovered, doctors prescribed radiation with full-body MRIs, where the patient is enclosed in a machine for forty minutes without moving. For Kalman, this presented an enormous challenge: He suffered from claustrophobia and avoided closed-in spaces, even trying hypnosis to cure it.

Yet Kalman was up for the challenge. Summoning his powers of thought control, he lay in the MRI machine, meditatively speaking to God and expressing gratitude for all his blessings. During the session, Kalman would start with his body, mentally reviewing each part from head to toe. Then he'd detail the virtues of his beloved family, friends and community.

Through it all, Kalman did not fear. He recalled the talmudic passage of Moses being arrested in Egypt and taken out for execution. As the sword came down, Moses' neck miraculously repelled the sword. He escaped and went on to lead the Jewish people.

In Kalman's mind, there is always hope, even with a sword on one's neck. "Everything is in God's hands," he said. "My thoughts are not the same as God's thoughts. The Almighty has a plan and is taking care of me. We are entirely under God's care and there is no other power than the Almighty. The way things turn out is meant to be – and best for me."

To strengthen his belief and calm his spirit, Kalman made a list of all the times that a situation looked hopeless, yet worked out for the best. He told a humorous story to illustrate this notion:

> A king's friend committed a capital crime. Though the king was obligated to uphold the law, he was loathe to sentence his friend to

death. To delay the inevitable, the king told his friend, "I'll give you one year to teach my horse to sing. If you fail, you'll be put to death."

The man was put in jail and was overjoyed. "Why are you so happy?" the guard asked. "You're condemned to death!"

"Many things can happen in a year," the man replied. "The king could die. I could die. The horse could die. Or I might even succeed in teaching it to sing!"

Such was Kalman's attitude: The future is undetermined, and anything is possible.

———❖———

Though diagnosed with cancer four years before his passing, Kalman kept it mostly secret. Initially, Shoshana knew, but not their children, nor Kalman's parents and siblings. Even toward the end, Kalman insisted that his elderly father not be told, as not to cause him unnecessary worry.

As the months went by, Kalman casually mentioned his "health challenge" to friends, but resisted sounding the alarm and asking for prayers. Kalman hoped to continue, as much as possible, to lead a normal life and be spared an overwhelming amount of email and medical advice. He didn't want people to treat him differently, seeing him as "sick and dying" and feeling sorry for him. He wanted to be fully engaged, and felt that the specter of a fatal illness would prove a distraction. He wanted to be normal… a little longer.

HEALTH OPPORTUNITY

Kalman's thoughts returned repeatedly to a teaching he'd heard decades earlier from Rav Noah:

In Genesis chapter 28, Jacob dreams of a ladder reaching the heavens. The ladder symbolizes a basic human condition: In life, we're either going up or down. There is no standing in place. Every difficulty is a means of elevating oneself. With willpower and discipline, we can overcome the challenges and grow, climbing higher each day. The choice is always ours.

Whenever Kalman saw a ladder, he'd ask himself, *What challenge am I currently facing? Am I climbing higher in spiritual level, or going down?* If ever the answer was "going down," Kalman would strengthen himself and climb from there.

⸺⸺◈⸺⸺

Despite the serious medical diagnosis, Kalman was remarkably calm. He understood there was no choice about the cancer – only a choice of how to respond: Either to despair and retreat from the world; or to be happy for the goodness he has, and enjoy the remaining time with family and friends.

Though in tremendous pain, Kalman took the illness as ultimately for the best. He wrote:

> The purpose of life is not "comfort." The Almighty did not put us here to cruise through life without challenge, only to die peacefully under a beach umbrella with a piña colada in hand.
>
> The purpose of life is to perfect our character and grow spiritually. God gives us challenges to grow. We can either view these as obstacles or as stepping stones. In life, pain is inevitable, but suffering is optional.
>
> In a worldview without God, where everything is ultimately random, then looking for meaning in life's events is hopelessly irrational. Yet if one believes that the Almighty created the world, cares about us and has an individual, direct relationship with everyone, then asking "Why did this happen?" makes good sense.
>
> Every challenge is accompanied by God's love and guidance. There are no "accidents." Everything that happens – "good" or

"bad" – is inherently meaningful, a customized message from the Almighty, a course correction to help us perfect our character and fulfill our life mission.

In processing his health situation, Kalman referenced the quote describing three types of people, in descending order of greatness:

- Those who make things happen.

- Those who watch things happen.

- Those who ask, "What happened?"

Kalman added to the top of this list: Those who ask: "Why did this happen?" Rather than complain or question God's ways, Kalman saw his illness as an opportunity to delve into the underlying spiritual cause. He explained:

> The highest form of living is to make your desire synonymous with God's desire. *"Gam zu l'tova"* – everything God does is for our good. Our job is to ask: *What is the Almighty communicating? What should I learn from this? What does God want from me now?* Even if we don't always understand the reason why things happen, nobody ever lost out by asking the question.

In the early stage of diagnosis, Kalman compiled a short list of priorities, vowing to focus relentlessly on those things for the remainder of his life. High on the list was closing the circle on his many relationships. During his decades as a rabbi, Kalman had spent hundreds of hours with dying people, and no one ever said, "I wish I'd spent more time at the office." But he'd often heard, "I wish I'd spent more time with the people I love."

Kalman lived with the clarity that when we move from this world to the next, we won't be asked about the quality of our home furnishings or the size of our bank balance. We'll be asked, "What did you accomplish? How did you grow? Who did you help?

Kalman was always focused on priorities, yet the illness put him in a different category. "A major illness pulls you out of the mundane," Kalman said. "You know what counts and what doesn't. You know what's nonsense and what's real."

HOLISTIC HEALTH

Over the years, whenever visiting New York, Kalman would meet his friend Walter at Le Marais restaurant for a thick, juicy steak. On one trip, however, Walter insisted on going to a salad bar.

"Salad isn't food!" Kalman said in exasperation. "Salad is what 'real food' like our steak eats. Salad is a promissory note that real food is coming."

Walter smiled and gently explained his conversion to a "raw organic vegan diet." He'd been to a holistic health spa on the West Coast and had lost fifty pounds. He'd strengthened his immune system, no longer needed to take insulin, and was filled with vim and vigor.

Kalman was the quintessential practical person. When he understood something to be right, he integrated it without hesitation. (One example: after reading that driving with headlights during the daytime reduces accidents, from that day forward Kalman always drove with his headlights on.)

After receiving his cancer diagnosis, Kalman decided that instead of "sitting back and waiting to die," he'd proactively seek treatment. He spoke with many people who'd received a grim prognosis, yet were alive, healthy, energetic and cancer-free – five, ten and twenty years later.

Kalman embarked on a health kick to strengthen his system and fight the disease. When he was told that cancer feeds on sugar, he completely eliminated sugar from his diet.

Kalman also began spending two-week stints at a holistic wellness retreat in California. He tolerated the organic-vegan food as a necessary concession to his health situation. But at the wellness retreat, what truly energized Kalman, the master conversationalist and relationship builder, was the opportunity to meet new people and turn strangers into friends. Kalman would circulate among the guests and sit with different people at every meal.

Kalman sat for hours, listening to dozens of people share their personal and professional struggles. His joyous, soft eyes invited people to open up about any subject, as he deftly read their emotions and body language. Everyone has a story and Kalman relished drawing it out in a loving way. "There must be a story behind this," he'd always say. "I'd like to hear that story."

A living model of pleasantness, empathy and wisdom, Kalman was the consummate spiritual adviser. He'd guide people to identify the core of their problem, then help develop a practical action plan for moving forward.

At the wellness retreat, Kalman met Ron Langley, a self-described "naïve Montana man." Ron noticed Kalman's kippah and, in the course of conversation, mentioned, "My mother was Christian, but she always spoke about her mother and grandmother – Jews who'd left Prussia in the early 1900s to escape persecution."

Kalman did a double-take, then reached out his hand and said, "Congratulations, Ron. You're Jewish!" Kalman invited Ron to Shabbos services and arranged for a bar mitzvah ceremony which, in Kalman's words, "would make it official."

"Rabbi Packouz was an exceptional human being," Ron says. "In only two weeks together, he became a very special part of my life."

Kalman attended the wellness retreat multiple times and became a favorite with the guests. Many enjoyed keeping in touch; one man sent Kalman a box containing a gold pen, fancy lighter and other expensive items. In typical fashion, Kalman generously donated it all to charity, the Miami Kosher Food Ko-Op.

THE AFTERLIFE

Kalman often thought about his Hebrew School question regarding the afterlife – the same question he'd asked upon first meeting Rav Noah. This inspired Kalman to educate people about proper Jewish burial. He wrote:

> Life is a gift from the Almighty. We are created with a soul and a body. The soul is the real you. The body, on loan from the Almighty, is a vessel that houses the soul.
>
> We care for the body to the best of our ability, eventually returning it to the Owner, as it says, "From dust you are, and to dust you shall return" (Genesis 3:19).
>
> Graves teach about life's finality and not to be over-focused on acquisitions or ego. Graves connect us across the generations with love and devotion – bonding parent to child, and grandparent to grandchild. Graves remind us that life is important and motivate us to consider our epitaphs. *What is my contribution? How will I be remembered?*

On the "afterlife question" itself, Kalman wrote:

> Our physical existence is not disconnected from the afterlife. Rather, the two are interlinked. According to our degree of connection with God in this world – to that same degree we enjoy God-consciousness in the spiritual afterlife.

Kalman diligently strove to strengthen this connection. During his illness, while in tremendous pain, he'd cry out, "Help!"

"What do you want?" those nearby would ask.

Kalman shook his head. "Nothing, thank you. I am talking to God."

GRIM PROGNOSIS

For four years, the cancer proved manageable. Then in May 2019, Kalman was scheduled to go on a long-planned cruise to Alaska with friends. The day before departure, the oncologist requested that Kalman come to his office.

"I'm leaving town tomorrow and not available," Kalman explained.

The doctor didn't mince words, "I highly recommend that you come see me immediately."

In the doctor's office, the oncologist shared dire news: "Your health is in mortal danger and we should begin chemo treatments tomorrow."

Kalman had been anticipating the Alaska trip for months and didn't want to disappoint his friends. "What will happen if I begin chemo in a few weeks?" he asked.

The doctor spoke bluntly: "Without treatment, there's a good chance that in a few weeks, you'll be dead."

Characteristically, Kalman remained optimistic. After his first chemotherapy, he reported, "All went well. No complications. No side effects... yet. I feel in vibrant health. Onward and upward!"

Kalman used the illness as a way to strengthen himself spiritually and inspire others experiencing challenge. He wrote:

> I am not suffering. I know that my malady comes from the Almighty, and that the Almighty can take it away. Though things are challenging, rather than the misery of believing that life is unfair, random and cruel, I choose to focus on the blessings and goodness in my life, with the peace of mind that it's all part of a grand plan.

"Trust in God" does not mean that everything turns out exactly how we want. It means that nothing happens by chance, and that everything occurs according to God's will. With our finite understanding, we cannot know the whole picture.

Is today a good day or a bad day? I believe that any day I look at the grass from the "top down" is a great day!

During those four years of endless pain and procedures, Kalman had much time to ponder, *Why me?* Not with an accusatory tone, but with a sincere desire to decipher the meaningful message from Above. He wrote:

Life isn't always easy. When people ask, "Why do bad things happen to good people?" they typically define "bad" as that which involves pain and difficulty. On the contrary, life's challenges enable us to grow. Trials make or break a person. The greater the ordeal, the more we attain in surmounting it.

Nothing in this world is intrinsically good or bad. We choose whether to view a particular challenge as good or bad – an obstacle or a stepping stone. Is the glass half-full or half-empty? (That might depend whether you're pouring or drinking...)

Life has a higher purpose. Our challenge is to perfect the soul by building good character. Every challenge lifts us above previous limits. The greater the challenge, the greater the opportunity to unleash the potential locked inside.

God never sends a challenge we can't handle. This effectively puts every challenge in the category of "achievable." The Almighty wants us to succeed and, like a track coach, does not raise the hurdle higher than we can jump.

Life's ups and downs are far preferable to a "flat-line" – indicating the person is no longer alive.

HOSPITAL HUMOR

Kalman subscribed to the theory that any unpleasant experience can be improved with humor. During his illness, he described the hospital food as "absolutely hilarious."

On one occasion, Kalman asked the hospital food service, "What's on the kosher menu?"

"There's a choice of meatloaf with mashed potatoes, Salisbury steak with mashed potatoes, or roast turkey and vegetables."

"I'd like the meatloaf, please," Kalman said.

"I'm sorry, we don't have that."

"Okay. I'll have the Salisbury steak."

"Sorry, we don't have that."

"No problem. I'll have the roast turkey."

An hour later, they delivered a chicken dinner.

———◆———

Another time, Kalman got a call from food service. "Sir, you ordered the chicken soup with matzah balls."

"No," Kalman replied, "I ordered the vegetable soup."

Food service was adamant. "No, you ordered the chicken soup."

"I really did order the vegetable soup."

"No! Chicken soup!"

At that point, Kalman asked himself, *Why am I arguing over a bowl of soup?* "Okay," he said, going with the flow. "Send me chicken soup."

"I'm sorry, but we ran out of chicken soup," food service said. "Would you like vegetable soup?"

DEATH WITH DIGNITY

Kalman spent much of his final months tying up loose ends and organizing things for Shoshana. Foremost was selling their house in Miami Beach. Kalman and Shoshana had their house on the market for three years and did everything possible to promote it. They eventually got tired of the whole thing and took it off the market. Three days later, they received an offer to buy their house – at the original asking price.

Kalman burst out laughing. "Okay, God. You're in charge. We sold the house when You wanted – and not a second before."

During those final months, Kalman spent hours in contemplation: "When my time on Earth is complete, what will I leave to my children? People pay a lawyer to create a will for passing on material wealth. But what about spiritual and ethical wealth? What I've learned about life, what is truly valuable, insights into character and relationships, how to use our allotted time."

Kalman thought a lot about the idea of "death with dignity." Popular use of the phrase conveys the right to choose the timing and conditions of one's departure, when life exceeds an "acceptable level" of personal suffering and burden on family and friends.

Kalman regarded "death with dignity" as a clever euphemism, conjuring up images of the Angel of Death arriving in a chauffeured limousine, wearing a tuxedo and accompanied by a string quartet, then rolling out the red carpet and escorting the person to the next world.

Kalman learned the true meaning of "death with dignity" from his friend Brent (Boruch) Brown, who was afflicted with ALS, Lou Gehrig's disease. Brent's body slowly became paralyzed limb by limb, as he went from a cane, to a wheelchair, to bedridden. From speaking with difficulty, Brent eventually could only signal with his eyelids.

Kalman wrote in tribute:

> There is meaning and purpose to how life ends. If life is only about physical comfort, then "death with dignity" is a comfortable exit. Yet what if life is more than that?

Despite enormous hardship, Brent chose to embrace life. By facing his challenges with courage, Brent lived with dignity, and achieved "death with dignity."

PUBLIC ANNOUNCEMENT

One month before his passing, Kalman updated *Shabbat Shalom* readers on his condition:

> I have stage 4 prostate cancer. I have very little energy or desire. About the only thing I desire is that my *Shabbat Shalom* gets out each week.
>
> Although I have a serious illness, I know the Almighty loves me more than even I love myself. Everything God gives me is for my best, which I accept with love and appreciation. The choice to grow closer to God, or move further away, is entirely within our hands.
>
> I am totally good with my health opportunity. I believe that God has an individual plan that is for my best – to come close to Him, to grow, to fulfill my purpose in life. What that plan entails, I await as it unfolds. Whichever direction it goes, I am just thankful.

Kalman decided it was time to generate as much merit as possible. To his hundreds of thousands of *Shabbat Shalom* readers, he wrote:

> Those wanting to do something in the merit of Kalman Moshe ben Devorah, please focus on expressing gratitude, and never miss an opportunity to do an act of kindness, no matter how small.

Kalman composed a simple, heartfelt prayer for people to say:

> "Almighty, Master of the Universe, who provides all good things, please grant a complete and speedy healing to Kalman Moshe ben Devorah."

As a teaching moment, Kalman shared advice on dealing with people who face serious medical dilemmas or other life challenges:

> Heartfelt compassion is deeply appreciated. Yet keep it short. Obsessive curiosity and asking for a complete medical history – though well-intended – is oppressive, depressing and depleting of energy.
>
> Use the moment of interaction to forge something meaningful. Try asking, "Is there anything I should know, or that you want to tell me?" This is a great kindness – not forcing a sick person to answer questions they'd rather not answer.

Some people, in an effort to be encouraging, would say, "You're looking good!" Kalman bristled at this comment, which to him sounded like, "Wow, I expected you to look sallow and on the edge of death!"

"You're looking good" also reminded Kalman of the adage: "There are three stages to life: youth, middle age, and 'looking good.'"

UNFINISHED KADDISH

Growing up in Portland, Kalman was the third of four children – two girls followed by two boys. Kalman's mother Dorothy was a classic Jewish homemaker – always home when he returned from school, and making sure that Kalman did his homework, took his vitamins and cleaned his room. Kalman's father, a witty insurance salesman, enjoyed telling Kalman, "The best decision you ever made was in the maternity room after you were born. You looked up and said, 'I'll take those two parents.'"

When Dorothy passed away from a stroke at age 98, Kalman said Kaddish for her every day in the synagogue. One day, while saying Kaddish, Kalman was overcome with emotion and began sobbing. Afterward, the rabbi went over to comfort him.

Kalman explained, "I want to properly honor my mother. Yet I'm so sick and unlikely to finish the year of saying Kaddish for her."

Kalman passed away four months short of finishing Kaddish for his mother – and arranged for someone to say it in his stead.

FINAL DAYS

Two weeks before his passing, when the doctors said there was nothing left to do, Kalman went into hospice care. Despite tremendous weakness and pain, he never lost perspective and clarity. When asked, "How are you?" he'd respond, "Thank God," serenely accepting his condition.

When Yedidya Packouz visited a week before his father's passing, Kalman was in an armchair with his feet propped up and eyes closed. Kalman was in unbearable pain, with even shallow breathing taking enormous effort.

Yedidya began tearing up and told his father, "It's really hard for me to see you suffer like this."

Without opening his eyes, Kalman shifted his head in Yedidya's direction. "I'm not suffering. I just feel awful."

In his final days, Kalman was in extreme discomfort and had mostly stopped eating. With no strength to speak, he'd communicate by pointing and gesturing. Now and then, he'd take Shoshana's hand and gently kiss it, channeling his pain into love.

Kalman never stopped trying to make people laugh. During those final days, on strong pain medication, he drifted in and out of consciousness. While visiting, David Packouz commented aloud, "Wow, these medicines really turn a person into a zombie."

Suddenly, Kalman's head popped up and his eyes bulged wide, staring straight at David.

"Whoa, weird timing," David said, shaken.

"That was intentional," Kalman muttered in a raspy whisper, before passing out again.

In his final hours, barely conscious, Kalman repeated particular phrases over and over, revealing the innermost recess of his consciousness:

- *Ein od mil'vado* – There is none besides God.

- *Yismechu b'malchus'cha* – Rejoice in God's dominion.

- *Ein Elokim zulasecha* – There is no God but You.

On Friday, November 15, Kalman was listless and his eyes were closed nearly the entire day. Shoshana never left his side. At 8:30 p.m., shortly after Shabbos began, Kalman suddenly looked up, opened his eyes wide and – with a bright light shining from his eyes – stared at something past Shoshana's shoulder.

Shoshana was startled and looked around to identify the source of the intense light. Yet there was none. It was the light of Kalman's soul, preparing to depart, shining through his eyes.

Kalman then uttered his final words: "Hi, Mom." Kalman's mother, Dorothy, who had passed away eight months earlier, was accompanying her son on his final journey.

On 18 Cheshvan 5780 (November 15, 2019), as devoted *Shabbat Shalom* subscribers sat at their Shabbos tables and read Kalman's inspiring words, a great light was extinguished. Kalman's pure soul left his physical body and returned to his Maker.

FUNERAL

Though Kalman's death came as no surprise, it left a shocking void. Kalman had filled so many roles: as educator, fundraiser, author, community leader, friend and family patriarch.

Tears flowed at the widely attended funeral in Miami. An additional 2,000 people attended via livestream.

Rabbi Yochanan Zweig, Rosh Yeshiva of Talmudic University, described Kalman with the exalted status of *"Adam Gadol* – a great person."

———⸭⸬⸭———

Kalman's body was flown to Israel for burial in Eretz HaChaim cemetery near Beit Shemesh. Kalman's ironic sense of humor was in evidence, even at the cemetery:

- Avraham Packouz said, "My father would want us to say at his funeral: 'Hold on a second – he's still alive!'"

- Hizkiyahu Packouz shared that he once asked his father how he'd want to be eulogized. Kalman replied, "Begin with: 'My father, my hero.'"

- At the burial, Rabbi Edward Davis of Hollywood, Florida, "heard" Kalman's voice say, "Nice day for a funeral, isn't it?"

As Rav Noah's loyal disciple, Kalman requested that his tombstone include the words: "He merited to hear Torah from Rav Noah Weinberg."

FINAL FAX

Deeply devoted to his *Shabbat Shalom* readers, Kalman prepared a "final fax" to be sent out posthumously. Not one to mince words, he titled the computer file: "Death."

Good morning! By the time you read this, I will be dead.

I've always loved that opening line – full of power, no beating around the bush... right to the punch line! However, my wife never had the same affinity for it. So I asked her, "How else should I start out – 'It was a dark and stormy night'?"

Kalman dedicated that edition of *Shabbat Shalom* to Shoshana:

My eternal gratitude for raising our family. Everything she does is with love, caring and joy. My thanks to the Almighty that she married me."

[As Rabbi Akiva said about his wife:] "All that I have accomplished, I owe to her."

With deadpan humor, Kalman also dedicated that week's *Shabbat Shalom* to his own memory. He then signed off with final words of advice:

Never leave a loved one or a friend without saying, "I love you."

I love you.

BROAD IMPACT

As a wave of messages and letters poured in from around the globe, Kalman's impact on the masses became increasingly obvious. Thousands had experienced firsthand his devotion to teaching Torah, pursuing peace and always thinking of others.

Soon after Kalman's passing, a first-grade class in Brazil was learning the biblical account of how Abraham welcomed guests. The teacher mentioned that a rabbi in Miami had died, at which point a number of children shouted out, "Yes, we know all about him! Just like Abraham's kindness brought people closer to God, Rabbi Packouz did the same."

One man wrote from Singapore:

> When I was becoming a *ba'al teshuva*, Kalman turbocharged the
> process. He became like a big brother to me. He genuinely cared
> and always had great advice.
> I know he is up there looking out for us all. His energy can never
> be extinguished; it just moves to a higher realm.

A friend from yeshiva days wrote:

> From the day Kalman walked into Shema Yisroel, he was clearly
> not just another student. His sincerity, insight and breathtaking
> honesty had an impact on students and staff alike. He quickly
> became someone I could turn to for insight, advice and encour-
> agement. And Kalman ensured that our relationship lasted for
> decades.

For nearly twenty years, Kalman took walks on the Miami Beach
boardwalk with his friend Stacy Richman, who says:

> Kalman carried a burden of responsibility, sharing in the happi-
> ness and the sadness of others. He was devoted to healing the soul.
> I will never forget Kalman's words of wisdom on a humid night:
> "When people lack clarity between right and wrong, I have an obli-
> gation to show them."

In a beautiful tribute, Stacy handed out twenty-five envelopes to
poor people. Each envelope contained money and a note that read,
"From your friend, Kalman."

Though most *Shabbat Shalom* readers never met Kalman personally, they considered him a trusted friend and a primary source of
their Jewish education. Readers wrote:

> • I never met Rabbi Packouz, but he wrote in such a skillful
>   way that it forged a personal conversation between us. He

will never know the impact he had on my thinking. I initially received his email by mistake. God knew what He was doing!

• For years, I thought that the purpose of life was to become rich and famous. I now see the futility of that. Rabbi Packouz found a way to extend himself, unselfishly teaching me that a successful life is based on giving. I aspire to be like him.

• Though it took me two minutes to initially subscribe to *Shabbat Shalom*, I was rewarded with twenty-five years of the most impassioned, erudite and illuminating words of wisdom. Rabbi Packouz is truly an embarrassment of riches.

• Years ago, I discovered Rabbi Packouz by accident. He was sending faxes to my office for a former employee, and I became the lucky recipient of these abandoned faxes. I loved them so much that I filed and saved them.

• Rabbi Packouz was warm, authentic and down-to-earth. He was always available to help, and whenever I'd email him about a difficult situation, he'd send back helpful advice. Rabbi Packouz was my connection to Judaism. He will be immensely missed.

SHABBOS PREMONITIONS

A few days before his passing, Kalman received an email from Robin Wasserman in California:

Dear Rabbi Packouz,

When we first became observant, our rabbi challenged us to add some Torah learning to our Shabbos table. Having no clue what to do, we printed out *Shabbat Shalom* every week and read it Friday evening during dessert.

Till today, we agree, discuss and argue over your weekly thoughts. We've learned so much, not just about the Torah portion itself, but how it's applied, and how to transmit these values to our children.

Favorite *Shabbat Shalom* phrases like "Good Morning!" and "Example, example, example" have become our inside family jokes. *Shabbat Shalom* is as much a part of our Shabbos table as the challah.

Though Kalman was on his deathbed, with barely enough strength to speak, he managed to send this reply:

Thank you for the beautiful and uplifting letter.
It's nice to know the impact one has.
Warmly, Rabbi Packouz

Robin was so touched that she printed out her original letter and the response. As she read it aloud at Shabbos dinner, the family had a strange feeling of Kalman's presence there with them.

Fast forward one week later. As they read aloud that week's edition of *Shabbat Shalom*, the family was stunned to learn that Kalman had passed away. After reading more details, they gasped and stopped. Kalman had passed away at 8:30 p.m. the previous Friday – the precise moment they'd spoken about him and felt his presence.

"We all got the chills," Robin says. "There is more to life than we know."

⟫◈⟪

Michael Marcus, whom Kalman greatly influenced, reports:

I began my Jewish journey twenty-three years ago and was blessed to become friends with Rabbi Packouz. Not long after, my children and I began traveling from our home in Plantation, Florida, to spend Shabbos with the Packouz family. This was a wonderful way to experience the warmth and beauty of Shabbos, and it continued for many years.

One of Kalman's customs was to light a single candle from the Havdalah flame before it was extinguished. This way, he explained, the light of Shabbos would continue into the week. We adopted this custom and have extended the spirit of Shabbos this way for over twenty years.

On November 16, 2019, we ended Shabbos with the joy of Havdalah as usual. When I went to light the special "Kalman Candle," to my dismay there were no candles or tea lights anywhere to be found. This was the first time in decades that we hadn't lit the candle, and I had a feeling inside that something was amiss.

A few minutes later, my wife went online. The first email she read was the news of Kalman's passing, just hours earlier.

Today, we continue the custom of lighting "Kalman's Candle," feeling his spirit with us in those special moments right after Shabbos.

THE POWER OF ONE

Looking back fifty years, the spark that transformed Kalman's life journey was his high school friend, Ron Balshine. Had Ron not been in yeshiva in Jerusalem, Kalman would have likely gone straight from the kibbutz back to Europe.

Ron, who remained Kalman's close lifelong friend, reflects, "We all have a role to play and I did my small part, at the right place at the right time. It's all the orchestration of God. We're just pieces in the puzzle."

One shudders to imagine the Jewish people bereft of Kalman's accomplishments: forty-two years of happy marriage, nine children and numerous grandchildren, *Shabbat Shalom Weekly*, the

Western Wall Webcam, the $15 million raised to fund Jewish education, the prayers prayed, the Torah studied, and the innumerable acts of kindness in all shapes and forms.

Kalman embodied Rav Noah's foremost teaching: "One person can change the world." True, not everyone is blessed with Kalman's unique intellect, charm, persistence, communication skills and knowledge – combined with extreme love, respect and compassion for all people. Yet we are all capable of continuing the mission and using every available tool to spread Torah's life-affirming message to a world yearning for authentic inspiration.

Today, the main street of Talmudic University's auxiliary campus in Pennsylvania is called "Kalman's Way," a reference to one man's honest and straightforward approach. It is a testament to the goodness that Rabbi Kalman Packouz brought to the world, and the thousands upon thousands of lives he touched and changed forever.

KALMAN'S WAY: LIFE ASSESSMENT

Kalman lived by the motto: "Know what you're living for!" This list of self-reflections can assist in clarifying one's mission and purpose in life:

- What do I care about most passionately? When do I feel that life is most meaningful?

- Who is my hero, and why?

- What higher value, cause or ideal am I willing to sacrifice for? Why is this important to me?

- Do I strive for constant awareness of my choices?

- If I could offer myself three pieces of advice, what would they be?

- What would bring me more happiness than anything in the world?

—⟫·◆·⟪—

- What are the most important relationships in my life? How can I nurture those?

- Do I regularly express my feelings to those who mean the most to me?

- What is one thing I can do to project more joy and positivity?

- What can I do to be more compassionate and giving?

—⟫·◆·⟪—

- What is my greatest strength? What is my greatest weakness?

- At some point in life, I dreamed of who I could become. Am I living that dream?

- What is my deepest aspiration? What project or goal, if left undone, will I most regret?

- If I knew I couldn't fail, what would I undertake to accomplish?

- What practical steps can I take to achieve that goal?

—⟫·◆·⟪—

- What are my three biggest achievements in the past year?

- What are my three biggest mistakes in the past year?

- What important decision did I avoid making in the past year?

- What is the most important decision to make for the coming year?

- If I could change one thing about myself, what would it be?

- What would I want said at my eulogy and written on my tombstone?

———◆———

- Do I experience God through the wonders of nature?

- Do I experience God through the genius of Torah?

- Do I experience God by appreciating the miracle of Jewish history?

- Do I experience God by seeing Divine providence in my life?

- What is God's purpose of Creation? What is my unique role in furthering that plan?

- Am I fulfilling Abraham's mandate to set a personal example and teach others about God?

Afterword

I first met my beloved friend, Rabbi Kalman Packouz *zt"l*, in 1991, when he was registering his children to attend our newly-opened elementary school. At the time, I was executive director of the school and those tuition meetings could sometimes turn unpleasant. But that very first meeting, we hit it off and it was easy to see what a special person he was.

We shared many similarities: Kalman had moved to South Florida to open the Aish HaTorah branch and spread the Almighty's wisdom, and I was focused on spreading Torah through our educational institutions. Both our jobs required taking financial responsibility for our respective organizations, and we commiserated and bonded over similar financial pressures. Kalman suggested that we meet weekly to strengthen one another. He was one of the warmest, most pleasant people you'd ever hope to meet; it didn't take much to convince me.

That was the beginning of an incredible 27-year friendship. I learned over the years that, aside from Kalman's gentle nature, incredible warmth and sterling character, he was brilliantly creative. He also had a wonderful sense of humor, always doing his best to cheer me up. In my opinion, his defining life attribute was a deep and abiding love for God and all humanity. He was endlessly kind and generous. If someone needed Kalman's help, he was simply incapable of saying, "No."

Notwithstanding all of Kalman's innovative contributions for the betterment of humanity and the Jewish people, his defining life's work was *Shabbat Shalom – Fax of Life*. I don't believe there's ever been a more widely-distributed weekly Torah publication. Through this, Kalman changed the lives of millions – all types of Jews and non-Jews alike. Today, some 300,000 people receive Shabbat Shalom weekly, and the numbers continue to grow. Every week, it is distributed in 300 synagogues across the world, and is translated into Portuguese, Spanish and (coming soon) Russian.

Every week, I have the cherished privilege of perpetuating Kalman's legacy by writing the *Shabbat Shalom* column. I am grateful for his entrusting me with this supernal project, and for giving me the honor of following in his footsteps. And I am eternally grateful to the Almighty for bringing Kalman into my life.

In 2020, my school bought a campus in the Appalachian foothills of Pennsylvania. We named the campus "Aishel," to commemorate the hospitality inn built by our forefather Abraham to promote awareness of the Almighty (see Genesis 21:33). This campus is designated to be a nexus of Torah study, spreading the beacon of Divine wisdom.

The main road running through the campus is named "Kalman's Way" – a nod to Kalman's chosen path in life: commitment to Jewish education, coupled with his gentle, kind, honest and wise "way." May his memory be for a blessing.

Rabbi Yitzchak Zweig
September 2023 / Tishrei 5784
Miami Beach, Florida

Acknowledgments

- Full credit to the Almighty for making everything possible.

- Rabbi Yitzchak Zweig, who encouraged me to write this tribute to our beloved friend Kalman zt"l.

- Yitzchak Winkler of Talmudic University

- Berel Simpser and Rafael Marlowe

- Shoshana Packouz and Avraham Packouz for insights and feedback. May this book perpetuate Kalman's love and wisdom, as a merit for the entire family.

- Estie Dishon of ED Press Solutions for expertly typesetting and shepherding the book's production

- Aviad Ben Simon for the cover art

- Yonoson Rosenblum for the invaluable research in his definitive biography of Rav Noah, *Torah Revolutionary*

- Eric Coopersmith for editorial consulting

- Aaron Dayan for audio recordings of Kalman

- Chantal Rubin for editorial input

- Google, for enabling me to voice-type large portions of this book, hands-free and from remote locations.

- My wife Keren, for all the wonderful years we've shared, and looking forward to many more.

In alphabetical order, thanks to the many people who shared recollections. Apologies to those inadvertently omitted.

Danny Aiken

David Ail

Stephen Baars

Ron Balshine

Avshalom Baskin

Carol Berger

Motty Berger

Rabbi Yitzchak Berkovits

Sam Bilmen

Aron Blatt

Marty Bogoratt

Josh Boretsky

Daryl Brenner

Chris Broward

Yaakov Burstyn

Edward Davis

Daniel Dembs

Gil Eisenbach

Marsha Epstein

Cathy Eufemia

Gerson Farberas

Chaim Feld

Vince Fermin

Steven Finer

Suzanne Gerard

Michael Gerson

Shoshan Ghoori

Nechama Greenfield

Yitz Greenman

Elazar Grunberger

Sheila Hecker

Dov Heller

Yisroel Herczeg

Chaim Hirsch

Steven Hirsch

Dovid & Rona Holzer

Richard Horowitz

Shimon Hurwitz

Shmuel Mordechai
        Jacobovitch

Yisroel Moshe Janowski

Boris Jovanovich

Jay Kaplowitz

Ben Karan

Chanan Kaufman

Chaim Kessler

Phyllis E. Koss

Murray Kowalsky

Dovid Kramer

Gershon Kramer

Zvi Kramer

Chana Lebovics

Eli Lebovics

Melony Lee

Dr. Brian Lerman

David LeVine

Barry Lynn

Mitch Mandel

Michael Marcus

Betty Matz-Gelsky

Andrew Mentch

Tom Meyer

Tzvi Nightingale

Bart Ostroff

Akiva Packouz

David Packouz

Elimelech Packouz

Hadassah Packouz

Hizky Packouz

Mindy Packouz

Yedidya (Jay) Packouz

Elisha Paul

Zelig Pliskin

Dr. Mark Pomper

Boruch Rabinowitz

Stacy Richman

Chaya Richmond

Yaakov Robinson

Daniel Rudofossi

Shalom Schwartz

Alexander Seinfeld

Nancy Sharff

Brian Sherr

Raphael Shore

Chaim Silberstein

Michael Silver

Carol Spellman

Asher Stein

Matt Sweetwood

Joan Swirsky

Rabbi Baruch Taub

Laura Tauber

Phil Tobin

Alon Tolwin

Ricky Turetsky

Shmuel Veffer

Judy Waldman

Robin Wasserman

Leonard Wein

Yehuda Weinberg

Chaim Willis

Yitz Wyne

Yonah Yaffe

Gedalia Zweig

Rabbi Kalman Packouz zt"l

A treasure who loved life, Hashem, his "flock," his family,
Torah, his "mission," his friends, the world.
He relished each and every encounter, with a joie de vivre
that inspired everyone he came in contact with.
I feel tremendous loss whenever I think of him.
Yet also feelings of great joy for having known him
and calling him my friend.
Not to mention a desire to emulate him and his mitzvot.
We lost a true giant,
but thank Hashem for the blessing of his life!
Miss you, Rabbi. Rest in peace.

Mark

To the memory of our dear friend

Rabbi Kalman Packouz zt"l

For helping to
guide us back to the observance
of our ancestral faith.

*Dr. and Mrs. Benjamin
and Ellen Befeler*

To

Slava

my beloved husband,
on his special birthday.
May you live to 120
and may we continue to share blessings.
Love you forever!

Gretchen

In memory of

Max and *Anita Karl*
and *Ernesto* and *Maria Secomandi*

Drs. Robert and Nilza Karl

In memory of

Rabbi Kalman Packouz zt"l

The ultimate teacher
who brilliantly brought Torah
and its worldly practical relevance
to attentive students of all ages and backgrounds
around the world every week.
May his *neshama* be elevated greatly
by all that we have learned from him.

Stan and Marla Frohlinger

I was first introduced to Rabbi Packouz in 1992 by an investment client of mine. "Shabbat Shalom Weekly" was just created and called the "Fax of Life" which at the time was the exclusive mode of circulation. To this day, I still look forward to reading it; of course, as an email and from Rabbi Yitzchak Zweig, whom Rabbi Packouz brilliantly hand-selected as his successor.

Over many years, Rabbi Packouz would visit our offices in Aventura weekly to teach Torah; often the Torah portion of the week and to just schmooze. His warm presence was always felt as was his larger-than-life smile whenever he greeted me. Throughout the years, we had random, yet meaningful, one-on-one conversations about Jewish life and life in general.

When my father of blessed memory passed in 2007, without a word of advanced notice, Rabbi Packouz drove over one hour each way from Miami Beach to my home in Boynton Beach to pay a whole-hearted and memorable shiva call. We sat and talked and he comforted me. Before heading back to Miami, he handed me the book, *Remember My Soul* with his personal inscription.

I miss you dearly, Rabbi Packouz.

May your memory be for a blessing.

Stuart A. Mehler

In memory of
Rabbi Kalman Packouz zt"l
For the great impact he had on those around him.

Lederer Family

In memory of
Rabbi Kalman Packouz zt"l

Dr. Gil Melin

I had the honor of meeting Rabbi Kalman Packouz zt"l
several times at *simchas*. The last time I saw him was at an
airport when he was flying home with his son.
He always had a kind word to say.
I enjoy reading his weekly *Shabbat Shalom* email.
May his memory be for a blessing.
May his family cherish the good times
they shared with him.

Joseph Roisman and family

Miami, Florida

In memory of

Rabbi Kalman Packouz zt"l

a true mentsch.
You inspired, guided, and enhanced our lives.
We will always remember your leadership
and devotion to our people.
Todah.

Miriam and Dror Zadok

In loving memory of

Ruth Scherer
Albert Scherer
Jerry Hecht and Marilyn Hecht

Karen and Mark Scherer

I met Rabbi Kalman Packouz zt"l in 1983
at a Shabbos dinner at Aish HaTorah in Yerushalayim.
I sat with Kalman,
heard incredible *zemiros* for the first time in my life
and became *Shomer Shabbos* immediately after that trip.
I also began a life long friendship with Kalman,
an extraordinary Jew who had a major impact on my life.
I miss him dearly. May his *neshama* have a huge *aliyah*.
May this book inspire countless Jews in the years to come.

Ricky and Pam Turetsky

Rabbi Kalman Packouz zt"l

was a continuous presence in my life for more than twenty years. I was never the best at maintaining long-term friendships, especially with other guys. But Rabbi Packouz would call me up almost once a month for lunch, or just stop by my office. Better yet, he would include me in his little special projects. I was the print shop and designer behind the "Window on the Wall" mousepad, microfiber cloth and holiday postcards. I also helped with the layout of the Rav Noah memorial book that Kalman made for the Weinberg family.

Rabbi Packouz strengthened my connection and participation in Judaism over a very long period. He introduced me to Aish audio lectures and invited me to annual Aish HaTorah conferences in Stamford, CT. After each visit, he would always say how much he loved me and what a pleasure it was to be with me.

Rabbi Packouz told me of the time he wore a light blue, button-down shirt to give a talk. After the talk, someone commented that it would be better if he wore white shirts, more in line with the "standard uniform." It bothered Rabbi Packouz that this person did not hear his words and seemed to only see the blue shirt. He related this event to Rabbi Weinberg, who told him to ignore the criticism. Rabbi Weinberg said that he himself was color blind, but not to worry, since blue was his favorite color anyway.

Like Rav Noah, Kalman loved each Jew as they were. He was "color blind" to what "kind of Jew" you believed yourself to be. He knew that within me was a Divine spark yearning to be revealed.

I miss him very much. With much love,

Michael Gerson and Family

Yitzchak Winkler

———◆———

Rabbi Kalman zt"l and Shoshana Packouz
were true friends to our family.
Kalman is greatly missed,
as are his weekly *Shabbat Shalom* wise words.

Julie and Sam Gold

———◆———

To Rav Kalman zt"l, who left the world
a better, happier and holier place.

Moshe and Beth Firestone

———◆———

To my beloved teacher and mentor Rabbi Packouz

Richard Wallin

———◆———

Diana and Oded Ben-Arie
Bob Burg
Michael Eleff
Eli Goldach
Ariel Herskovitz
Steven Hirsh
Elisha Paul
Joan Swirsky
Judy Waldman
Pam Weiss

Rabbi Kalman Packouz zt"l

was a role model of kindness. I reached out to him due to my father's illness and without my asking, the next day he dropped off at my front door two books, of which one was ArtScroll *Tehillim*. He inscribed it: "In the merit of your prayers and the Psalms you read, may your father have a full recovery." I read it daily, providing the inspiration and prayers to not only help me, but also of my departed my father.

Rabbi Packouz is of blessed memory.

Steven Hirsh

About the Author

Rabbi Shraga Simmons, co-founder of Aish.com and co-author of *48 Ways to Wisdom*, was Rav Noah Weinberg's ghostwriter for twenty years.

Shraga is also co-founder of HonestReporting, and author of *David & Goliath*, the definitive account of anti-Israel media bias (2012).

Shraga currently produces books, films and curriculum on universal Torah topics, including the series of "LifeWisdom" booklets.

Originally from Buffalo, New York, Shraga holds a degree in journalism from the University of Texas at Austin, and rabbinic ordination from Rav Noah Weinberg, Rav Zalman Nechemia Goldberg, Rav Yitzchak Berkovits and the Chief Rabbi of Jerusalem.

Shraga lives with his family on Moshav Matityahu.

Contact him at: rabbi@shraga.com

Shraga Simmons and Kalman Packouz